Render Me, Gender Me

BETWEEN MEN ~ BETWEEN WOMEN
Lesbian and Gay Studies
Lillian Faderman and Larry Gross, Editors

Render Me, Gender Me

Lesbians Talk Sex, Class, Color, Nation, Studmuffins . . .

Kath Weston

COLUMBIA UNIVERSITY PRESS   NEW YORK

Columbia University Press
Publishers Since 1893
New York   Chichester, West Sussex
Copyright © 1996 Kath Weston

Library of Congress Cataloging-in-Publication Data

Weston, Kath, 1958–
     Render, me, gender me : lesbians talk sex, class, color, nation,
studmuffins ..., / Kath Weston.
          p.   cm. — (Between men–between women)
     Includes bibliographical references.
     ISBN 0–231–09642–9
          1. Lesbians—United States—Identity.   2. Lesbians—United States—
Psychology. 3. Lesbians—United States—Attitudes.   4. Sex role—
United States.   5. Gender identity—United States.   6. Stereotype (Psychology)—
United States.   I. Title.   II. Series.
     HQ75.6.U5W47   1996
     305.48'9664—dc20   96–14888

Designed by Linda Secondari
Printed in the United States of America
c 10 9 8 7 6 5 4 3 2 1

for geeta, with love

Contents

Acknowledgments

To the women in these pages, who took a chance on a cultural anthropologist. To Janaki Bakhle and Suzanne Vaughan, for keeping me this side of meltdown and calling me back into my name. To Young-Ae Park, for walking into the desert to find whatever it was we found. To the Bad Girls—Celia Alvarez, Tressa Berman, and Gloria Cuádraz—for reminding me that exiles (like activists) are made, and not by job markets either. To Julie Erfani, for returning me to writing class/race/nation when living them was hard enough. To my writing buddy, Tim Diamond, for having the old-fashioned audacity to insist upon a better world. To my cousin, B. C. Cliver, whose narrow escape from studmuffindom had to show up in a book title somewhere.

To Nico Colson-Jones, who convinced me I was wrong about a lot of things but right about dreams. To Julie Cordell, who laid out for me in death the power of the word. To Carla Schick, who helped set up the second round of interviews and whose work with the Women's Writers Union fed poetry to my prose. To Kristin Koptiuch and Kara Tableman, for those magnificent dinners. To Steve Kossak, for the little room with a view that ushered me through chapter 8. To Pamela Feldman-Savelsberg, for the story. To Lisa Márquez, amid the storm clouds at Acoma, for inspiring me more than she knows. To Susan

Cahn, Ed Cohen, and Wendy Patterson, for the calm. To Cheri Thomas, for understanding the difference between being in contact and being in touch. To Esther Newton, for Graceland and showing me a few of the ropes. To Sheila Friedeman, for pointing out the obvious when it wasn't.

To my great-aunt and godmother, Irene Heidenway, for always being by my side. Oh, right, and for the gift of irreverence. To my baby sisters, Lynda Foster and Jeanne Lisse, who swear to this day they taught me everything I know. To my mom, Darlene Weingand, and my dad, Wayne Weston, who never let me fall for the line that working people don't read books.

To the activists of the National Writers Union, especially Sarah Bewley and Elaine Perry, for getting me in that writerly way. To my agent, Charlotte Sheedy, for her steady encouragement and no-nonsense advice. To Lori Jervis and Marcie, for help with the interview transcription. To Lisa Kammerlocher, for dropping reference after reference into campus mail. To Deborah Bright, for the "tour" of the slide archives that led me to the work of Gaye Chan.

To the National Science Foundation and the Rockefeller Foundation, for funding the research that led to this book. To the Center for Advanced Feminist Studies at the University of Minnesota and the Center for Advanced Studies at the University of Iowa, for shelter and support. To the Spring 1995 Queer Theory class and the Faculty/Staff Discussion Group on Lesbian and Gay Studies at Wellesley College, for some lively feedback on the "Chameleon" and "Guessing Games" chapters. To the faculty and students at Princeton who attended my presentation "Writing High Theory for Its Discontents" and commented on the "Copycat" chapter. To Arizona State University West, for granting the leave that allowed me to edit the interviews. To the women of the Lesbian Herstory Archives, for doing what they do best.

A book that wends its way through so many differences and identities owes a lot to the people who take the time to critique it. To John Comaroff, Renato Rosaldo, and Sylvia Yanagisako, for reminding me to ask when difference makes a difference. To the late David Schneider, for a metacritique that will outlive many manuscripts. To the friends and colleagues who willingly subjected themselves to earlier drafts, including Lawrence Cohen, Judith Halberstam, Yasumi Kuriya, Ellen Lewin, Radhika Mohanram, Geeta Patel, and Judi Weston. My missteps are my own, but there would be many more if it weren't for these folks.

In a tribute to the butch at heart, Geeta Patel got me out of the muck more than once when my wheels were spinning. My thanks to her for showing me more about nuance in a day than I'd learn on my own in a lifetime. Who would have thought all those signs for utopia weren't leading to a way out?

Render Me, Gender Me

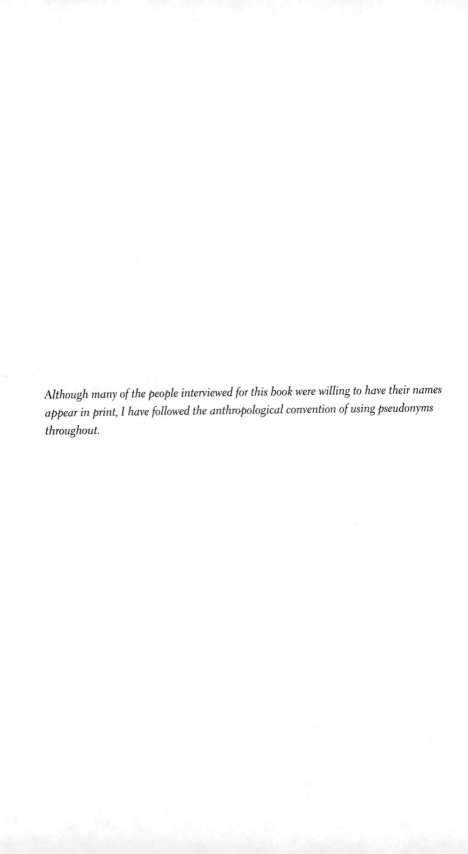

Although many of the people interviewed for this book were willing to have their names appear in print, I have followed the anthropological convention of using pseudonyms throughout.

First Takes

The last passengers raced across the lounge to catch the afternoon flight to New Orleans. Amidst a barrage of loudspeaker announcements, tourist posters, TV monitors, and airport food, I was filled with anticipation. Several weeks earlier a heterosexual colleague I hadn't seen in years had arranged this rendezvous to introduce me to her seventeen-month-old daughter. Over the phone my friend reported with pride that her child had mastered the cultural logic of gender at the annual anthropology meetings. Little Daria now divided strangers into two groups: women became "Mama" and men "Papa." My friend considered her daughter's recourse to kinship terms understandable, given the many ways that family relationships in the United States incorporate gender.

I soon glimpsed my visitors stepping off one of the moving sidewalks that crisscross the airport like conveyor belts in a transportation factory. Threading her way through a tangle of legs, bags, and briefcases, Daria rushed toward me with a toddler's wobbly self-assurance. "Papa!" she exclaimed as I lifted her into the air and she grabbed a fold of my leather jacket. Her mother looked abashed. "Well, maybe my daughter hasn't *quite* mastered gender," she said apologetically. "Don't worry," I replied with amusement. "Daria just has a few things to learn about the nuances of butch and femme."

In day-to-day life people move through the world acting as though they know exactly what they mean by feminine and masculine, boy and girl, mama and papa, butch and femme, stud and fluff. But like Daria, they use these terms to think their way through situations without necessarily thinking their way through the implications of separating the world into two discrete camps.

These first takes involve more than "mis-takes." People know that dichotomies such as "man versus woman" oversimplify the world. Many are careful to qualify their terms, and some set out to escape labels altogether. But they generally find themselves swept back into a confrontation with categories that do not even begin to convey what it means to be gendered "me."

Halfway through the interviews for this book, I began to think that some of the most sophisticated theorists of gender in the United States were out walking city streets. Narrator after narrator pointed out ways in which women can be differently gendered from one another (and men from men). They drew attention to historical changes in the construction of gender that timeless categories such as "masculine" and "androgynous" cannot convey. They zeroed in on ambiguities that make one woman's butch another's femme. They insisted that an exclusive focus on gender obscures the very aspects of race, class, and nation that give gender shape.

Render Me, Gender Me is a book of personal narratives designed to complicate contemporary discussions of gender. It is also designed to be humorous, disturbing, fun, and thought-provoking, the sort of book that can be assigned in a graduate seminar or read aloud to a girlfriend before turning out the lights. In my commentaries on the interviews I spend more time generating questions and introducing complexities than seeking definitive answers or building models to explain it all. Woven into the text are theoretical clues that suggest some unaccustomed ways to approach the topics of gender and identity. Readers who like their theory "straight"–with fancy footnotes and analytic chasers–will have to wait until the publication of *Unsexed: Gender on the Edge of Identity*, a work in progress that will provide not so much a sequel as a companion volume to this one.

In the pages that follow, I am less interested in genders–Woman and Man–than I am in processes of gender*ing*. Anything and anybody can be gendered in a variety of ways. Marketing departments sell everything from breakfast cereals (Special K, GI Joe) to hair coloring (Just for Men) to briefcases ("hard" and "soft") by using gendered distinctions to differentiate products. When it comes to people, gendering can shift across the course of a lifetime: the rough-and-tumble country girl grows up to be a high-fashion model, the fifth-grade bookworm learns to operate backhoes and cranes, the unemployed autoworker remembers the bravado of younger years, the shy boy from the back of the class becomes a sought-after date and dance floor sensation. Different social and historical contexts also open different gendered possibilities. A woman in shirt and pants would go unremarked in most suburban shopping malls in the United States today. Dress her in the same outfit and put her in a 1920s farm field, a 1930s sit-down strike, or a 1940s defense plant, and she would be making another sort of social statement.

To add to the complexity, gendered relations are filled with contradictions and inconsistencies. Jokes abound about the "masculine" one who can't handle a screwdriver and the "feminine" one who likes to call the shots in bed. Puzzled looks greet the what-shall-we-call-him one who looks like he could pack a mean punch but refuses to hit. And then there is the variation in what counts as feminine or masculine from time to time, group to group, place to place.

Power relations in the wider society guarantee that things are seldom simply gendered, but raced, classed, and sexualized as well. Occupations, fashions, sexual practices, styles, bodies, gestures, and chores are all coded with respect to social location. A person cannot don a generic suit of clothes in order to transport herself into some color-blind, class-free, neutral and neutered space. It makes a difference whether her shirt is woven of rough or smooth fabric; black, pink, or print; scoop-neck, banded collar, or button-down. A silk evening gown signifies differently than chinos or a polyester knit. What she wears and how she wears it will help mark her as church lady, homegirl, class tourist, elder, recent immigrant, fancydancer, passing woman, WASP on holiday, or a camp version of any one of these. Her access to material resources and placement in social hierarchies will influence whether she feels as though she controls the constellation of symbols that locate her or whether she feels assaulted by stereotypes.

The idea that people continuously negotiate gender can apply to anyone: heterosexuals, bisexuals, lesbians, gay men, queers, even people who don't use categories of sexual identity to order what they do in the world. So why make lesbians the focus of a book on gendered difference? Placing "same-sex" relationships at the center of an attempt to rethink gender makes the modes of gendering more obvious. There's less temptation to believe that bodies tell you all you need to know about the meaning of words such as "masculinity" and "femininity." Or that biology supplies the fixed template upon which culture works its variations. Or that gendered differences are always male-female differences.

I conducted the interviews for this book from 1985 to 1990 as part of an ethnographic field research project in the San Francisco Bay Area. All of the women in the otherwise diverse interview sample identified as lesbian or gay. Of the forty women whose interview excerpts appear here, approximately one-third were women of color and two-thirds were white. More than one-third came from a working-class background, with almost half employed (or unemployed) at the time of the interview in what could be described as working-class occupations. The majority belonged to the "new gay" and "queer" generations who came out (in some sense of the term) subsequent to the gay liberation and women's movements of the 1970s.

Most gay women in the United States are familiar with words such as "butch" and "femme" that describe gendered differences in same-sex relationships. Some detest these categories, believing that they perpetuate stereotypes about lesbian sexuality. Some describe a deep, lifelong identification as one or the other. A few see themselves moving at will between butch and femme. Others rarely use the words, reserving them for certain people or special occasions: the woman who does a certain type of "man's work," the lover dressed up for a night on the town. Some of the same women who say they can't be bothered with butch/femme can be found using the terms to joke, tease, describe, or disparage.

Like the androgynous rock star, the adolescent who's "a real flamer," the welfare mother, the corporate executive, or the church lady and unemployed autoworker of earlier paragraphs, butch and femme are representations. As representations, they create an image of a certain kind of person, a figure that is raced, classed, sexualized, and gendered in particular ways. In the United States, the executive tends to appear in the mind's eye as heterosexual, male, white, and middle-class, even though the ranks of corporate management include Chicanas, Pakistanis, Filipinas with a range of class backgrounds and sexualities. The unemployed autoworker is more likely to be pictured as white and the welfare mother as African-American, despite the fact that most welfare recipients are white and a sizable proportion of the work force in the auto industry African-American. The image of a fancydancer tends to locate American Indians in timeless tradition, outside any class system. (No matter that the fancydancer in question has to wake up early the day after the dance to go to work.)

Of course, if you happen to occupy one of these categories yourself or have a first-hand acquaintance with someone who does, the associations that come to mind might differ. But you still have to grapple with the ways that representations peg you as a certain type of person, order the institutions that order your life, and make your dreams seem either worth pursuing or just plain crazy.

Representations do not do a very good job of depicting the specific people assigned to cultural categories. If you put four self-identified femmes in a row, you may find it hard to determine what they're supposed to have in common. Watch your perplexity grow as your gaze jumps back and forth from one woman's red pumps to another's gym shoes, and from each individual woman to representations of "the" femme. If "butch" brings to mind nothing more than a hackneyed picture of some truck-driving diesel dyke, you probably won't know what to make of the paradoxical figure of the studmuffin. As precious as she's butch, a studmuffin could be you (depending) or me at a moment when butch collides with femme. Watch that *macha*'s feelings turn delicate when you tease her for taking gender too seriously or for lapses in studly deportment.

Sometimes people resist attempts to box them into any particular gendered category. Mixing and matching clothing from "opposite" genders may cause enough consternation to stop business-as-usual at the local barber shop. But there's more to gendering than pleasure or playful resistance. What if the stranger who judges someone "too butch" is an employer turning away an applicant from a much-needed job? Suppose the same employer unknowingly hires a queer because he assumes that women who want women cannot be femme or brown or both?

You might think that the interview format, with its focus on an individual life, would make it difficult to understand the part played by society and history in forming the ways that people think, talk, and do gender. But embedded in the tales people tell about gendering are observations about communities, nation-states, even the global economy. In a society where to be represented at all is to be gendered, a focus on gendering provides a "way in," a place to start tracing the operations of power, one facet of an entire prism of social relations.

Everyday people are also everyday analysts. Like me—the intrepid researcher with library and tape recorder in tow—most of the women I interviewed wondered what to make of gender. For each story in this book about the color coding of gender categories or a midlife butch crisis, there are additional passages in which people try to explain the world as they see it. I have deliberately edited and organized their interviews to call into question the concept of identity. Lesbians who consistently named themselves "androgynous" or "butch" or "femme" appear alongside lesbians who used these terms sparingly or not at all. This strategic juxtaposition shifts oral history away from chronology toward montage in order to disrupt cultural assumptions about what makes women women, lesbians women, and gay women gay.

The back-and-forth movement between interview and commentary in the pages that follow opens a space for you, the reader, to gender yourself alternately as storyteller, anthropologist, traveling companion, theorist, voyeur. You can read each interview segment separately, or as part of a chapter organized around a theme, or in sequence from cover to cover. Through sometimes wild and always various guises, *Render Me, Gender Me* invites you to walk the fine line that weaves difference together with desire.

4

5

Chapter 1   Guessing Games

Can you always tell one when you see one? Of course not, but that doesn't keep people from trying. In the United States, the shifting sands of gender are sculpted, in part, by the widespread belief that lesbians can be identified at a glance. "Is she or isn't she?" people wonder. To back up their speculations, they look for clues, confident in their ability to infer sexual identity directly from bodies. And these guessing games are far from a heterosexual pastime. Gay women and men play too.

In most cases the clues people seek are not about sexuality per se but about gender. Rather than ask whether anyone has ever spotted So-and-So kissing another woman, people are more likely to assess her gay potential based upon the timbre of her voice, the way she occupies space in a room, the boyish cut of her clothing, or her "nontraditional" job. Using gender to infer sexual identity is not a new gambit in the high-stakes game of representation. During the first half of the twentieth century, psychiatry gave credibility to the notion that homosexuality is accompanied by gender inversion (exhibiting "traits" of the "opposite" gender). Lipstick lesbians aside, most popular representations still depict "real" lesbians as masculinized women, assuming all the while that everyone agrees upon the meaning of "masculine."

Even after So-and-So's gay identity becomes known, or at least assigned, the speculation doesn't end. Players regroup for Round Two. Now the questions revolve around how she genders herself lesbian: Is she butch, femme, neither, both, androgynous, or (in hushed tones) "one of those halfway middlers"? Less discussed, but no less important, are the ways that race, class, age, and ethnicity thread through these ostensibly gendered categories.

Guessing games are a constant reminder that gendering involves much more than claiming an identity. They point to deep-seated cultural assumptions, including the notion that the world is made up of two fixed genders and that individuals display a consistent set of gender "traits." Via the categorizing moves required to play the game, people become engaged in the process of creating gender. They also learn to twist and bend received notions of what makes someone "that kind" or "that way."

Only one of the four women in this section considered herself butch or femme. Yet all four women used these categories to explain past events, present relationships, and everyday encounters. So don't be too quick to dismiss femme and butch as outmoded stereotypes, or identities only a few lesbians claim. Who knows? They might just provide a starting point for rethinking gender.

Marta Rosales: "God, If I Ever Meet One of Them!"

"I remember growing up, and my father would say someone was *marimacha*. 'Marimacha,' he said; you know, 'You *dyke*.' And I always used to be so afraid. *Marimachas* were just like awful abominations. I thought, 'God, if I ever meet one of them!' My idea of a lesbian was someone who was in leathers, and they were really tough. Very tough and mean."

Before she moved to the Bay Area from Southern California, Marta Rosales said she "didn't think there were [*marimachas*], really. I know they talked about them. There was one—but she wasn't Hispanic—at my dad's work. *She* was over *him*. Ha-ha! It was great, now that I think. Damn! All the men were scared of her. This was the stereotype I had: she wore steel-toed boots. She wore men's straight-legged jeans. Wallet in her pocket. These little Hawaiian shirts that she'd roll up. She had these nice arms—nice arms, oh! I still remember that! She had this real curly hair, that she kept with gel. I mean, *this* was a dyke to me. My dad would say, '*La marimacha* Pat.' I was so afraid of her.

"When I was fourteen and a half, I started working with my dad. And here was Pat, who didn't like anyone. She liked my father, for some strange reason.

She respected him as a worker, but he looked down at her for being a dyke. He'd say, 'Good morning, Pat,' and she'd say, 'How ya doing?' and then I would just run away! But that was the only dyke I ever really knew. And she was in such a position of authority. She was in charge of everybody else."

Marta described her younger self as "very untraditional. I wasn't like my sister. I wasn't like my brother. I was fascinated with bicycles, and I used to take them apart and put them together. I showed my brothers how to ride their bicycles. I showed my brothers how to *fix* their bicycles. Then I decided I wanted a scooter, and that wasn't enough, and I got a motorcycle. Here's this Hispanic family, the *girl* buying a motorcycle. 'Oh, what people are gonna think!' And I said, 'I don't care what people are gonna think about me, Dad. I decided to get a motorcycle.'

"Then I used to wear my little 501s and tool around on my bike. I was really happy. But people then started asking me. I didn't have a boyfriend [after] high school. They would come up and say, 'Are you a lesbian?' I said, 'No, I'm not. I am not. I don't know what you're talking about.' I was real heavy into denial. What I used to resent [was] not so much that they would think I was gay but because they were stereotyping. Because here was this woman, who had a motorcycle, who wore jeans and was so nontraditional."

When Marta moved to the Bay Area to continue her nursing education on a scholarship, a friend introduced her to a lesbian who "broke down a lot of stereotypes. Even when I first started coming to the bars here, if someone was very butchy, it was like, 'Oh my god!' But she broke down all that. She had her master's in criminal justice, and she was intelligent. Oh my god, this woman had an IQ!"

For Marta, talking about gender meant talking about her Mexican-American upbringing. "We had a lot of family down there, and we'd always get together for the big celebrations. I didn't want to grow up, seeing what these women do. There are more now that aren't Catholic, but the majority [are] very religious. You're going to grow up to marry a man and cater to a man. ([Although] that may not be so much the thinking *now* . . . the [Mexican] culture, with the American [culture], it's mixing.) You're going to learn how to cook, you're going to learn how to be a good mother, and you're going to learn how to do everything for someone else except yourself.

"Here's Marta, who everybody just looks up to, and is so 'good.' This whole Madonna complex, really! I remember being in classes with aunts and cousins. They'd always come back to my mother: 'Rosa, this girl of yours!' My mother put up with me. I think that [my mother] would want me to be different. Because she so supported my being individual. I was the only one in the family that also stood up to my father and had arguments with him. The clock said seven o'clock and he said it was six. I said, 'Father, this clock says seven.' And then he said, 'No. I say it's six, it's six.' And I'd say, 'No. It is seven.' Things like that. You don't question men in Hispanic culture."

When it came to the categories femme and butch, Marta felt she had "a little of both. I can't say one or the other, because I really go in spurts. I think I'm more butch and very much in control, but I have very feminine qualities, in another way. But on that butch/femme distinction, is it do you just have oral sex? Some people don't like dildos. Some people don't like anything about that kind of role playing. When I was in senior year [of college], about two years ago, they said, 'God, you know, you're really butch.' And I thought, well, what is being butch? 'Oh, that means when you're more controlling, or you're more aggressive.' And I'm aggressive in some things, but, oh gosh, I'm just not in other things."

Over the years, Marta had come to associate the term "femme" less with sex or clothing and more with "the emotions, and the dependency. I've always had a vision that femmes are so much more dependent. Dependency's not bad. You need to need someone. You can't just do it all yourself. A lot of people will tease. They'll say, 'Oh, you're such a femme.' And I'll say, 'Oh, you're right. I guess.' I never get upset if people call me a femme. Because I'm very nurturing. I'm very dramatic. I'm emotional; [my lover] Toni's not. But people who *really* know us will say, 'Toni's the femme and you're the butch. Because you're the one that really runs the show underneath.'

"Let's say I was with someone who was just as emotional, or even more dependent, and very into helplessness. Then I think they would see me more as butch. But I do get helpless. There's some things I cannot do, and I rely on Toni. And there's some things that she just can't do, and she relies on me. I think we're a pretty good balance. She sometimes tends to be a little bit on the butch, but I think I'm attracted to qualities like that, also. Which makes me think I'm more of a femme. Even though I have *both* characteristics, if you wanted an answer to categorize myself am I butch or am I femme, I would say femme.

"Even if I were to be in a bar, and say I saw someone come in. Someone had jeans on, with a little sweatshirt like this. I would say I would be more attracted to that person than someone who came in with wool slacks and a nice silk shirt. Because that's more down to earth, also.

"Two years ago, three years ago, someone would have said I was a butch because I was sitting on a motorcycle. Here I am, this little thing on a motorcycle, with the jacket and the helmet. You look at me and think, 'Oh, my god, what a *dyke*! That butch!' It was hilarious. Or people would just be flabbergasted. 'You drive a motorcycle? *You*, Marta? You're so quiet!' I said, 'I like motorcycles. It has *nothing* to do with that.' And I used to laugh! I said, 'Toni, people think I'm such a butch because I drive a motorcycle! And you know better!' So I said, 'I know what I'm going to do. I'm going to buy a pink helmet and tool along.' She says, 'Don't you dare!'"

Sid Stein: "I've Seen Some Pretty Curvaceous Butches"

"I don't think I've ever been taken for a femme. Except once, when I went [with] a friend of mine who's butch to a wedding for somebody who she worked with. They took me as a femme there because she seemed butcher than me, and they just figured one of us had to be a femme. So I won the femme award.

"When I first came out in the 1970s, it was sort of uncool to be butch or femme. But I was clearly butch in the relationship that I was in. And we used to play with it sometimes. You know, we'd get dressed up to go out. She would wear little lacy things and I would dress in a tie. In relationships I was mostly attracted to femmes. But it was like you weren't supposed to have roles. You were supposed to be evolved from that sort of thing in 1976. I never said I wasn't butch. I just thought, 'Well, you can't act like that.' I didn't think, 'Well, now I'm real androgynous,' or something. I thought of myself as 'butch et cetera.' Later on, when things relaxed a bit, I was more clearly defined.

"Some of it is obviously dress, the way we dressed. But that's just really superficial. And some of it's body language. She was very feminine in body language and I was much less so. And then some of it is the way that emotional issues were dealt with. She tended to be much more open emotionally, much more wanting to talk about stuff. And I tended to be much less that way: 'It's all right, I can deal with it.' Or, 'It's your problem.'

"I think with lesbians it's easier to fool around with being butch if you're femme than it is for women who identify as butch to fool around with being femme. I mean, it's frightening for me to think about wearing a dress. It really is. [Or] putting on makeup. And I know that she didn't particularly have a hard time putting on my clothes or not wearing makeup. I can certainly picture femme women picking up butch body language rather than vice versa.

"For me, to be feminine is to feel real vulnerable. It's frightening. It feels degrading. It's confusing. So, I wouldn't do it. I guess it's not the same for women who are femme." Looking at her past femme lovers, Sid saw "some of the vulnerability. I don't think it's degrading at all. It seems like it's natural. It's just that for me it would be. I'd be forced into something that's not me.

"I think, you know, some of it has to do with [being] molested when I was growing up. And I think that, in a lot of ways, I was treated as the boy in the house. My dad talked about me as if I was a boy, his son, and we did boy stuff together. I really attached to that: that was a safe time, to be around my father, but when I was a girl it wasn't safe. Being treated like a girl, female, anything like that is very uncomfortable for me, because it makes me feel unsafe.

"Sometimes I still have a hard time with having a body that's pretty feminine. Breasts . . . I have hips, thighs . . . I have a feminine body. I think sometimes if women can't tell I'm a butch it's partially because my body type is fairly feminine. But I've seen some pretty curvaceous butches. Who made me think they weren't butches!

"I've talked to a lot of women who are butch dykes. They'll talk about not wanting to wear shorts. But I don't see shorts as feminine, particularly. Men wear shorts. I've certainly seen a lot of butches wear shorts, and they didn't particularly look like femmes simply because they were wearing shorts. But [for] the women I've talked to, it's [about] revealing parts of the body. They're more likely to be more feminine parts, you know.

"I didn't wear women's clothes until the last couple of years. The fact that I can do that now says that something's changed. My job makes it more changed. [Before entering management] I never shopped in a women's store. I buy fairly androgynous clothes, but to me, if it has buttons, it's a woman's jacket! When I first did it I felt, really, like people were going to laugh at me: a butch trying to dress up in women's clothes. I looked real strange. I felt strange. But now I don't feel strange, and I don't have to come home and change out of it, either.

"I didn't want to be a girl when I was a kid. I thought it was some kind of cruel mistake. I didn't want to have a penis, but I wanted to be a boy. I mean, I wanted to be a boy because I thought they had more exciting lives. I never really liked boys. I just didn't want to have breasts and get my period and all that stuff.

"It changed in my teens. At that age I started thinking maybe I was a boy, by accident. I had read something about where the kids who were hermaphrodites, they sex them at birth, and sometimes they make mistakes. They say, 'Okay, this is a boy,' and they make a mistake and it's a girl. So what do you do? And I thought, 'God, what if that was me? What if I really have male chromosomes and I was really a boy?' I was afraid of that. At that point I really didn't want to be a boy [any more].

"Your role is created when you're a kid, and that's what you are. I think everyone is a little to one or the other [butch or femme]. To me, it doesn't matter what you dress like: you are a role. I have a friend here, an older woman in the city, and everyone thinks that she's butch because she dresses real butch and she's aggressive. And to me there's no way this woman is butch, because [of] her body language. It's just the way she puts her hands on her head, you know? It's just little gestures like that, that say, ah, that's a real femme gesture. She came up in the bars in the era when roles were pretty well defined. Then, she was a femme. [Now] she's slicked back her hair, wears a tie and big boots. But she's a femme.

"I think that butch/femme is beyond what we see ourselves as. Beyond what we want to be, really. I have a friend who goes back and forth. She's a butch. She can say she's a femme; she's a butch. She'll go through a period where she'll say, 'I'm really a femme at heart. You don't understand: I think of myself as femme.' 'Okay, you're a femme at heart. Great. But you're a butch.' But we're not going to fight about it. Now she's a butch again, and she'll probably want to be a femme again for a while. The funny thing is, with her nothing even changes. She looks the same, dresses the same, does everything the same.

"I had a friend when I was in college . . . she was straight-up butch. And she was under a tremendous amount of family pressure and life pressure. We parted ways and the next time I saw her she was in nylons and heels and makeup. I honestly felt that she lost her mind. It was frightening. You know, it looked so unnatural to me. I felt really sad. She was dating men, too. I mean, the whole thing was really sad. She's a butch. She's still a butch. She wore makeup; she's dating men. But she's butch at heart. And all that makeup isn't going to change it.

"Sometimes people don't know what I am, because they picture butches being a lot harder than me or a lot different than me. [They take me as] one of those 'in the middle.' They have a whole different picture of what a butch is. I'm not that, so what am I? They don't know."

How did Sid think she differed from this standard representation of a butch? "Well, I'm not particularly handy. I don't fix shit. I think people don't see that image of butch as liking to read, being kind of intellectual. [You're supposed to be] into that kind of heavy stuff, which I think is a misrepresentation of butches, but nonetheless, people have this image of butches that they are construction workers and hang out in bars and ride motorcycles. I don't ride a motorcycle. I tried to. I got scared, so I didn't do it.

"Middle-class privilege gives one the privilege to pass a little bit more in this culture. I don't pass for straight, but I pass in other ways. I'm acceptable in certain ways that I know women who were raised working-class who are butch are not acceptable. I went through a drug program here. It's a big program, so there's a few lesbians there. Two of the lesbians were pretty butch. They had a harder time in the program than I did. People were less accepting of them. They had a little less class.

"I have these friends from Los Angeles. We used to talk about cultural differences: that maybe Jewish butches were a little different, because Jews' education is so emphasized that a lot of times people were not particularly good athletes. I mean, that's a generalization, but . . . Do good in schoolwork, read a lot, have good conversation, be able to argue. That kind of stuff was what was important in my family and [to] a lot of other Jewish dykes that I know. So consequently we didn't learn to fix things, and I didn't ever play a sport. I hated sports. I don't want to play softball. So I think those kinds of things make different kinds of butches."

Louise Romero: "They All Say I'm Femme, So I Go as Femme"

"I didn't think I was ever going to work. I was just going to have babies. In fact, I didn't worry about anything, because I always thought, 'Oh, I'll get married, have kids, and the guy will always bring home the money.' Cook, clean the house, maybe a little part-time job doing something. Now it's like I really got to keep a flow of steady money in my pocket, money in the bank above that, where I didn't think I really was going to have to take care of all that stuff on my own. [After coming out] I knew definitely, no one's going to support me.

"I had a boyfriend [in high school]. We had planned to get married and everything. But he was real pushy. Actually, he was real abusive. He didn't like me smoking cigarettes, or he didn't like me working on the cars. He went, 'It's not ladylike! It's not ladylike!' I go, 'But I want to!' 'It's not ladylike!' All he wanted to do was fuck all the time, and I'd tell him to go stick it in the light socket.

"I was trying to get rid of him. Meanwhile I was having an affair with this woman, thinking, 'Oh my god, what is this?' I didn't know I was a lesbian at the time. I just couldn't believe how attracted to her I was! When we first met, we didn't like each other. We almost got in a big fight. She hung around with the little hoods. I had this hat on because it was raining, and she took the hat and threw it on top of a pole. I called her a bitch and I said, 'Get my hat down. Who do you think you are?'

"I was real new. I'd just started high school, just got out of Catholic school, didn't know anybody because I didn't go to public school. So this woman did this, and I was real stubborn. I wasn't about to back down. Finally she shook the pole; the hat came down. But people were standing around: 'Hit her! Hit her! Hit her!' And it was like, 'Go ahead and hit me, bitch!' She never hit me. She just turned around and walked away, and then the next day she came up to me and started talking."

In her late teens, Louise's friend married. "She's always been into sports, so she knows a little bit of self-defense and she was showing me some moves. We were wrestling around. She said, 'Oh, you're not so tough!' All of a sudden I had her pinned down and I just kind of made a pass at her. She responded, and we started making out. Actually, we made out for a *long* time. It was kind of intense, because I was lying on top of her. Then we were staring at each other. And then when I realized she was looking at me, I eased up, and she didn't push me off. I mean, she could have, because I let go. So it was more like I let go and at the same time she was pulling me toward her.

"And then her husband drove up and we just sat there. We weren't doing nothing; we were really scared. The next day we talked about it and we decided we liked it. We did it again. We'd go to the movies together. Our boyfriends would go to the snack bar and we'd make out in the car, or other kind of shit like that!

"Then finally I broke up with my boyfriend. I wasn't happy with guys. There was always things you couldn't do because you were a woman. And plus, I didn't like doing it. I didn't like that penis in me. It gave me an upset stomach! I found women's bodies are so much softer. Males seem to be so hard. They tend to be more rough or something. Even with my first boyfriend, I wasn't really attracted to him sexually. It was no *desire*. I wanted to feel orgasms, but I didn't want all this other stuff that came with it!"

Louise enrolled in beauty school, where she met two gay men. "They were the only ones that I knew. I came out to them eventually. I go, 'I can't go out to the bars because I'm not twenty-one. But I want to meet some women!' 'Oh, honey, come with us. They'll never know.' So we did.

"Philip was dressed in drag, and he brought his doll head. We had these little mannequin heads that you work on in beauty school. He dressed me pretty butch. I mean he stuck this leather jacket on me, stuff like that. I looked young then. I don't know how I got away with it. There were hardly any women [at the bar]. There was something like five women that were heavy-duty into more of the butch-type role. It was all right, but they didn't *speak*! They just sat there and drank. It was kind of intense. How do you approach all this? But at least I knew there was women out there.

"I was really happy, because I didn't have to worry. When I'd go to the women's bars when I first came out, I'd wear all this low-cut, sleazy stuff in style. You know: disco. See, I always worried about being around males and my tits and stuff. A lot of times I go out, I like to wear low-cut blouses, or I love not wearing my bra. I'd wear my T-shirts with my tits hanging out. I could dance and move around and I didn't have to worry about anybody grabbing me or trying to rape me or shit like that.

"I also never felt that [intense racism] among lesbian women in the community. Even if they're racist, they're not trying to be! That's what's funny. You know, they might say something, but I know it's no bad intention, or [that] they hate people of color. Because they just weren't taught, they just don't know.

"But sometimes they just think they know everything. I seen this one [white] woman with this [other] white woman talking about something that has to do with a *black* woman, and I think, 'Well, god, I don't even know shit like that. How am I supposed to know? I'm not black. You're not black. Why do you think you know everything?' This woman is such an asshole! She'd best learn to keep her mouth shut, that's what I tell her. Those kind, I just won't bother with. Unless I want to. If it feels safe, I'm willing, but if it doesn't feel safe to me, I won't do it.

"Most of my friends, they all say I'm femme, so I go as femme. Look, see, I've always been the same. I haven't changed my dress. I do like real pretty dresses: evening gowns, low-cut things. I do. But I hate high heels, so I can never wear those. I think male clothing is made better. Male clothes are more practical to wear, more convenient, more comfortable. If you think wearing T-shirts and Levis are butch. . . . I like dressing up and putting on makeup, too, when I go out. So I don't know if you consider that femme.

"In bed I've never had any butch/femme roles. I've heard about a few stories of women doing that, but I don't like doing that. Sometimes I'm a little aggressive, sometimes I'm not. Sometimes I like the opposite, sometimes I don't.

"I did date a woman that dressed rough and always marched around with the muscles. As a matter of fact, she was a boxer. She had muscles like this! Of course, rode her motorcycle; always in the [gay pride] parade on her motorcycle. When she was at home, she swishes in the kitchen. She'd always cook and she'd swish. I said, 'You're so butch you swish!' The butcher they are, [the more] they have this little act. It's like they're such little, little, wimpy little things! That's what I've found. They're afraid of flies or something.

"The same thing with my other friend. She loves to pretend she's a butch. My best friend. She'll dress up and wear the tie and the whole bit and love it. She likes her lovers to wear dresses. And she's this little thing, can't even lift a hammer! 'I have the femmes do that.' I said, 'Oh, yeah, right.'"

Carolyn Fisher: "In Five Minutes, I May Want to Wear a Dress"

"My parents will say they're German before they say they're Cherokee Indian. So as I grew up, it was more being German than being Indian, from whatever reason they had. I think because society looks down on Indians as being drunks, as being lazy, no-good. Then when I was in junior high school I had gotten beaten up because I was German, because we had watched a Holocaust movie. I got teased a lot. That's when I started becoming more proud of being Indian. Just because of the way society said, 'Germans are mean. Germans are no-good people. Look what they did.' And listening to my great-grandmother talk about Indians. It really excited me. It made me proud of it. It was like Indians basically did good, to where the Germans basically were mean and rotten people with bad tempers! But now I'm proud of being both.

"You do applications, then if you put Indian they think you're full-blooded Indian, and if you put white . . . I don't like to put myself in the white category. Lots of times I don't feel white and I don't *look* white. If people ask me I'll tell them. A lot of people tend to think that I'm Latin because of my dark hair, my eyes, my complexion. So that's usually how people know who I am, is because they think, 'Are you Latin or Italian?' 'No. I'm German and I'm Indian.' It's not as important as people knowing that I'm gay. It is a big part of me, though.

"The people that I went to school with didn't dress up, so it made it easy for me to fit in. I think it had a lot to do with being in the country. You walk out and you get all dirty. Everybody basically wore jeans and casual things. The country's not really into fashion. There's nobody to be fashionable for! A lot of women [there], they *look* like dykes. But there, they just think you're an athlete. They think you're a tomboy. You're country! That's what you are, you're country.

"I think I learned a lot of things about myself [from coming out]. More things started coming to me. Like when I was younger, instead of playing with dolls I was out playing cowboys and Indians. I felt a relief. I felt like now this is who I'm really supposed to be. And now I don't have to go around and put makeup on if I don't want to.

"For me, it's like with a lot of gay women. You could just *look* at them and you go, 'They're gay.' Because it seems like a lot of gay women wear a lot of the same things. The jeans and flannel shirts and T-shirts. They just have that air to them. And that's how I feel like *I* am. I feel like a lot of people look at me and just say, 'She's a dyke.' And that's okay. I feel good with that. But I was a different person coming out of me, when I came out. Because when people used to say, 'Well, you're just a little dyke,' it's like, 'No! I'm a tomboy! I'm a tomboy, I'm *not* a dyke!' I think I got mad because I knew it was true.

"It was my attitude. The way I dressed. It was far from feminine! An 'I-don't-give-a-shit' attitude. This is who I am, and fuck you! Now that I look at it, it was more of a carefree attitude. More of a rough, tomboyish attitude. I wasn't out to impress people, *especially* men.

"My mind talks all the time. I have shit going through my mind all the time. I could *imagine* being with a woman, but then it was like, what am I going to do after that? How am I going to get married and have kids? I'm going to get hassled my whole life. Once again I'm going to be in rebellion. And once again I'm going against the grain of society. It was a hard decision, society-wise, for me. And when it really happened—when it came down to me knowing for sure after being kissed—it was like, yeah, this is what I like. I don't like men touching me, but I like for a woman to touch me. It was *reality*. And if people don't accept you, screw them! They're not your friends.

"I came out when I was around eighteen years old. I didn't know *no*body! In the straight community it doesn't seem like they [mind going] across age that much. But when you get to the gay community, what I've run across is, once I tell someone I'm nineteen years old, then it's like, 'Nineteen years old! You're too young. I don't want to mess with it. You got that energy that I can't deal with. It's like being with my little sister.' That's probably the hardest and most frustrating thing that I've come across. It's made me think twice of my sexuality.

"Come on, what is age? To me, age doesn't mean a lot. They're numbers. It's life experience, not age, that counts. And it's someone's heart, how good their heart is. How honest they are. Where were you when you were nineteen? I bet you were dating someone older. Because for me, it's hard to find people my age that's come out.

"I like dark-complected people, Latin people. And just casual. Not real feminine, not real butch. Somewhat like me. Athletic, intelligent. Just recently I used to be dating a couple of white girls. Which is really unusual, because of their backgrounds. 'Wow, I never went through this before! Going with a white girl.' And I had this thing in my mind to where lesbians aren't rich. Rich people aren't gay. Because I grew up having money. At first it was like, 'Oh, now you can't be gay!' But then after a while, the more it started sinking in that, yeah, I am gay, that meant that I had to break loose and do it on my own. That would mean that I'm not rich. And as I started meeting more [gay] women, there *was* women who were financially well-off."

After moving to San Francisco Carolyn had to support herself for the first time in her life, so she enrolled in a job-training program that placed women in blue-collar trades. "I could never picture myself working in the Financial District wearing a little dress, or sitting behind a desk doing paperwork all day. It'd drive me buggy! I want to be out moving around, being physical and building things and taking things apart.

"I don't like to go out with people who are really femme, because they want you to dominate them the whole time. It's like someone giving you all that power, and I'm not into that. And then I don't like someone real butch, because they intimidate me. I've met some really butch women, and it's like almost looking at a man. I don't like that.

"I think another part of why I'm gay is that I hate for someone to dominate me. Sometimes it's okay, but not all the time. I mean, I tried going with men when I was gay, and it was opening doors for me, walking me home. Ugh! Don't do this to me all the time! I don't like the old-fashioned way of dating. I feel like things should be equal. And that's the way most of my relationships have been.

"Most of the women I go out with could go either way. They like that equalness. And I enjoy that. Some people tease me: 'You are butch, but then you're not. You just can't make up your mind.' I don't feel like I should *have* to make up my mind with something like that. In five minutes I may want to wear a dress! Who knows? And in the next five minutes, I might want to just get totally butched out. I want that freedom to be able to do what I want. I find in the lesbian community there's a lot of labeling. You're a preppy, or you're butch, or you're femme. Why should I have to go to that? If I want to be casual, that's who I am.

"I've always been a little bit different than what people wanted me to do, and what people were supposed to do. If people were supposed to wear their hair long, I'd wear mine short. Coloring my hair, chopping it all off. I think it *would* be hard for me [to wear makeup and jewelry], because of the way a lot of the community sees lesbians as dykes: as rough and tough and motorcycles and leather and leaning to the butch side. But knowing my personality, I'd probably be like, 'Fuck it if you can't take a joke!'"

18

19

Guessing Games: Double Takes

Mari (Mary) + *macha* (the feminine of macho): a specifically Latina, and implicitly working-class, rendition of "dyke." Gossiped about but rarely glimpsed, *la marimacha* embodies an entire range of assumptions about what it takes to make a lesbian. To Marta Rosales's youthful eyes, *la marimacha* Pat was the only gay woman around, visible because she violated gendered expectations. More uniform than wardrobe, Pat's clothing conformed to classic representations of the 1950s street dyke. From her steel-toed boots to her slicked-back hair, her appearance flew in the face of prescriptions for middle-class white womanhood. Marta's reaction to Pat—fear strong enough to make her run away and hide—is a common one in stories that set up a confrontation between childlike innocence and representations of the Other. That first "real live lesbian" trots on stage as big bad butch, an intimidating creature of another order. But in Marta's case, childhood terror mixed with a retrospective dose of desire: "Nice arms, oh! I still remember that!"

Such is the power of representations that when Marta attempts to measure herself against the standard set by Pat, she can't find a place for herself in the picture. Do I have to wear chinos and roll up a cigarette pack in the sleeve of my T-shirt to be a lesbian? Do I have to be Anglo? Do I have to be tough? Do I have to be like her? If I'm attracted to women but a far cry from all of that, what am I? Marta was not sure whether *marimachas* really existed or whether Pat qualified as *marimacha* ("there was one—but she wasn't Hispanic"). *Marimacha* is culturally coded Latina, not just a Spanish translation of "dyke." How could Marta visualize herself as *marimacha*, if the one individual who seemed to bring the category to life was white?

Rather than attempt to regender herself to conform to these representations, Marta slowly began to modify her idea of what it meant to be gay. Encounters with different kinds of lesbians encouraged her to revise some of her original impressions. Imagine: a lesbian with a college degree (that is, not working-class) and "an IQ"! An entire range of gendered possibilities emerged.

Once it becomes obvious that not every lesbian is best described as *marimacha*, gendering recasts itself as a matter of intrigue and an open question. People avail themselves of new categories that elaborate gendered differences. As Marta tried to sort things out, she wondered what made someone femme or butch. Dress? Behavior (timidity, speech patterns, aggression)? Sexuality (oral sex, penetration, assertion, seduction, who's on top)? Emotions (passivity, expressiveness, independence)? Anatomy (the shape and size of breasts, hips, thighs)? Gesture? Occupation? Gender-coded activities? The "evidence" for classifying someone as one or the other tends to take the form of a set of standardized examples: tree-climbing; motorcycle-riding; wearing makeup or high heels; taking out the garbage; initiating sex. In the course of wondering whether particular individuals met these criteria, Marta also puzzled over how to interpret the criteria and even which ones to apply.

One of the first things people figure out when they begin to hazard a guess is that most "real live lesbians" (or heterosexuals, for that matter) do not fit neatly into gendered categories. Guessing games rely upon a problematic tendency to treat people as though they possess a consistent set of gendered "traits." But the world is not so easily divided into masculine and feminine, butch and femme. Louise Romero said she knew gay women who claimed they had never met a femme who worked on cars. In other words, they would define someone who engaged in that (butch-coded) activity right out of the femme category. How was Louise to reconcile the apparent contradiction in her love of mechanics *and* low-cut dresses? Louise's friends called her femme. Was she caught in a framework that forced a choice between two gendered terms?

Marta certainly felt trapped between representations. People found it hard to believe that she rode a motorcycle because they viewed her as quiet and responsible, a "good girl." For Marta, it was "this whole Madonna complex" that rendered her an enigma. The admittedly oversimplified notion of a Madonna complex—which posits "the Madonna" and "the whore" as the two basic positions open to Latinas—runs gendering through ethnic identity. Madonna and *marimacha* just don't jibe. But where did that leave Marta?

To complicate matters, many things are not gender-coded in any straightforward fashion. Sid Stein's comments on some butches' reluctance to wear shorts offer a case in point. In and of themselves, shorts are neither masculine nor feminine attire. Both men and women wear them. Only the feminization of bodies brought about when a particularly revealing article of clothing highlights hips and thighs brings this item into the realm of guessing games.

Then, too, there are aspects of the gendering of heterosexual relations that do not find a counterpart in butch and femme. Although it is not uncommon for older men to go out with younger women, Carolyn Fisher found the pain of rejection by older lesbians who considered her too young to date so intense that it "made me think twice of my sexuality." Louise, who had always expected a man to support her, did not transfer that expectation onto her female partners. And at the same clubs where Louise was taken aback by the silence of women she later identified as butches, she remembered the freedom of dressing as she pleased without worrying about someone raping her or refusing to take no for an answer. Their remarks provide another indication that the gendering of lesbian relationships stands in a complex relationship to gendering in the larger society.

People do not carry around gendered traits like a portable CD player or display them like the message on a favorite T-shirt. Gendered traits are called attributes for a reason: people *attribute* traits to others. No one possesses them. Traits are the products of evaluation.

Take the butch who's fond of bubble baths. If her secret passion becomes known, her friends *could* use this potentially discrediting piece of information to reclassify her as androgynous or femme. But they are much more likely to use it to tease her. Why? People tend to assimilate new material to the story already in place about an individual. Friends end up portraying the bubble bath as the humorous exception to the rule, rather than deciding that someone was a pseudobutch or closet femme all along.

But instances of recategorization do occur. When Sid toyed with the idea that anatomy should override dress or behavior for the purposes of assigning gender, reclassification became the name of the game: "I've seen some pretty curvaceous butches. Who made me think they weren't butches!" But she spoke with wry self-consciousness, since she had just finished describing the coexistence of her own butch identity with a "feminine" body.

People can subject attributes to endless interpretation and reinterpretation. Although women often cited initiating sex as a butch trait, seduction (surely a mode of initiating sex) qualified as femme. Disliking or declining sex was up for grabs in the gender sweepstakes. Players debating the finer points of butch/femme could have it both ways, calling upon one-dimensional representations of untouchable ("stone") butches who live for their femmes' pleasure, or "old-fashioned" femmes who lie there and take it.

Even Sid, who believed that butches "just are," also believed that butches are made. Growing up Jewish, she maintained, creates "different kinds of butches": "Sometimes people don't know what I am, because they picture butches as being a lot harder than me or a lot different than me." Although Sid contended that a lesbian did not have to be a jock to be butch, she realized that some people questioned her butch identity because she failed to conform to their preconceptions about what a stud should be. Her strategy? To call for more varied, culturally sensitive accounts of what it means to be butch.

Trafficking in the abstractions of gender traits artificially isolates gender from class, race, sexuality, ethnicity, and context. But none of these is discrete. When Carolyn first arrived in San Francisco, she had the impression that "rich people aren't gay." It took her a while to realize that she had fallen for a stereotype that links sexuality to class. Come to find out, queers are not all either unusually wealthy or down-and-out habitués of back-alley bars. In attempting to apply these images to her own situation, Carolyn remembered thinking that she couldn't be a lesbian because her parents owned their own business. (Surprise!) Likewise, when Marta predicted her attraction to a woman in sweatshirt and jeans over another in wool slacks and silk shirt, she was talking about a desire that combined class with gender and sexuality. Either outfit could come across as butch.

To grasp what's going on here, you need something more than gendered terminology, because forced dichotomies such as butch versus femme do not accommodate multiple lines of identification. With the single word "untraditional" Marta drew together race, ethnicity, gender, and sexuality in a way that underscored the shock value of her punchline: a Mexican-American family in which the *girl* buys the motorcycle. For Carolyn, childhood memories of playing cowboys and Indians became double-edged tools for figuring out "who I'm really supposed to be." How—or whether—she read herself into the category

"Indian" raises a host of questions about power and identification, even in play.

In Louise's account there is an important slippage between the initial claim that she had never encountered racism among gay women and her later allusions to racist incidents. "She'd best learn to keep her mouth shut," Louise advised regarding one white woman. "Those kind, I just won't bother with." A recurrent theme of safety and threat links Louise's discussion of her relations with men in general to the passages about relating to Anglo lesbians.

Informing all these discussions are elements of race, class, and ethnicity already built into the gendered representations with the widest circulation. Louise's rendition of femme departs radically from the middle-class assumptions built into Marta's first impressions of femme ("dependent, and very into helplessness"). For Louise, defending herself in a schoolyard scrap was perfectly compatible with femme, because in her working-class neighborhood, the ability to fight didn't necessarily mark you as a tomboy or dyke. Many people said that butches were supposed to be physically active, construction worker types—all the things that Sid, with her fear of motorcycles, was not. By reworking butch to encompass the intellectual as well as the athlete, Sid interpretively linked education to Jewish identity in a way that counters images of butch as white, Christian, working-class. Street theorist that she was, Sid could not help but note the irony of using oversimplified representations of what's Jewish to counter generalizations about what's butch.

Coining the phrase "butch et cetera" was Sid's way of expanding the term beyond the fuzzy edges supposed to mark the boundaries of butch. There are other strategies to close the gap between self-perception and gendered representations. A person can edit inconsistencies out of her narratives, like the woman who goes into great detail about her softball team and her welding trade but who "forgets" to tell new friends that she was once a high school cheerleader. A person can try to locate herself along a continuum from "more butch" to "more femme." Like Louise, she can accept other people's evaluations for what they're worth. Or she can launch herself into perpetual motion like Marta, tacking back and forth between femme and butch. In that case, she may define herself relative to a lover. The old adage that opposites attract, combined with the assumption that butch and femme are always defined *as* opposites, explains how people could take Sid for femme when she appeared at a wedding alongside an even "butchier" friend.

Women also argued for paying attention to context. Just because driving a motorcycle is a butch signifier, Marta protested, does not mean that everyone's interest in motorcycles relates to gender. According to Carolyn, rough mannerisms might indicate a country girl rather than another dyke-in-the-making.

(Note, though, that the urban/rural contrast, like all dichotomies, oversimplifies by representing every city dweller as a white-collar worker with a desk job who never has to worry about getting her clothes dirty.) Their comments underscore the importance of asking what things mean and noticing how meanings shift, rather than treating people as collections of petrified "traits."

If you're going to play guessing games, you might as well enjoy yourself. Marta's story about a pink motorcycle helmet drew a lot of laughs because she juxtaposed the color that symbolizes femininity with the machine that signifies toughness. After all, the woman saw herself moving between femme and butch. Why should she pretend otherwise? A "masculine" symbol here, a "feminine" symbol there. . . . Let that pink helmet be a lesson to anyone who tried to stick her with a matching set of gender traits.

Sid had no more interest than Marta in tying up gender neatly with a ribbon and a bow. As a child she wondered whether she might be a hermaphrodite. Often people who are intersexed possess a version of both male and female genitals. But "I didn't want to have a penis," Sid insisted. "I just didn't want to have breasts and get my period and all that stuff." So she bent the medical literature to her own imaginative ends.

Louise derived her pleasure from counterexamples. "You're so butch you swish," she admonished her date, a woman who enjoyed cooking in the privacy of her own kitchen after flexing her muscles in public. Marta took delight in the turnabout that placed *la marimacha* Pat in a position of authority over Marta's father. A complicated negotiation of gender, race, class, and sexuality characterized this relationship: "She respected him as a worker, but he looked down at her for being a dyke." A Chicano worker answering to an Anglo boss challenges little about the power relations that structure labor markets in the United States, but a lesbian (and a butch one at that) supervising a man in a blue-collar job is turnabout indeed. Carolyn thought she would have a hard time wearing makeup and jewelry precisely because the most common representations of gay women are masculinized. Yet she responded with a power play: It's my prerogative to challenge your expectations of me and throw them back in your face.

In contrast to these anecdotes of playfulness and transgression, much of the repartee about gendered differences is organized by the erroneous presumption that people can be determined to be absolutely, unequivocally, essentially, irrevocably butch, femme, androgynous, or what have you. There's lots of cultural reinforcement for tracking down one's "true" self (whatever that means). But even four narratives give ample indication that people are not that consistent and their identifications aren't limited to gender. Why, then, continue to play the game?

A hidden stake in guessing games is the power to claim the insight or expertise to determine who's who. Take Sid's friend—the one who called herself femme but whom Sid insisted upon characterizing as a butch dressed up in women's clothes. Did Sid catch something her friend missed when it came to gender? Or was Sid's friend whatever she considered herself to be? How about the woman who says she doesn't like the way that the terms "femme" and "butch" flatten out her experience, but whose friends argue that "anyone can tell" she plays fluff (femme) to her partner's stud (butch)?

These are questions of voice and authority endemic to identity politics. (Compare Louise talking about white women talking about African-American women: "Even I [as a woman of color] don't know shit like that. . . . [Anglo women] think they know everything!") Are people the best judges of their own minds and experiences? Who can speak for whom? Just how transparent is experience, anyway? Rather than being self-evident, isn't "experience," as historian Joan Scott has argued, open to conflicting interpretations?

When all is said and done, no one has the inside track on the gendering of lesbian relationships. There is no consensus about what makes someone butch or femme, because there can't be. The search for gender traits is never-ending, because there are no traits lying in wait to be discovered. But that doesn't make gendered categories such as femme and butch meaningless. Gendering is produced in social interactions and shaped by representations. Louise rejects a boyfriend who pressures her to stop working on cars. Carolyn searches for words to describe her first date with a white woman. Marta imagines gendering herself differently in relation to different lovers. Sid ranks body language over dress as an index of gendered differences.

Guessing games may be part of the process of creating and recreating gender, but that does not account for their popularity. What seduces people into looking for an authentic answer to the questions, What are you? and Who is she, *really*? Some of the power and much of the enjoyment lies in the playing of the game. Like Carolyn Fisher, many people have minds that talk all the time when they try to place one another with respect to gender. Where they find their answers and what they use as evidence have as much to do with history as with idle talk.

Chapter 2 Metro Retro

What better way to debunk the myth that all lesbians are male wannabes than by rejecting "roles"? During the 1970s lesbian-feminists attempted to convince anyone who would listen that butch/femme was nothing more than a twisted imitation of straight relationships. Outdated and oppressive, "roles" had become a thing of the past. The new buzzword was "androgyny," a celebration of sameness and gender-blend that presumed "women-loving-women" had a common gender which automatically gave them something *in* common. Few spoke about the possibility that relationships between women could be differently gendered. When they did, they usually held those conversations in secret, sometimes no more than the self speaking to the self.

This dismissal of "roles" as an unwelcome carryover from the 1950s had an impact on queer communities that extended well beyond lesbian-feminist circles. Many are the stories of the travails that awaited a woman in heels who dared to walk into one of the lesbian bars of the period. But just when butch/femme seemed to be a thing of the past, the so-called butch/femme revival of the 1980s hit urban areas on the East and West coasts. Activists and academics launched the sex wars, heated debates about butch/femme, sado-masochism, and other marginalized aspects of lesbian sexuality. The relationship between sexuality and power came under new scrutiny. Categories such as "femme" and "butch" that once represented an accommodation to heterosexuality now appeared to have subversive potential. Precisely because statements about gendered differences in same-sex relationships were disconcerting, they could signify in-your-face instead of in-your-place.

Some said butch/femme had emerged from a decade-long closet, having been there all along. Some said butch/femme had assumed unpredictable and unprecedented forms. When Carolyn Fisher in her torn-up jeans characterized gender as a free-for-all, as much about switch as swish, she seemed to typify this new thinking: "In five minutes, I may want to wear a dress." By the mid-1980s gender was back with a vengeance, and with it, new opportunities for pleasure and resistance.

Or so the story goes. But should this microwave version of the recent history of lesbian sexuality be taken at face value? Why are the 1950s associated so strongly with "tradition," that imaginary baseline of a time-without-change from which change is supposed to start? Why do certain gendered practices get assigned to the 1950s and 1970s, others to the 1980s or 1990s, but hardly any to the 1960s? What gets left out? Is there any room for class and color in this sanitized telling, except as an afterthought? What about the relationship between gendering in lesbian "communities" and gendering in the larger society? Or the impact of the telling itself?

Doesn't every story about a past help construct a "tradition," a "community," an ours and a yours, a now and a then, a time when things were supposed to be better and a time when things were worse? At stake are issues about not only how gendering has changed but also how narratives remake gender as they remake history. And whose history will it be? A history for white girls? For feminists? For people of color? For queers of all colors? For churchgoing rebels, litigating lieutenants, tax payers and tax resisters? For women with phrases that chip away at customary notions of occupation or ethnicity or politics? What are the consequences for gendered identities such as "androgynous" and "femme" when so many stories take the form of a journey from here to there? And just why are so many storytellers eager to mark themselves off as different from the ones who came before?

Julia Benoit: "Now She Has Long Nails and Nail Polish"

"One day I came home [to the army barracks]. I had the best area, because I had taken as many lockers as I could. I had a little chair there and my stereo. I walk in. She's sitting with this woman on her lap and they're making out on my chair! I'm going, 'Hmm, that was two women, and they're in my area.' I wanted to run and tell somebody. I thought it was exciting. So I said, 'Do you mind? Would you move?' And then they went to bed! The lights were out. My bed's right here, and her bed's right there. I hear them kissing, and I can't believe [it]. I just thought it was rude. I mean, if it were two men, or a man and a woman, I would have thought, 'They shouldn't be doing this when I'm here. Couldn't they wait till I fall asleep?' I don't think I heard too much more than that. But I thought, you know, here I got to see some homosexuals!"

The woman in the next bunk, whose desire for women caught Julia by surprise, was married. Nothing like Julia's friend J. T., who had entered basic training wearing T-shirts and jeans. J. T. was "different than the other girls. I mean, she wasn't girlish, and she liked to have fun. I was attracted to her. She was a little flirtatious. Not flirtatious; I guess it was just a playfulness with another girl that I didn't experience before. When I found out she had a boyfriend, I was really surprised. He was not this person that you would think anybody actually would go out with. And so I remember thinking that it was a front: she wasn't really boyfriends with this guy."

Shortly after Julia's release from military service she had a three-way affair with a married couple. A few months later she accompanied a friend to a lesbian bar. "I do remember going, 'Oh, I suppose I'm a femme,' and feeling a little resentment. Because I was going on appearances, and I was convinced that anybody there is going to think I'm a femme. That made me uncomfortable, thinking that. 'Oh, everybody thinks they can pick me up.' Because I had long hair, not a very tough build, I guess, and the clothes I wore were not real butch."

Like many white women who came out into lesbian-feminism during the 1970s, Julia soon cut her hair. "Even though I [later] changed a lot of the way I dressed and carried myself, I really feel like the way I changed was not because I wanted to fit into a more butch role but because in realizing my feminism I let go of a lot of things that I had been socialized into. Things that I didn't like, so why should I [do them]?" She believed that her new haircut made people take her more seriously. But she still felt "put down" by her girlfriend's roommates for being "too much of a femme."

"[Back then we were] looking at men as the enemy. [We had] the idea that you have to be careful every step, from not wearing nails because they made you less capable of doing something, to not wearing necklaces because it's a good way for someone to grab you." By the mid-1980s, Julia's "new" style had altered only slightly, but her old girlfriend's appearance had "changed so drastically. Now she has long nails and nail polish and she's completely femmed out! Doing things that we had felt very radically against in our younger years, as feminists."

Melissa Simpson: "No Self-Respecting Butch Would Have Worn Lingerie in 1972"

"In the 1980s at some point a discussion of butch/femme started being possible again. That was not possible with any kind of freedom in the 1970s. I think in the 1970s, those of us who thought of ourselves as butch and femme thought that we were sort of throwbacks to a heterosexually identified world. There was something a little bit bad about us. That the real good feminists and lesbians totally had nothing to do with butch/femme roles.

"Part of [the lesbian-feminist analysis of] butch/femme was that we were imitating, which is such a superficial explanation for a pretty complex phenomenon. That was the line, always: well, they were just imitating heterosexual roles. You can read that in a half dozen books that were written between 1970 and 1980. 'She just wants to be a man!' And that's funny, you know . . . I don't think I've ever known any butches who wanted to *be* men. That never seemed what it was about at all. In fact, most of them didn't *like* men very much.

"I felt the difference in the Bay Area when I moved back here in 1984. Somewhere between 1980 and 1984 there had been a shift in the Bay Area in people's willingness to identify as butch or femme, and talking about it, spoofing the roles, dressing up that way. For the first time I saw women wearing nail polish, women wearing dresses, women wearing spike heels and hose, women wearing lipstick. That would never have happened in the 1970s. Not in the groups that I was around.

"See, butches had always all along been able to spoof their roles and dress up. Butches all along wore tuxedos, wore men's slacks, men's shoes, etc. But femmes, if you were in the movement, femmes never felt free to wear dresses, etc. I can remember the first skirt I wore to a lesbian event: a Judy Grahn book party opening in 1981. And how much courage it took for me to do that. How nobody else was doing that in my group at the time. And how much comment it elicited."

Leaning back into the pillows on the sofa in her office, Melissa Simpson paused to reflect upon the path that had taken her from midwestern origins to one coast and then the other. The daughter of a self-employed mechanic, she had grown up poor and white in a rural area where her love of books left her feeling like she never quite belonged. Education offered a way out. After completing course work for a graduate degree in the late 1960s, she moved east with her husband and two children.

"I had always thought that I liked men far better than women, that women were stupid and trivial. I had always been in [academic] departments in which there were no other women, or very few other women. So I had spent my life around men. And to find out that women were exciting, interesting, attractive, enjoyable, was great. So I decided I didn't want to be married any more, and that I wanted to be independent and be on my own and see if I was a lesbian.

"The lesbian world at that point [c. 1970] seemed to be divided up into butch and femme. At least in the bars. I had to start thinking about who did I identify with psychologically. When people would say, 'When you were little, did you identify with Robin Hood or Maid Marian, or did you identify with Peter Pan?' I always identified with the *female* character," she laughed. "So I *thought* of myself as femme."

In the women's groups Melissa joined, "There was a lot of talk and a lot of thinking about butch/femme and roles. We weren't your androgynous 'there's no roles; we don't talk about roles' type feminists. *Our* group wasn't. I think that's largely because of the influence of two or three 'old gay' women who were in the [group]. If there hadn't been that influence, we would have probably been more like work boots, jeans, and work shirt type people. But we weren't. We weren't downwardly mobile. We weren't hippies. We were part of a more spiffier crowd.

"Out of twelve of us, all of whom went on to become leaders of other women's institutions, nine people identified as butch. Three people identified as femme. And there was a definite feeling in the early women's movement, as far as *I* was concerned, that being butch was better. That *real* lesbians were butch. And that it was better not to identify as femme. It was better to try to be androgynous. Women in the bars were very identified along butch/femme roles, and there was no problem whatsoever. But women in the bars were not feminist. My primary social group weren't women who were in the bars.

"At that point I didn't feel good about identifying as femme. So I would not have said I was a femme out loud much to anybody. I mean, I thought that secretly. My lover thought that. My lover thought that she was only attracted to femmes. But I wouldn't have been very vocal about that identity.

"The first five years that I was out, I felt like there was something wrong with me that I was femme and identified as femme. I spent a lot of time *trying* not to be that way: trying to have larger gestures, trying to have a longer stride, trying not to look like a girl, trying not to run like a girl, trying not to throw like a girl. There was a lot of positive stuff [in the women's movement] on carpentry and softball and nontraditional jobs and roles for women. I think that it was hard for women who identified as femme to feel good about themselves in that situation. At least it was hard for *me*.

"It's an interesting issue I'm sure that you will wrestle with all the way through the book: How is it that psychologically women pick up on whatever cues there are, however subtle they are, that says, 'This person is butch' and

'This person is femme'? I mean, when I look back on my life I think I almost always choose femmes as best friends. And yet I find other femmes extremely attractive. I don't know if I can say this across the board, but I don't feel sexually attracted to people that I identify as femmes. And *rarely* do I find other women attracted to me unless they identify themselves as butches.

"There's a wide variation there of how strongly *identified* with being butch they are. I think that butch identity in this culture is a much more difficult one than a femme identity. It stands so far apart from the feminine role. So I think that you might have a butch who the world would say would be very butch, but she might not identify, or feel very good about that, and so try to appear more feminine.

"One of the women that I lived in a communal house with was an 'old gay' woman who had been butch but who had fallen in love with somebody who was butch, which you could not do [at that time]. So she became femme. When you saw pictures of her when she was femme, she had a beehive hairdo and heels and stockings and the whole business. And I swear, she was the butchest person that I knew. I mean, she looked like a man! In the picture, she looked like a woman. Although if I'd been around her physically, she might have looked like she was in drag. I don't know. It could have been. But what was so startling to me was that you wouldn't have seen that wide variation, I don't think, between a middle-class butch and a middle-class femme in the 1970s. They would have been closer, on either side, to androgyny in terms of the physical, gender-identifying way they dressed.

"There used to be a joke among working-class women that a middle-class butch would be a working-class femme. I think that there's some degree of class differences in how butches and femmes present themselves and think of themselves. And what's important, what traits are important to a butch. Or probably even a femme.

"I think there are a lot of middle-class butches who don't see physical competence in the world as part of their butch identity. So they don't think that doing carpentry or being handy around the house is an integral part of their butch identity. They might be good at that or not good at it. I think that among working-class butches, it becomes more central to seeing yourself as butch. That may be because working-class people work more with their hands and middle-class people work more with their minds. So that a middle-class butch may think of her competence in the intellectual area or whatever as more important.

"For the first time in my life, now, I'm involved with a middle-class woman. And I find myself much better at what I had considered typical butch tasks than she is. I'm better mechanically, etc. And that's really a difference.

Because when I was with working-class women, they were always better at those kinds of tasks that had to do with physical competence.

"How *I* identify myself as femme is very different than how people *see* me. I think that people see me as fairly androgynous, and toward the middle in terms of how I dress, etc. But I think *I* would probably identify myself as more femme than other people see me as. So I would probably put myself more like three or something [on a scale from one to ten where one is femme]." I asked Melissa whether she perceived any class differences in terms of the people who viewed her as more androgynous than femme. "Yes, that's probably true, now that you mention it. I think, yes, that middle-class women would be more likely to see me as androgynous. In fact, I think that sometimes in terms of the way that middle-class butches dress, that they might dress closer to the way I do, than I am to the way working-class femmes might dress.

"A lot of working-class women that *I* was around in the 1970s had a less refined way of dressing that looked less female than middle-class butches. They might have been more likely to have been mistaken as male. And for a lot of butches that I knew in the 1970s, that was important. They didn't want to be seen as traditional women. They thought of traditional women, and heterosexual women, as weak, and they didn't admire them.

"I think that butches, generally speaking, are conflicted about femmes. I think that on the one hand, they look up to anybody who can pass, or has the ability to pass, as straight. On the other hand, I think they *hate* that. They hate that they can't pass, don't want to pass, have pride that they don't, can't, and look down on somebody who can. So it's a very conflicted feeling. I'm always surprised when I find out how much self-hatred butches have. How I *perceived* them as identifying seemed to have a lot more pride in it than what I hear them saying lately.

"In the early 1980s you would hear people say, 'Well, you don't see the butches going back to being straight, or going back to men.' Well, that's not true. I happen to personally know a number of butches, including one of my ex-lovers, who have gone back to being with men. But I think the general perception was that femmes were less trustworthy, that femmes had an easier time passing, that femmes could go back to being straight in a way that butches never could. That a path toward heterosexual privilege was cut off from butches."

When I asked Melissa if her sense of self as femme had ever fluctuated in relationship to different lovers, she smiled. "No. And you know, I think it's because I have some investment in thinking of my lovers as butch. My present lover seems to think that I think that she's a lot more butch than *she* thinks she is. So I don't know whether that's because she doesn't want to be as butch as I think she is, or because I really *need* to see that. There's something sexually more interesting to me about women I identify as butches. I see it as being more closely related to desire, sexual desire, than it is related to sex roles.

"I don't know how being femme relates to what you do in bed, because . . . I mean, there is that old saying of 'butch on the streets, femme in the sheets.' And the meaning of that always was that women who were more aggressive in their external lives were more passive in bed. I would say that in every relationship that I've been in, I've been more sexually aggressive than the butch that I was with. I've probably taken more initiative around sexuality, been more open around experimentation around sexuality, probably determined the tone of the sexual relationship more. I don't know if that's typical for femmes at all.

"I mean, at one point I thought [butchness] was about that physical competence in the world, but then my lover now is so incompetent in the world, it's not that, clearly! Boy, it is really elusive. It really is. It's something about difference, but I don't know what it is. Because I don't think there's any single set of behaviors or way of being that I can point to and say, 'Oh.'

"I don't think that my internal experience of thinking and feeling myself to be femme has changed much over the years. And my behaviors have changed a lot. I mean, I'm a whole lot more competent in the world now than I was twenty years ago when I came out. Sheer living! Maybe if I had a husband who supported me, I wouldn't be! I have never felt, myself, that being femme cut off any possibilities for me at all. Now, I have known butches who have felt that, being butch, they couldn't 'x.' And I think I have more stereotypes about who butches are than I do about femmes.

"Among 'old gay' women of a generation before me, who they were in terms of butch and femme got set earlier in life, and it got set more rigidly. I've definitely seen people become, quotes, 'less butch.' And by that I mean I've seen people gain a wider range of feeling that was available to them, [so] that other people would put them more on the feminine side. As a result of feeling okay about themselves, a result of personal growth, going to therapy, whatever. I've seen people become less rigid, more willing to try out new things that they might not have tried before. Like more willing to wear lingerie, which no self-respecting butch would have done in 1972. I think there's that fluidity in *behavior*. I don't know to what degree there is fluidity in self-identity."

"I've never thought of myself as particularly feminine. The fact that I'm small—you know, I have small hands and small feet or whatever, short—it seemed to be that people would think I was feminine. But *I* had never thought of myself as particularly feminine. I'd *always* thought of myself as femme. But all the butches I've ever been with have thought of me as feminine. And they found that erotic, they found that attractive. So I don't know."

Raye Porter: "Honey, You Can Do That Yourself"

"Women are starting to feel good about being femme and being butch, and being out there and socializing, and having a good time with it. It's not so terrible. A lot of the behavioral stuff that was not good is no longer expected or tolerated. I could not see myself going out to a bar and walking up to someone who was quote-unquote 'butch,' and ask them, can I dance with their lady. I mean, *that*, to me, is not what I would do. Or be an escort type. That kind of relationship where, 'This is my woman. You better not ask her to dance.' You know, fetch and carry, let me go get the coats, let me drive the car, let me light your cigarettes. 'No, honey, you can do that yourself.' What people call that role stuff where you identify like *down* butch. Absolutely not. I never could act like that because somebody would shoot me if I tried! And anyway, I don't even think it's necessary.

"I haven't read a lot of lesbian history, but my feeling of what I can just remember is that at certain times, those roles were necessary for people to be able to identify themselves as lesbians. Also for mutual protection. Also because that was what the standard was and that was what other folks were doing at the time. As times changed and we gained more freedom and we came out more, we didn't have to do that, behave that way.

"But how do you tell somebody that? Unless you're a close friend. [Then] I can sit around and we can kick it, and I can share that with them. It's really nice to be able to act as a mentor for young lesbians of color who are coming out. It's an opportunity for them to get an idea that [it's okay to] do whatever you want. I think they've been given the wrong story."

At the age of 40, Raye jokingly called herself "the last of the true butches." Why, I asked, was a butch identity so important to her if times had changed since the early days of butch/femme? "Coming out and then being in touch with myself as a butch was like freedom: freedom to act the way I always [wanted]." Raye's foster parents had considered activities like bike riding improper for a girl from a religious household in a "close-knit black neighborhood" in Northern California. "I may have worn dresses and have tried to do like I was brought up to, but I never felt comfortable. I would always see myself in a whole different way than the way I was acting.

"It took me a while—it takes us all a while—to really settle on that [butch identity] and say, 'This is who I am and I'm going to feel comfortable with that.' There was a time when I felt bad. I mean, people can make you feel *bad*. When prevailing opinion in the lesbian community is that you are fucked up, then that makes you feel bad. I never thought of changing. I thought about maybe hiding out in the house and maybe not going out as much, and not being social, only socializing with people who were a lot like me.

"Before I grew dreads, I had very short hair. I've had people say, 'Oh, Mr. So-and-So,' or something like that, to me, which is not very nice. Doesn't make you feel very good. It was just someone who hadn't looked close enough. It denies who you are. It makes you feel like someone just doesn't even see you.

"I know there's certain jobs that I would never be able to get, no matter how competent I am. I would have to change who I am, the way I am, in order to get those jobs. I'd be there a week and they'd throw me out on my ass. They'd say, 'What's this woman doing with her feet up on the desk with a skirt on?' So, in that way, I'm discriminated against because of the clothes I wear. At this point in my life I would say I'm absolutely not willing to make that trade-off. Now, I'll tell you this: if I needed to [change] for the child, that is the only way. If my daughter needed something.

"As society changes and the mood becomes more conservative, or there's a witch hunt, I would change to survive. But that's the only way I can see myself changing. Only as a survival mechanism, but not because I want to be more accepted. Because as long as the folks around me, my friends, the people I work with, of course my daughter, if those folks accept me, then everybody else can go to hell. I have food, I have a place to stay. If they don't pay my rent, I don't care very much about what they think. So it's hard, but you know, it can't be helped.

"I've been places where every woman in the room, *every* woman in the room, had on a dress except for me. But I went anyway. I dressed the way I dressed. But it does make it difficult, and sometimes your issue and the people you represent suffer for it, which isn't fair."

In another sense, though, Raye believed that a butch presentation had operated to her advantage in her work. Before an important meeting, she would consciously visualize herself as stud. "It's like, 'Okay, I'm ready. Kick ass and take names. This is it. I have my shit together absolutely.' It's a level of self-confidence, it's a level of tone in your voice, the way you walk into a room, how people perceive you as being *business*. And this is bad, but I could go into a room and be prepared, and a woman I work with who's femme could go in the same room, and people won't pay her any attention. Absolutely none. But they will defer to me and say, 'Well, Raye, what do *you* think?'

"Raising a child on welfare and being treated the way I was, I always said that if I ever got an opportunity, I'd go back and I'd make those people pay. They'd wish that I had never gotten out of law school. Every day of my life I'd think, 'I'm going to change the way that poor women are treated.' Now [that I have my law degree] one of the things is the way people who come to my office see me. It's humorous, because I think they wonder, 'Who the hell is this little lesbian?' They can't quite get it. 'You're a lesbian but you have a daughter. How can you have a daughter if you're a lesbian?' You have to explain it.

"My daughter is a lot different from me. I always wanted her to have a basketball scholarship to a certain school. My daughter never played basketball. She's very femme, long fingernails, the makeup, the whole nine yards. Early on, when she was younger, obviously we had a few times when she wanted me to dress up and change the way I looked to come to school or to an open house, and I wouldn't do it. I was real clear with her. I guess there was a year that I didn't go to any parent-teacher things. Then she got a little older, and she said, 'Mama, would you please come? I don't care, just come. I like the way you look. It's all right.' And after that, we didn't have any problems.

"You know, most kids just think of you as their mom, and she thinks of me as her mom. Of course, she'll tell you, 'My mom's a butch. God, look at my mom: my mom would never wear *that!*' She certainly knows my taste better than I do. But still, when she was sick, I was there. When she had major decisions to make in life, I was there. I work hard, I've taken care of her, and that's what counts to her.

"I have a good friend who's a little older than me who was very much someone who would not think of washing a dish or changing a diaper if there was a child around. But for me personally, I've always had to be a self-reliant person. I grew up in a situation in foster homes where we were expected to cook and clean.

"I remember one relationship I was in, and the woman I was in the relationship with was very femme, and *her* expectations of what I should do around the house were quite different from what I was used to doing. It was like, 'Okay, I'm gonna move the furniture in the living room.' I'm supposed to come and move the couches and chairs and shit. I'm going, 'What is this? I'm supposed to do all of that and you gonna stand over there and point while I move the furniture?' I did it because I was in love. 'Yes dear, you want me to carry those clothes out to the car? No problem.' But it was strange.

"In couple relationships with women who were really, really, really femme, that sort of forces you to be more butch, only because you're trying to satisfy their concept of you. The relationships I've felt the worst in were with women who are really wanting me to be butcher, because they're femme and they want that kind of relationship. I feel real uncomfortable in those kinds of relationships, actually. Because most the time, I'm just a slug. I am who I am and I do what I do, and I really don't want to be forced to be butcher in a relationship to make someone feel femmier, or to set up that role.

"I've been in a certain relationship where sexually I was supposed to be the aggressive party. The woman I was with wants to sort of lay there. I was supposed to do everything. I obviously hadn't any sexual desire myself except to satisfy her, and that's what I worked toward, and that was not good.

"I think with another butch it's much easier sexually to experiment, to do different things. Both parties can say what they want. There's not that idea that 'I'm a vessel waiting to be filled.' I *hate* that. I really hate that. It causes major fights. It's like, 'Oh no, girlfriend, I am *not* doing this all night! No, no. You are gonna have to do something yourself. Roll over, please!'

"I just think with another butch it's not like that, because it's a shared experience," Raye explained, gesturing toward the sound of the television in the other room where she and her lover had been watching a football game when I arrived. "You can be as aggressive or passive as you want to be in a given time. It has this almost simple quality to it. It does have a little bit of, 'Ooh, we're doing something *wrong*.' You know, 'Ooh, two butches!'

"A lot of times with women who are femme and think that way, even if they understand that sex is mutual, making love is mutual, [it's still] very passive, very passive sex. If you are too aggressive and you're being too butch, it's frightening, and then you get into the 'male-identified' and all this stuff again. When you're in a relationship with someone like that, it makes you feel like they don't see you as another woman. It's like they see you as a woman—they want you to be sort of like a woman—a man/woman, or something. They want you to be a woman who acts like a man, rather than a woman who acts like a woman. That's uncomfortable. That's more than uncomfortable: it's unfortunate.

"In my own experience—that's all I can talk about—with other butches, there's room to be aggressive, there's room to be gentle, there's room for mutual satisfaction. It's not just, 'Me, I'm gonna lay here until I come and then I'm gonna go to sleep.' But then again, I have friends who are butch who would never think of [being touched]. 'Don't you even talk about going down on me! Are you *crazy*? I'll *kill* you!' Yes indeedy. Absolutely do not want that: 'Don't touch me. That's not your role.'"

The important thing, Raye believed, was to have a fixed identity. "I don't think you can be a butch for a night. I think you can try to imitate a butch for a night. Because certainly I think, if I ever had that feeling, I could put on a dress and high heels and go out for a night. But it wouldn't change who I was, basically. I think that if you had never met me before, and you saw me that way, I think you would have some indication by the way I conduct myself that, 'Hey, hmm. What's this thing doing in a dress?' The femmes, I don't think any of them could be butch for a day, and the butches couldn't be femmes for a day. Please! The femmes would gang up on them and run them out of town!

"As long as lesbians and gay people are oppressed, I want folks to make a commitment. I don't care if you're straight. I don't care if you're a lesbian. I don't care if you're gay. I just want you to be something, because when the shit hits the fan, I want to know which side my friends are on. I think people who can go back and forth so easily will tend to do that when push comes to shove. They'll choose a side that's not going to be in the middle of the crossfire.

"Being African American and being decisive, knowing who you are, is that part of [being butch]? Because of racism and because of class, one of the things you have to do is you have to have a consciousness. You have to be conscious of who you are in the world. You also have to know culturally who you are, and then you have to go out and you have to *do* something. Your conduct must display that you have knowledge of this. So I think that's part and parcel of it, is that you have to know who you are in this country.

"I think working-class folks and I think people of color are much more likely to *have* to make a decision [about being femme or butch] because of what they've experienced in the past. When you have privilege, you don't *have* to decide. You can be whatever you want to be. Here today, gone tomorrow.

"African Americans who are not in touch with their culture and not in touch with who they are, are people who are having the problems, who are having a difficult time surviving. Because of skin color no one's going to mistake you, and if you don't know you're black and everybody else does, you're in a shit's creek without a paddle. If I'm out there in the world, and everybody else thinks I'm butch and I think, 'Oh, I'm just one of [the girls]. I'm not femme, just fish'—bad term, I hate that term, but you don't mind, do you?—you're gonna get *slaughtered*. You're gonna get slaughtered.

"Once you decide this is who I am, this is what I'm doing, then you can conduct yourself that way, and you can defend that position, and people will have to deal with you straight out. But as long as I'm muddled in my thinking, it muddles everybody around me, and it makes it hard for me to survive. Once there's no oppression you can be whatever you want. Same thing I taught my daughter. I said, 'Look, if black people weren't oppressed, you can go out and be a beach bum. As long as black people are oppressed, you owe an obligation to your race to get an education and come back.'"

Metro Retro: Double Takes

If young women of color have gotten the wrong story about fluff and stud, as Raye Porter suggested, it is not because there is a right story. It is because standard accounts of the gendering of lesbian relationships do not deliver a story *for them*.

In Melissa Simpson's chronicle of the 1970s, butches and femmes make a brief appearance as "throwbacks" to an earlier time. White lesbian-feminists equated "stud" with bar brawls, domestic violence, objectification: an entire slew of things that bad boys do and good girls don't. Those fightin' butches of yesteryear were heroes for another time and place, not for now, when lesbians ought to know better. "You were supposed to be evolved from that sort of thing in 1976," Sid Stein recalled with irony.

Among the lessons of the radical feminism of her day taken to heart by Julia Benoit: don't be "caught dead" in jewelry. A man could be lurking around any corner, waiting to throttle you with decorative implements of your own destruction. Looking back from the vantage point of the 1980s, white women such as Julia and Melissa realized that prescriptions for "androgyny" had translated into anti-femme as well as anti-men. But at the time many idealistically headed off in search of a gender-free space.

During the 1970s many lesbian-feminists took it upon themselves to wipe out inequality in lesbian relationships. Or, more precisely, *gendered* inequalities: the kind supposedly represented by butch/femme. It seldom occurred to them that their vision of progress from the old days of butch/femme to a more "enlightened" androgyny could embroil them in legacies of racism.

With its denim shirts and painter's pants, the lesbian-feminist version of androgyny asked lesbians of color to adopt an Anglo style, and a working-class one at that. In Julia's story the old lover who undergoes a femme makeover stands in for lesbians "now" and "then." When Julia's ex dons heels on the heels of the 1990s, her transformation to high femme personifies a larger historical shift away from androgyny, if not a return of butch/femme as the same. Yet she is implicitly raced white, right down to the chain that graces her lovely neck. Why? Because wearing jewelry does not, in and of itself, mark a masculine/feminine divide for homies or rappers or Diné (Navajo) silversmiths or latter-day chic.

And what about the story's fantasy of the heterosexual menace around every corner? Although the threat of rape and attack is real enough for lesbians, discussions of "male violence" among white women too often tap into fears of urban "crime," an increasingly politicized term that associates violence with poor men of color. Embedded in Julia's story is another history for white women: not necessarily a bad thing, except when it relies upon racist images or passes as a history for *all* women.

The apparently race-neutral model of evolutionary gender change had some insidious effects. Why would any self-respecting African-American queer want to locate herself in an up-out-of-the-jungle tale of evolution from a less advanced (butch/femme) to a more advanced (androgynous) state? What had popular notions about the survival of the fittest done for black people lately? The evolutionary elevator supposed to take people to the top generally left people of color to languish on the ground floor, with African Americans lucky to find shelter in the basement. In histories that equate change with progress or evolution, "advanced" too often means "white."

Eventually, the evolutionary model began to go the way of all dinosaurs. A few brave souls complicated the story by racing it, classing it, sexualizing it, and relating it to developments in the larger society. They began by asking what was so inherently progressive about androgyny. Even the white lesbian-feminists who called themselves androgynous never agreed upon the meaning of the term. Was the idea to "balance" masculine and feminine, or to do away with gender altogether? And how could they hope to agree? Gendered categories have no life apart from culture and class and the situations in which people bring gender into play.

Melissa claimed that her working-class background allowed her to detect nuances of femme and butch in middle-class white lesbians who otherwise presented as androgynous. Don't forget the old saying, she grinned, that pegs a middle-class butch for a working-class femme. Context is everything. Trapping mice has little macho cachet for middle-class professionals with the money to call an exterminator, or for people whose religious beliefs condemn killing animals.

Gendered African-American hairstyles, as Raye observed, might or might not gender signify to whites or Asian Americans or Latinas, just as, after years in the foster care system, Raye did not perceive cooking and cleaning as particularly gender-coded activities. But what about the centuries that coerced African-American women into domestic work and slavery? If Raye had located these tasks within a raced and classed history, the same cooking and cleaning might have carried undertones of subordination into discussions of self-sufficiency.

Who were these lesbian-feminists who proclaimed butch passé yet still chopped off their hair, who considered women in mascara uniquely susceptible to going straight, who convinced Julia to give away her bracelets, who got Melissa to practice throwing "like a boy," who reduced Raye to hiding out in her own house, who called women with cigarettes cupped in their hands "androgynous" when another decade might have labeled them butch? Well, at the time, they were Julia and Melissa and (occasionally) Raye. By calling for androgyny, lesbian-feminists hoped to bring about greater freedom for women. But in the name of emancipation from a restrictive gender regime, lesbian-feminism ended up producing its own gendered imperatives.

Sometimes androgyny looked like a watered-down version of stud, in which butch was better, fluff was betrayal, and *marimachas* still looked like the "real lesbians." Why should the lesbian-feminist uniform of the 1970s have taken the shape of work boots and overalls rather than, say, hyper-femme? Why did it take nearly a decade for the disgruntled to wonder whether so much sameness necessarily made for equality?

By the 1980s many lesbians were eager to leave androgyny behind. Raye began to carry a torch for the importance of taking a stand upon a gendered identity and a name. In a dog-eat-dog world, she thought it was dangerous to believe in a melting pot of gender. (We're all androgynous here. Can't we just get along?) Look at Julia, reluctant to adopt the terms "butch" or "femme," but filled with resentment that lesbians who perceived her as femme considered her sexually available. Although Julia described herself as far from "girlish," power differentials led some people to believe they had the god-given right to pick her up. And those power differentials had to be taken seriously.

On the job Raye worried that her butch presentation had the potential to hurt her clients' cases. Yet she also believed that a studly stance made her opinions command respect. When all was said and done, Raye would rather have had people in the office defer to her than ignore her as they had more feminized coworkers. And who knows how much their reaction was colored by the combination of race *and* gender *and* sexuality packed here into the term "studly"?

If the road through Androgyny ran nowhere near the Promised Land, perhaps lesbian-feminists had been too quick to dismiss butch/femme. Speaking as "the last of the true butches," Raye began to rewrite the lesbian-feminist morality play. Butch/femme relationships today are perfectly capable of fostering equality, she argued, if not fostering equality perfectly. Women of the 1980s who advocated butch/femme implicitly responded to the lesbian-feminist critique of "roles" as nasty and oppressive and bound to hand femmes a raw deal. Then they set about transforming what would count as fluff and what would count as stud.

A lot had happened between the bar raids of their parents' day and the pride parades of their own. For starters there had been major shifts in the economy. Never underestimate the impact of the phenomenal numbers of women entering the workforce in the years after World War II (though race and class hierarchies ensured that not all these women would have access to the same income or the same jobs). Fashion had embraced military drag, chola, unisex, Afrocentric, Eurostyle, and more. Corporations had even begun to use girl-on-girl advertising to market products to lesbians.

Out was the "old-fashioned" butch described by Carolyn Fisher: the compulsive lighter of cigarettes and opener of car doors. In was a new generation of studs reputed to be less intimidating, more fluid in dress and attitude and behavior. Stories consistently associate the hard-core butch, adamant about her prerogatives and territorial about her woman, with the 1950s. Her counterpart, the nouveau butch of the 1980s and 1990s, could turn up in the lingerie department and had no problem rotating the chores. After years as a lesbian Raye felt the freedom to grow out her hair into now stylish shoulder-length dreads. Melissa finally admitted to handling tools better than her middle-class butch lover.

Butch/butch and femme/femme relationships that would have been a no-no in the 1940s or 1950s achieved a modicum of acceptance by the late 1980s. (Compare Melissa's story of the "old gay" woman who had to switch to fluff just to get the stud she wanted.) Butch/femme relationships previously associated with the working class seemed newly accessible to anyone. Gender bending, which mixed contraries such as leather and lace, displaced gender blending on the social scene.

But even this revamped community history, condensed from interviews, raises more questions than it answers. Clearly history does not move forward in a straight line down a one-way track called Evolution or Progress. So to curve that line into a circle that says what goes around eventually comes around again (this time in the form of a butch/femme "revival") doesn't help much. In Melissa's and Raye's version of gender change, lesbians jump on an express train that runs between past and present and stops at only two stations: the yesterday of rigid butches/helpless femmes and the today of enlightened butches/empowered femmes. Their accounts flatten all the nuances of change into a single "past" (home to the "traditional" femme, the "old-style" stud). And what do you have when you disembark but another fairy tale of unmitigated improvement?

This particular time train is easy enough to derail. First of all not everyone seemed to have boarded the train. Julia's ex-lover might have undergone a gendered transformation, but Julia herself had not. Flannel shirts and jeans still tumbled from her dresser drawers. And there seemed to be limits to nouveau butch fluidity. Why else would other lesbians seem surprised after learning that Raye had a daughter? Femmes are still more likely to be targeted as the appropriate ones to bear kids. Raye's aside to me when she used the pejorative word "fish" also hints at the endurance of power differentials between femme and butch, with "femme" still the devalued term. "But you don't mind, do you?" she continued, inviting me to engage in the kind of "just among us butches" repartee that walks a fine line when it comes to dissing femmes.

And how much had things changed? Melissa would certainly have taken issue with Raye's portrayal of "classic" femmes of the past as sexually passive. (Not that a few weren't, but surely all those women encouraging their butches to flip were showing *some* initiative.) Tremendous variation existed in butch sexuality, too, from untouchable studs, to butches who liked it on the bottom, to studs who might kiss and tell but never flip and talk, to studs who resolutely kept butchness out of the bedroom.

Does butch/femme signify the same thing today as in years gone by? Maybe the butch/femme revival of the 1980s was no revival at all, not even a return of the repressed, but a nostalgic appeal to *beliefs* about the way things used to be. After all, what would there be to revive for the Latinas in the Southwest who continued to patronize "roles" bars throughout the "lesbian-feminist" 1970s? To call it a revival obscures changes in the meanings of gendered terms and whitens lesbian history. Placing androgyny at the center of the story can have a similar effect.

Melissa characterized the 1980s as the decade in which lesbians learned to spoof butch and femme. Yet Sid Stein described wearing a tie "just for fun" during the 1970s, the decade usually associated with androgyny. Standard histories portray lesbian-feminism as a movement of middle-class white women from the 1970s. Yet Raye with her law books and Julia in her army fatigues are reminders of class and race differences within the movement that carried over into the 1980s. Not to mention the legions of women who continued to call themselves androgynous at century's end.

In 1990 adopting a term like "stud" made good political sense to Raye. As she saw it, gendered identities are not set in stone but provisional, ready to be taken up or laid down as historical circumstances demand. Resolving the question of whether people are born femme or butch is neither here nor there. The important thing to resolve is never to close your eyes to the consequences of entering life at the bottom. With a host of institutions working to keep you there, freedom from identity categories—"I'm beyond labels!"—becomes an illusion only privilege can sustain.

Oppression based on gendered differences, Raye argued, is just like oppression based on race: "Because of skin color no one's going to mistake you." Precisely because they are oppressed, Raye believed that people of color of all classes and working-class people of all colors need to adopt identities, if only for their own protection. "Butch" gave her a place from which to stand and fight.

In an unjust society Raye advocated what Gayatri Spivak has called strategic essentialism. Operate as though you are one thing through and through, a model of consistency and conviction, even though you know damn well life is more complicated than that. Sure, "femmes" can build bookcases, "lesbians" may sleep with the occasional guy, and "white people" may come from families with African-American or Filipino ancestry. Spotlight the consistencies, downplay the discrepancies. Act for all the world, if not yourself, as though each identity you claim is natural and inescapable and quite simply "who you are."

What makes it strategic is this: you stake your claim to a particular identity as a conscious, even political, choice, realizing all the while that there's nothing automatic about it. Butch-identified as she was, Raye believed she could alter the way she gendered herself. Anything subject to claim is also subject to change. But why bother? So long as she and her daughter had food on the table and a place to stay, she saw no reason to switch. Political conditions that threaten your survival are one thing; shifting to meet social expectations or a lover's desire is quite another.

Raye's philosophy of identity is as different as can be from the gender-blind version of androgyny that pretends we're all the same, or at least equidistantly different. Its strength lies in its insistence that, in this society at least, color and class and sexuality matter. But it's all too easy to isolate these terms by speaking of each separately. Raye discussed her daughter's femininity in one place, the social consequences of her daughter's darker skin in another. What would the same conversation sound like if she had put the two together, talking specifically about African-American women, or African-American daughters? When she looked back over her personal history of class mobility, she recognized in her clients a younger version of herself. Yet Raye had lived her twenties as a black lesbian mother on AFDC, which must have been something more than the sum of "poor."

In her defense of strategic essentialism, Raye compared the history of racism to the history of homophobia ("no one's going to mistake you"), when in her own life these histories had not run on parallel tracks. Nor could they work themselves out as analogies, because Raye—like all of us—has only one body through which multiple identities play. She cannot wake up to class today, gender tomorrow. The hierarchies that attempt to carve these categories deep into her skin will be there waiting for her in the morning.

Do you have to take a stand on identity in order to work for change? According to Melissa, identity holds no special key to gender. Whether your partner identifies as femme or butch or androgynous or none of the above is irrelevant to how you see her and what will turn you on. Outside the bedroom, strategic essentialism remains complicated in its effects, because it can unwittingly incarcerate you within the very categories used to oppress you. "For precisely as long as the jailer hears your moaning," James Baldwin once wrote, "he knows where you are. The sound of the victim's moaning confirms the authority of the jailer, the keeper of the keys." Why give people who seek your demise the tools to track you down and pin you down? Like identity, ambiguity retains its own advantages for survival, as well as its charms.

Chapter 3   Baby Pictures

Talk to someone in the United States about gender for more than twenty minutes, and you're likely to walk away with a childhood story. Many of these anecdotes have as much to do with sexuality as gender. The big bad butch starts out as a mischievous little roughneck. The tomboy turns into a dyke. The three-year-old princess seems destined to plan a (straight) wedding trousseau. Embedded in these tales is a gender inversion model of homosexuality: the mistaken belief that queers inevitably display gendered "traits" associated with the "opposite" sex. In contrast, budding young heterosexuals can be spotted by their "gender-appropriate" behavior. Catch 'em every time.

You might think that lesbians would want to dismiss the tomboy-grows-into-a-dyke narrative for the stereotype it is. But by drawing upon the inversion model, a woman can use gender to argue for the "realness" of her gay identity. How? She slips continuity into her descriptions of the ways she has gendered herself over the years. She reminds you that her first words were, "Play ball," but forgets to tell you about the time she tried out for cheerleading or homecoming queen. The earlier her examples of boyish behavior, the better. She contends that she is now as she always was and ever more shall be. The more consistent, the more "natural," the more authentic, the more convincing.

Stories about growing up gendered can help her claim a timeless sexual identity as a dyed-in-the-wool lesbian.

If childhood stories offer any guide, a femme is a femme and a stud is a stud. Or are they? As it turns out, not all gay women buy into the gender inversion model. Some tell a different kind of tale. They recognize the centrality of tomboys to accounts of growing up (to become a) lesbian but insist that they personally never climbed a tree in their lives. On the other hand, they say they know plenty of tree-climbing women who are happily living out their lives as heterosexuals. And those heterosexuals aren't required to "explain" their sexuality, with or without references to gendering. Like Marta Rosales, they turn the expectation of gendered continuity on its head by calling attention to the motorcycle-riding youngster who grows up to be an occasional femme. Or they point out how hard it is to account for lipstick lesbians if all you have in your head are pictures of a miniature diesel dyke.

Are lesbians who call themselves butch best understood, in the words of one, as "tomboy survivors"? To what extent does "the tomboy" operate as a raced and classed, as well as gendered and sexualized, figure in childhood stories? How often does the tomboy grow up to be someone who calls herself androgynous or fluff or faggoty or beyond the reach of labels or even (gulp) straight?

Is gendering usually consistent across a lifetime, or is consistency an impression produced by the stories people tell about those formative years? Does something called socialization set a course for life? Or is gender no more reducible to early childhood experience than it is the lump sum of so-called gender "traits"?

What to make of women who flash their tomboy credentials to explain their love for women, yet denounce grown-up gendered identities such as "(bull)dagger" or "stud"? How do femmes penetrate a storytelling genre that celebrates the baby butch within? And what about the whole idea of gender inversion? Could it be that childhood memories chronicle something more complex than simply "crossing" between two fixed gender positions, or staying put?

Edith Motzko: "I Won't Grow Up. I Don't Want to Be a Man."

"A friend of my husband, after talking with me one evening, said that most of the time a woman will compliment a man in conversation. I was more in competition rather than complimenting him. It's the way I've always been. I have a very heavy masculine trait, because I was my father's son.

"I grew up out in the Avenues [in San Francisco], which is typically middle-class. We lived in a cold-water flat. Golden Gate Park was my back yard. I could climb fences and shoot slingshots better than most of the boys in the neighborhood. I was the oldest of five, with quite a few responsibilities. My dad was always working. The only way I was able to ever spend time with him was to go on a job site. So I learned the trade of carpentry and fell in love with it.

"My parents got me a coonskin cap, and I had shotguns and water pistols and all the rest. I built model cars and airplanes. But they permitted me that much because it was a craft type of situation. They bought me a little tool kit when I was a kid. Took the saw out of the box so that there wouldn't be any short legs on the tables and chairs. Forgot to take the screwdriver, and I took the set screws out of all the doorknobs in the house! They all had to be rethreaded.

"I had a crush on a girl who lived across the street, named Valerie. I'd sit in my house and look at her, sitting on the front steps with all the boys. I couldn't do anything [about it]. I was raised a Roman Catholic, and there's quite a stigma involved in homosexuals. Even at that time I considered myself bad, black, evil, dirty. All the negative things. Heaven is something to look forward to, and hell is something we carry around in us every day.

"It got real bad at one time. When I was thirteen, I contemplated suicide to the point where I strapped a shotgun to two chairs and actually pulled the trigger the first time without any shells in it, and then sat there with the shells in it and thought about it for a long time. I decided that God put me on this earth for a reason. And I was gonna be damned if I wasn't going to find out what that purpose was first, before I decided to blow my brains out. So I put the shotgun away, put the shells away, and trudged on through life: my teen years, my twenties. And stayed in the closet.

"When I was in high school, there was a softball game going and I had to play. My turn came to bat. I had played baseball with the guys growing up, so I knew what to do. My stance at the bat . . . there were a couple wisecracks made [about] how I looked just like a guy. So I hit the softball into the fence. I sat down and I didn't play again, ever. Because I couldn't handle it. So I just let it go.

"It was real tough in the locker room. Mandatory showers were difficult for me. I just had to keep myself from going crazy. I kept my head in a corner and didn't look. As much as I wanted to. Because it would have just brought too much trouble. Other people would have noticed, and that of course is the biggest fear: of being found out. I had my girlfriend at school and we would double date. The only problem is, she would be in the front seat and I was in the back!

"In my early twenties I got pregnant and had a baby. About six months later I met a man and married him. I stayed with him fifteen years. [Even then] I would want to be with the girls. Never with the guys. I'd spend a lot of time with [girls] without any physical contact, without any talking of my feelings for them. I would do silly things. Buy them flowers once in a while. Send them cards. Even a hug, that would have been the ultimate for me. It would have been enough. As it was, I settled for companionship and friendship and spending time together.

"Because of the way I felt about women, I would not accept the fact that I was a woman. Because when I did, that made me wrong. In [my] journal I had written at one point, 'I won't grow up. I don't want to be a man.' And I *didn't* want to be a man. But I couldn't be a woman in my mind, either, because I loved women.

"I was fighting with society and the things that I was taught and brought up to believe. I'm a survivor, so to survive I had to be straight. Because I saw what happened to people who were gay as I was growing up. I grew up here in the city, so I knew what was going on. San Francisco's very liberal. I was involved with the coffeehouse beatniks, with the flower children in the Haight-Ashbury. If you're a little bit different, society just wants to destroy you. They put you down for anything and everything. So to be safe, I lived in a house that I said was my castle, which was actually my dungeon. And I kept myself locked up. I was a woman at home with her children. And I was straight. People came to believe that.

"Because I lived in a glass house all my life, I never threw rocks. So there was no reason for me to ever be prejudiced against anyone, whether they be gay or straight or black or white or yellow or green. That's what I tried to teach my children, too. Not to see a person for their color, or what they do, or how they behave, but just because they're a person. Learn to like them, give them a chance first before you start making judgments. Because there's a swishy queen walking into the room, don't say, 'Oh, that faggot's no good.' That's not the way to do it. Give him a chance!

"I had been in an apprenticeship class to the carpenters. Just before I slipped a disc in my neck, I'd met this woman. Walked into the bar across the street when we were on break, having a drink, and she walked in. She was the sun and the moon and the stars and everything I'd ever dreamt about. And she was gay." That encounter gave Edith something to contemplate during the long weeks in cervical traction. "When you're in traction, you can't do anything. You're totally immobile. You can read, or you can think. When I came back, I had finally accepted the fact that I was a woman, and I liked it." She decide to separate from her husband.

"Most of the guys I've worked with for the last seven years, since I've been in the trades, they all still think of me as very straight. They want me to go out, and I won't go out with them. I have a 'boyfriend' now. That really sticks in my throat when I have to say it. [My lover] will get very carried away sometimes and leave little marks on my neck. And I get teased about that at work. 'Oh, you're seeing *him* again!' And I said, 'Yeah!' If I could even just say 'my lover.' But even that [word] has such connotations, that they would just automatically [know].

"Carpenters are so macho, so tough. They're like the last of the cowboys. One guy wanted to know what I was doing after work, and I said I go to this bar. He wanted to know what bar, because he was going to come and see me and buy me a drink. I said, 'You wouldn't be comfortable in the bar, because it's a women's bar.' He says, 'Oh, one of *those*.' I said, 'What do you mean, one of those?' His whole attitude was, you know, very very heavy-duty chain and leather dykes in the bars. He says, 'Oh, you like to go and get hit up by women.' And I said, '*Nobody* hits up on me.' He says, 'Oh, well then, you're hitting up on them.' I looked at him and I said, 'No, but that's an idea.' He almost fell off the scaffold!

"I'm always really hard. Very, very butch. [My lover] notices it. She says I talk to [my roommate] one way, but I talk to her in a different voice. So much softer and easier when I talk to her, when I talk to [other close women friends]. That softer part of me comes through. But this masculine trait of mine has always been so valued and so thick.

"[Growing up] I was the strong one in the neighborhood. At one time one of the boys fell out of a tree in the park and knocked himself unconscious. I wasn't at the park that day, but the guys came to *my* house to tell me what had happened so *I* would go and tell his mother. Because they couldn't do it. But I could do it. I could do anything, in their eyes.

"I worked all day on a job site one time with a broken finger. I hit it with my hammer at like 7:30 in the morning. I just thought I'd smashed it. I told the foreman at lunchtime I needed to go to the doctor's after work and have him punch a hole in the nail, because my finger had swollen up twice the size of what it should have been. I went to the doctor's after work. He said, 'How did you work all day with a broken finger?' I says, 'I didn't know it was broken.' I also passed out cold when he said it!

"I haven't changed. I'm still me. If I walked out of my house to my pickup truck and I put it under my arm and carried it across the street, these kids in the neighborhood would not blink an eye, because that's me. If I walked out on the street with heels and a skirt, they'd go crazy, because that's not me!

"[In the] mid and late 1950s, the military had survival runs on the newsreels, on the television, where they would drop these guys in the jungles and they'd give them just basic survival tools. I asked my father one time, I said, 'How would I do?' He said, 'Well, if they dropped you and a pocket knife and a safety pin,' he said, 'you'd probably spend two weeks longer than anybody else and come out gaining about forty-five pounds.' That's the kind of confidence that he had in me, because of what I'd learned through him. These guys are all coming out, they'd show them coming out skinny and all raggedy-assed. Not me! I would have come out gaining weight, new set of clothes! Having this big brown bear pulling it out on a cart that I built myself.

"At this moment, I'm in debt up to my ass. But I'll make it. I'll pull through without any problems. I will survive, because I am a survivor. The hardest thing I ever had to do in my whole life was to wait for my first lover."

Yvonne Taylor: "You Can Never Take Naps Together Again"

"Arlington County is several miles from Washington, D.C. A long time ago it was split between the black part of Arlington County and the white part of Arlington County, so I grew up in a black neighborhood. The land that I grew up on, my family had had since 1867. It's part of a plantation that was split up.

"I feel like I was a little girl, and I had all the little girly qualities. But I also liked to play football, and I played with my brother all the time. Not only that, but I stood up for myself a lot. I was really focused on reading and going to school. I grew up always knowing I was going to go to college. I was not athletic. Ballet was what I did.

"When I was really little, there weren't girls in the neighborhood, so my mom started taking me to ballet when I was four. So before I started school, I'd know what girls were, so I would relate to them. I learned to be more of a girl. I've been thinking about it lately, about how *weird* it must have been. Here I am, four years old, and my mom takes me to ballet once a week. We drive all these miles into Washington, D.C., really far into this one part of the city. Now I realize we went there because the ballet schools that were in Virginia I couldn't go to, because they were probably segregated. This was 1964, or 1963. I mean, when I was a kid, I had no idea.

"When one little girl moved into the neighborhood, we used to fool around a lot. We were supposed to be taking a nap once. We must have been seven and eight. My grandmother walked in. She heard us because we were laughing. She was so flipped out, she said, 'Okay, you can never take naps together again.' I'd never seen her so upset. And just shocked. She said, 'This is our secret. You can't even tell your parents.' This thing that I had done, or this way that we had been, was *so* horrible I couldn't even tell my parents. Oh, did I feel guilty! I felt guilty forever! I told my mom about it. I broke my promise to my grandmother. I'm sure somewhere inside, that's kept me from being sexual with women for so long. It kept me from coming out somehow.

"I was this really, really good kid. I didn't do anything. My brother did drugs, and he'd run away from home, and he wrecked cars, and he'd get arrested because he was with gangs of kids shooting BBs. He did all these things, and I was just really perfect because he was so awful. I saw all this pain my parents went through, so I was like, 'Oh, I have to be really perfect.'

"I was totally into Jesus, and he was going to save me. See, there's one thing that really was a catalyst for my becoming a Christian, and that was, I was raped when I was thirteen. But I never told my family at all. I didn't tell my family until a couple years ago. When I went to college, I woke up my first morning in the dormitory and I didn't read the Bible. All of a sudden. 'Okay, I don't need to live that way any more. I'm kind of on my own.'

"I went to an all-girls high school. The headmistress and the dean of students, I'm *sure*, were dykes. They were both so powerful. The headmistress was always making these anti-male comments. I'm sure that she was one, because she was basically a separatist, [though] she may not even call herself a separatist. For me, that's what a lesbian was, was Miss K. She was really *butch*! It frightened me. I couldn't even conceive of myself being lesbian.

"I'm definitely second-generation middle-class, or third-generation on my father's side. Owning your own land and stuff. Black people who were middle-class had these certain values. My dad, in the end of the 1940s, went to school in California because that's where he could go to school and get the kind of education he wanted. My mom went to school in the East. Their whole vision was much more to be assimilated, to fit into America and be Americans. The formula for being alive is to learn how to fit in. That means, if you're a middle-class black, you learn to be white. Or at least in certain circumstances.

"I remember my father used to tell me, 'You're American *first*.' He didn't say, 'You're *black* American first.' He said, 'You're American first, and everything else is second.' And [now] it's like, I'm a woman first. And I'm a *black* woman first. And I'm a black *lesbian* first. There are all these things that are first before I'm American! For me. But it took me a long time to figure out. Learning to be proud of myself as a black woman was a part of coming out. It was all at the same time, all these different things."

Teresa Cruz: "Everybody Wanted to Get Close to Mercedes"

"When I was five years old—this was in Cuba, I was born in Cuba—it was first grade and we were doing Sleeping Beauty in this play. It's an all-girls school, right? The girl that was Sleeping Beauty I had this crush on and I really wanted to go and kiss her. They didn't have the prince yet, so I volunteered to be the prince. My mother made me this prince suit and I swear to god I felt like that was my mother's first mistake! Little did she know that that would lead to other things.

"There was this girl there who had a lot of charisma and charm. Everybody wanted to get close to Mercedes! During recess we'd go and make out behind the bookshelves. I loved to play outside in the trees and with the boys. I was into soldiers. The typical toys at that time. My brother would get annoyed with me. 'You're not a boy, get out of here! Why are you doing that?' I'd say, 'I want to do it. Let me alone.' We were very close, too, because since we moved around a lot we were each other's best friends. So even though it bugged him, he would let me.

"My parents were both very liberal when we were growing up, in terms of politics. I know that they were very much into the revolution and they fought for the revolution. I would say like 95 percent of the Cuban people were in favor of the revolution when it was happening. Fidel was supported by the middle class, and my parents were part of the middle class. My parents, they were very much into socialism but they were not Marxists. They were not pro-Soviet. So what happened was that after the revolution, also because of their class background, they lost more than people who didn't have everything.

"After 1960 Cuba aligned itself much more with the Soviet Union, and a lot of things happened in terms of freedom of expression and freedom of religion and freedom of a lot of things that were curtailed at the time. My parents were very afraid that this was leading into a really huge dictatorship. There was this big propaganda also going on from the right wing, which was saying that Castro was going to send all the kids to Russia and train them to be these little communists. It was like a panic. So they left.

"We left with the second wave of refugees. My father was a doctor. Doctors were very much needed so they closed the borders to doctors. My father had to falsify passports saying he was a student and do all this stuff [to get out of the country]. Then we went to Latin America. And then when I was twelve we came here to California. So there was a lot of uprootedness in my life after that.

"I was a victim of history. I always wonder would I be the same in terms of my life—not in terms of my sexuality, I know [that] would be the same—but would it be the same if I was in Cuba. Because of who I am, because I'm gay, I've also been very affected by the gay oppression in Cuba. My god, would I have ended up in jail if I had been gay in Cuba?

"Already by the time I was, let's say, ten, I knew that the word "queer," which in Spanish is "*maricón*," was a negative, and that it had to do with boy and boy, and girl and girl. So I knew that I had to not say anything. I never thought of it as bad. I just thought it was different. I knew that I liked girls and I knew that that was different.

"But later on, I did have moments where I wanted to just be like other kids. One of the reasons that I felt I wanted to be just like other kids [was] because I felt this responsibility from my parents, because I'm the only daughter, to give them grandchildren. In Cuban tradition the men are supposedly the ones that run the family. Of course, the woman is still running the family, but you know what I mean. Forget about careers. You're supposed to just get married and have kids and take care of your man.

"I knew there was my brother, but I felt that there's something about a girl having [the baby]. The man is not the one that's pregnant, so it's different for the grandparents. I don't know if that's just cultural or not, but I know that I felt that because I would give life, it would be more important that I would be the one. Also, in Cuban culture, there's this thing about the son will not always be the son but the daughter will always be the daughter. Like the son might go away but the daughter will stay. Even after she's married. So that gives the grandparents an opportunity to be around and see their grandchild or grandchildren. I always felt a sense of responsibility around family. That's the way I was raised.

"When I came here to the U.S., from the time I was twelve to fifteen, I was having a lot of cultural problems—adjustment, the changes. People wanting me to be white American and me not fitting in, and [me] wanting to be white American and my parents saying, 'You're Cuban and you have these traditions.' Meanwhile, while all this was happening, I knew that I was a lesbian. More and more and more I knew that that was who I was. So I was having a lot of problems. When I was fourteen I started to take a lot of drugs, a lot of acid, a lot of everything. It was a really bad period. Started doing a lot of delinquent kinds of things: stealing and stuff like that.

"When I came to the U.S. and when I came out there was a lot of stuff I rejected around my culture. 'I'm going to be like any other American, and I'm going to fit in.' Because there was this thing, and I didn't know what to name it. The way that people treated me when I was Cuban, when they knew I was Latina, I didn't like it. Either I was exotic or I was below them, like less intelligent, less sophisticated, less capable of doing things. Also, they assumed my class: that I was poor because I was Latina.

"People are people, but it's more than people are people. There are some differences in culture and class and race. I whitewashed myself and I tried to melt into the white American way. When I turned twenty-one, after I broke with this lover, I went back and I lived with my parents for a year. I got back in touch with a lot of things that I had left. Realized that, 'My god, these are my people, this is my culture, this is so much a part of me. No wonder I had this problem with this person, because it was cultural.' When I rejected men, I didn't want to have men in my life, and then when I saw who I was, I didn't want to have Americans in my life. 'I don't want this, I want to be with Latinos.' So that was my second coming out.

"My life now is so different than when I was that age. A lot of my friends are people from other countries, a lot of Latin Americans, and Americans who are really aware and conscious and knowledgeable about the world. I feel a lot of times Americans are so limited in their world view. They only see their little space and they can't understand what's going on in another country, because they don't even know where it is! To me, that's amazing. The Americans that I know are really incredible people, the white Americans that I know, that are my friends. But at that time a lot of the white Americans that I was hanging out with were not that way. They were ignorant.

"Their views about Latin people were off the wall. They had no idea what they were talking about. I, of course, never feel racism as a dark-skinned Latin person would, because I'm light-skinned. So I never had that problem. I had the other problem, which was invisibility, where people would assume that I was white, and when I would say that I was Latina they would say, 'Oh, but you don't look Latina. Are you really Latina, really?' Like they couldn't figure out why I was Latina because I wasn't dark. They thought every Latin person in the world was dark-skinned, which is not true."

While Teresa was trying to make sense of differences in the construction of race and place that she encountered in the United States, she fell in love with a high school classmate named Tracy, with whom "nothing [sexual] ever happened. Then I met this girl who was already graduated from high school. She sold drugs. She was Chicana, and I knew right away she was a lesbian. I don't know how. I just had this feeling [that] I really need to get to know her.

"Then after that I had a lot of problems at home and I ran away from home. I went and looked for her. I had heard that she had moved out of her parents' [place] and had her own apartment. She was at that time engaged to this marine, and he was there. He starts saying how before he changed her, she was a bisexual, but now she was no longer a bisexual. So I went [to myself], 'Aha, she is! I was right!' I couldn't wait until he was going to go, because you know [marines] go a lot. When he left we just started playing around, tickling each other, you know how it is. We were getting closer and closer and we made love. That really was my first long-term relationship. I was with Patricia from the time I was fifteen till twenty.

"I didn't know the lingo at all. I remember that night when we made love I thought it was really funny because I had this thing in me like I wanted to kiss her like a man. I thought I had to kiss her like a man, right? So I went like this, and she turned me around and she said, 'It's my turn to be the dyke,' and I went, 'What?' I didn't know what that meant. We were both trying to be butch! She was the one that really introduced me to gay culture.

"When I was a little kid I always thought, 'Why didn't God make me a boy, because I like boys' things, I like to do the things that boys do, I like their freedom.' Then when I came out I always saw that I liked feminine girls. Not feminine, but you know what I mean? I didn't like masculine energy in women. But with feminism I realized a lot of it was that I wanted freedom to be treated as a human being and boys were treated more like human beings than girls. So I really rejected [butch/femme] roles after that. I said, 'This is bullshit.'

"And then later in my life, I started to realize that there is an energy sometimes between women that is masculine and feminine, and it's attractive. With [my last lover], for instance, I was more masculine. We just had that chemistry. With past lovers, some lovers, I've been much more feminine. In my twenties I was still searching a lot as to what my identity was. I know what my identity is now. And I accept all of it: the part of me that's butch, the part of me that's femme, the part of me that's a giver, the part of me that's a taker."

L. J. Ewing: "A Very Tomboy Thing"

"I'm sure that the first time I ever heard the word, I knew it was about me. I was a pretty forthright tomboy. I was real active. And I lived in a pretty rural town, so I had a lot of roaming room. Up and down, lots of hills and trees. I dealt with lots of animals—not so many people.

"I remember [the grown-ups] talking about how, when I was a baby, they couldn't put me in dresses. I crawled a lot and I would just get tangled up in dresses. They couldn't keep them on me, so I always was in little pants. I don't think I really got a whole lot of pressure to behave differently till getting closer to, say, twelve or so. I wasn't allowed to wear boys' shoes. That's where my mother drew the bottom line. I wanted high-top sneakers. I couldn't have those. I could wear Levis and t-shirts and everything else that boys wore.

"Other pressure came in sports, being told I should stop beating the boys. And probably a little bit from my grandmother, who lived next door, who the summer I turned twelve told me now I was going to learn how to sew. So I spent the summer at the sewing machine. That was a very strong attempt at socializing me properly. Now I know how to sew!

"During the period where I was fighting to have my hair short, the person

I used as an example of somebody who had their hair short—and it was okay for *them* to have their hair short—was a woman who was the vet's wife in town. My family being involved with animals, the vet was a respected role model. So I won the fight to get my hair cut, and after I did that, then there was a girl who was maybe a year or two older than me who accused me of having a crush on this woman. Which was a fairly interesting concept! I did think [the vet's wife] was pretty neat.

"Coming from a working-class background, I had some very strong formative role models. Strong, independent, self-supporting women. Even though most of them married, I always got the line that you had to be independent, had to know how to take care of yourself, because you never could count on a man to do it. Or to do it right! So you were going to have to take care of it. I think that was a help.

"On the other hand, some women I know from a higher class background went to girls' schools where there were *always* lesbians. In private schools they were sexually segregated. There was a lesbian tradition and a lesbian community in those schools. No matter how hidden and fucked up, they *knew* there was something there. So that maybe slowed me down a little bit. Although I wasn't slowed down awfully! I really can't speak for people who are not white folks. I'm sure there are some differences, but I wouldn't presume to speak to those.

"There's [still] a lot of the tomboy in me. A lot of physical activity, physical strength. Feeling confident about your body and what it can do, feeling good about your body, is a very tomboy thing. And trusting your body. Not being alienated from your body in your movement. It can be a very lesbian thing, also. Maybe in terms of roles, too, if you think in terms of "butch" and "femme," it could be an aspect of that. I don't know for sure. I came out at a time when people didn't practice roles real strongly, so I don't have a real strong [butch or femme] identity. But I think sometimes that there may be something to it.

"One time somebody said, 'Well, the bottom line is, if you can make love one time more in your life, would you rather make love to another person, or would you rather be made love to?' That was her bottom-line *sexual* definition. I have no hesitation saying I probably would rather be the one who was making love *to* somebody. If I had one last time to do it! If there's some truth to [butch/femme], that is where I would understand it for myself. On the other hand, I don't really divide the world up in that way all the time.

"I don't know if butch/femme really relates to masculine/feminine or not, or if it's its own case. When I was a kid, and I knew I was a tomboy, I had to stop and think about, well, would I really rather be a boy. I knew I was a tomboy; I had to think about what it meant. I don't think anyone ever posed that question to me, but when I thought about it I thought, no, I wouldn't really rather be a boy, because a girl could both wear dresses and wear pants. Boys will probably get a much harder time if they wanted to go running around downtown in dresses. Except for boys' shoes, I could get away with boys' clothes. Plus, I could choose to have a baby or not if I wanted to. For that reason I thought that women could do more things with their bodies and it probably was a better thing to be. That's how I'd been thinking in terms of it being okay to be female, it being the *best* thing. So I don't know if butch really related to masculine."

Connie Robidoux: "You Emphasize the More Physical Aspects of Your Story"

"I played street sports, but I was not real athletic. I was *not* a tomboy. I was much more of a girl, a little girl. When we played make-believe, my sister was always the prince. *She* was the tomboy. I was oftentimes the princess, or some other character like that. We did a lot of roleplaying growing up. If you want to call it butch/femme, definitely!

"I always wanted to be sexual with women. My first sexual experience *was* with a woman. It was with a girl, my sister. When we were little we would sleep with each other. We had separate beds, and I would crawl into bed with her. We never did anything genitally, that kind of sexual. But what we did was, we would roll our bodies together and we'd take off our clothes and we'd be real sensual with each other in bed. And it's interesting because we're both lesbians now. My first lover was my sister! I loved it. I felt like it was cut off for me because at one point she rejected me. She said, 'No, I don't want to do this any more.'

"I had a girlfriend—not a lover, I mean a friend—when I was around eighteen, and I fell in love with this woman. There was no way that anything was going to happen because we were both very Catholic, and at that time I was still a practicing Catholic. We used to spend an awful lot of time together. It all came to a head one night. I slept over at her house and we used to sleep in this double bed. My whole body language was so pulled into myself. Still I'm not a real assertive person physically, in terms of another person. I tend to be more shy. But then I was not only shy; I was like a board!

"We talked half the night. She was kind of feminine but not really. She had long hair and she used to wear hiking boots and jeans. She'd wear flannel shirts and stuff like that, but she had a femininity about her that was really there no matter what she did. She carried it with her. I remember responding to her and thinking that I must be more butch. Really thinking this: well, she's more feminine than me, so I must be the butch. And so it was up to me.

"This one night we finally went to sleep and I had this dream. No, I didn't have a dream. What I did was, in the middle of the night, I swung my arm and I punched her right in the nose! In my sleep! She woke up and I woke up, and neither of us knew what happened. I just rolled over and went back to sleep. And in the morning she said, 'Do you know what you did last night? You rolled over and punched me in the nose in the middle of the night!' We just laughed and laughed, and I never said anything. Because I knew it was my frustration that was coming out really strongly."

Connie believed that portraying an active, aggressive younger self is "always a plus in the [coming-out] story. 'Oh, yeah, yeah, you were a tomboy.' Or you emphasize the more physical aspects of your story when you tell it. I got a lot of that pressure to be more [that way]. I feel a lot of that kind of expectation, still: [to talk about] the way that you were assertive, or played softball as a kid, or climbed trees." Did Connie ever find herself playing up those elements of her childhood when she talked about being gay? "Sure, of course. Of course. So that feeds into the whole myth, then, right?"

Rose Ellis: "I Wonder Were They Like That All Their Lives"

"Where I was, there was nobody else gay. And it's pretty much black where I grew up at, except for the white owners. My time was spent around black people. When we got big enough to be out in the fields like everybody else, we were out there. So as far as I can remember, I've been working. If not there on the farm, it's been cutting grass for other people all day, and making three bucks in a day. I never had the thought of getting married. I was never going to lay at home and let some man take care of me. I wanted to work. That's the only thing about my life growing up that I don't regret, is because it made me not lazy today. I don't mind working.

"My grandmother lived on our land, also on the farm. Up the road. We could see the house from where we lived. We all grew up together with my two youngest uncles. We never was allowed to go and play with friends that much. If we did, we only could stay a certain amount of time. And being in the country, time we walked over that friend's, we had maybe twenty minutes—maybe an hour—to play and had to be back home. So sometime I didn't bother to go. But if we did and we'd get back late, then that's where the beating comes in. If you're a minute late.

"I remember fifth grade. One day I carried this woman's books, but she didn't know why. I knew why, yeah: because I liked her. So she was my secret girlfriend. If I had told this person, if I had said, 'Oh, I like you for a sexual reason,' or whatever, it would have got back to my mom and I might be dead today. But my girlfriend and I, we used to kind of play. Sometime we would just fake scenes, like I would put my hand on her leg and some such something. You know, rub her leg like this. It was like a joke. We would laugh from it.

"After I got up to about eleventh grade, things started changing. My stepfather and [my mother's] relationship started splitting up, so I was able to go out. I think that's after I had left to stay at my grandmother's. I felt like I'm sick of this abuse, and being treated the way I did. I wanted to leave. I didn't want to live there any more. I didn't like the life there. If I was rich and was abused, I could have had money and ran away and probably came out sooner. Just run away, fly away."

After graduating from high school, Rose left the South. "I came out when my son was eight months old. I decided because I wasn't really settled and I didn't know what I was doing, didn't really have a good job, that it was best that my kid stay [with his father]. Because his father still lived with his mom and his sisters and brothers. All his family lived right there in that town up the street from each other. The papers got him as sole custody. So that pretty much decided that, about the kid.

"When I lived where my son is now, I worked at a VA hospital as a nursing assistant. During my time there, there was this woman, or girl, or whatever. She was just turning eighteen, and she worked there part-time, in the kitchen. We had to take the patients their dinner, and that's when I'd see her. I knew I was attracted to her, and I was trying to find ways to get close to her. I asked her to go to a movie with me. Eventually she came to spend the night at my house. I was the aggressive one in this case, because she was straight. She told me later that she was scared. See, we were just friends, and I made the move of just trying to make love to her. She didn't fight it. And she was the type that was kind of a tomboy, but she liked the boys, but she never did anything with the girls. I guess I brought her out at the same time I came out.

"I didn't think about no sin. No, I did not! All I thought about is, what bar we going to next! I never believed in the God that they tell us to believe in. Like how do you know God was white? They would preach us this 'don't do that and don't do that.' But they'd turn, and you'd see them, and they're doing it!

"Down there in the country, you're country. You know how country girls are. They're just different from all that daintiness. It wasn't until *after* I got into the lesbian community that I found there's these stereotype things. Me, being a tomboy, and now, even though I'm not into roles or anything like that, *but I* would consider myself butch. And I am attracted to women that are feminine *only*. Women that are butch turns me off.

"I was in Amelia's [a San Francisco lesbian bar of the late 1970s-1980s] the other night. I was just looking at these women coming in all hard-core lesbian. I wonder, were they like that all their lives? I don't know anything about it. But I *do* know for a fact that some lesbians weren't like that, and then all of a sudden, there they go, looking all tough, and trying to present themselves as being lesbian. That bugs me. Why can't you just be your*self*?

"If you're feminine, that don't bother me. But some of the women that are on the butch side, I've seen them before, and then I see them again, and all of a sudden they're hard-core butch. And they weren't like that before. Why they got to dress like this now? Why can't they still care about how they look? They wear the raggedy jeans—some of them, not all of them—and the sneakers and whatever. Faded jackets, that type of thing. What if they go out to dinner somewhere nice? Are they going to dress like this all the time? Some of them do, I think.

"It doesn't take *that* to make you look butch. If it wasn't for the hair or whatever feminine characteristic, you would think they're men. It's when I see them change, that's when I know they're not themselves. Why can't they just be . . . be a woman? You still a woman, right? I'm butch, but I dress nice, but I dress nice *different*. But they don't. You know what I'm saying? I don't try to present myself as being a lesbian, the way I dress. I dress just the way I like. My clothes are nice, but I could say a woman that is femme would not wear my clothes."

Baby Pictures: Double Takes

Ho-hum. Another lesbian childhood chronicle of softball games. Or schoolyard scraps. Or running around the neighborhood playing gang-bangers. Or righting wrongs as el Zorro. Tomboy stories are among the most predictable, repetitive, even boring parts of life histories collected from late-twentieth-century women who grew up to call themselves some variant of "gay." But the very repetitiveness of these accounts can tell you a lot about the place where gender meets sexuality, age, nation, race, and class.

Looking for "signs" of homosexuality in childhood may be the ultimate guessing game, as North American as football, garage sales, drive-ins, or designer ice cream. And when people look, they are more likely to point to gender than sexuality per se. Edith Motzko believed she could have uncovered her "true" lesbian identity much earlier in life, if only she had paid attention to (gendered) clues from her past. She portrayed her younger self as a holy terror. Her childhood stories work hard to create continuity: the girl raised as her "father's son" grows up to do the father's job. Gendering stays the same, and so does class. It's not much of a leap from the play screwdrivers of her youth to the ten-pound tool belt she later wore as a carpenter. The tomboy grows into a dyke, right? Except, of course, that Edith was thoroughly ensconced in a heterosexual marriage when she first walked onto a construction site.

Tomboy stories feature stock elements that are supposed to provide "evidence" for sexuality claimed as an adult. Conflicts with parents erupt when narrators refuse to wear frilly little dresses or lust after short hair. For the purposes of establishing lesbian identity, only "boy" toys will suffice: guns, knives, model cars, cowboy hats, coonskin caps. These playthings do their gendered work for a particular time and place. A chemistry set would not necessarily signify "boy" outside the United States, or to every generation.

In the stories, childhood games are as gendered as they are conventional. Bandits and princes and cowboys outnumber witches ten to one. If narrators remember "playing house," they recall taking the peripheral part of "the daddy." No hopscotch or double-dutch for this crowd. Sports, yes, but only team sports really make the grade. Puberty dawns as a period when adults try to rein in their little gender rebels. Poor L. J. Ewing, chained to a sewing machine for an entire summer with not a shred of heterosexuality to show for it.

Once in a while stories explicitly link gender to sexuality. Teresa Cruz, for instance, joked that cross-dressing in a school play at the tender age of five eventually led to "other things." Rhetorical devices that signal gender, such as braggadocio and the dare, lend plausibility to tales of a passage from tomboy into dyke. Edith's "in your face" description of hitting the softball out of the park conveyed the same picture of "boy" competence as when she imagined walking out of the forest a self-made woman with bear and cart in tow.

More commonly, tomboy stories establish continuity with the past by telling tales about gender now and then. One motif in Edith's stories is strength. Way back when, strength made her the only kid in the neighborhood with enough guts to tell her buddy's mother about his injury. Today strength means that not a single kid on Edith's block would be surprised to see her shoulder her pickup truck and walk off down the street! Born to be bad? Born to be butch? These stories do not offer an explanation for homosexuality so much as they naturalize the popular association of lesbianism with "boy" attributes and "male" terrain.

If anything, femmes have a greater stake than studs in establishing the "realness" of their lesbian identities. For decades they have labored under the suspicion of going straight at the drop of a hat. Femmes don't look mannish, so people don't assume they grew up boyish. Because markers of gender inversion are in short supply in their everyday presentation, they cannot argue that gendering and sexual identity march together through a lifetime in any lockstep fashion. Does memory supply "feminine" lesbians with the same rich vein of material for legitimation that it provides self-proclaimed butch or androgynous types?

Femmes (broadly conceived) had several strategies for talking about childhood when sexuality was the topic. There were "switch" stories, like the one related by Marta Rosales, in which they depicted themselves as girl-boys who grew up to become something other than butch. A few attempted to make "tomboy" signifiers compatible with something called femininity. Rose Ellis echoed more femme narrators when she characterized country girls as "just different from all that daintiness." This rural/urban contrast left no room for streetwise city girls, ready to roam and ready to fight, but it very effectively undermined the equation of femininity with frills.

Many of the women who considered themselves "feminine" never tried to cast themselves as lapsed tomboys. Like their counterparts, they told stories that established gendered continuity from now to then, but in a femme key. At the age when Edith was outside playing ball, Yvonne Taylor enrolled in ballet classes. Connie Robidoux recalled playing the princess to her sister's prince. Both Connie and Yvonne went beyond gender to appeal directly to sexuality with stories of early sexual experimentation.

References to childhood sex play are more numerous than you might expect if you approach these stories with (middle-class, white, nineteenth-century) assumptions about girls' youthful innocence, sexual passivity, or late-developing interest in sexuality. Sexually explicit anecdotes are not confined to femmes: look at baby Teresa lusting after little Mercedes. Nor do these anecdotes always describe physical encounters. A highlight of Rose's young life involved the opportunity to "start in her head" with a secret girlfriend. Of course, what counts as sexuality (as opposed to curiosity, warmth, or affection) may shift under the influence of hindsight or storytelling conventions. But when such tales come from the lips of femmes, sexuality does what "cross-gendering" can't: it projects the lesbian identity claimed as an adult back into the farthest reaches of memory.

Does this mean that femmes overturn the usual story line of once a tomboy, always a lesbian? Hardly. Girl-girls such as Yvonne and Connie often reinforced the tomboy survivor narrative by emphasizing the ways in which they were never sports-minded, or "active," or running around in clothes ready for the laundry basket. Connie could have used the story about punching out a childhood friend, if only in her sleep, to portray herself as a protobutch to be reckoned with. Instead, she depicted herself as shy and unassertive, consistent with middle-class Anglo notions of femininity. When Connie said she played street sports, she felt compelled to add, "I was not real athletic." Although Yvonne mentioned dance lessons and football games with her brother, she, too, was quick to characterize herself as no athlete. By opening their accounts with references to sports, Yvonne and Connie distinguished themselves as a different sort of lesbian while keeping the tomboy-turns-into-a-dyke narrative intact.

It's hard to get yourself across as the kind of lesbian whose life departs from the conventional story line. Because "the tomboy" is a raced, classed, and nationed figure, the task becomes harder for some folks than others. Is it mere coincidence that white girls were usually the ones to tell tomboy stories in their most standardized form?

Edith and L. J. tended to look right through their whiteness, speaking as though they had no color at all. The comforts of living white in a racist society allowed them to disregard their own racial location in ways not available to people of color facing a white interviewer. Yet race and culture are embedded in their narratives. When they mentioned cowboy hats and coonskin caps, they did not go on to talk about the Mexican sheepherders or the African-American cowboys and buffalo soldiers who historically worked the frontier, but about light-skinned TV heroes such as Daniel Boone and The Rifleman who played to the fantasies of a particular generation.

To the degree that "tomboy" implies a certain flexing of the muscles, it also tends to be (white?) working-classed. Teresa distanced herself from the term, with its overtones of athleticism and its disregard for social graces, in the course of describing what it meant to come from an upper-middle-class Cuban background. Yet she picked out a boyish, if not especially *tom*boyish, incident (playing the prince) to establish the timelessness of her desire for women. Edith, in contrast, slipped almost effortlessly into "tomboy." Like many working-class whites in the United States, Edith called herself middle-class. But she grew up in a cold-water flat with a father who earned his money doing skilled manual labor. Her class location as an adult depended upon the gendered transgression of picking up a hammer in an occupation that forced her to be "tough as nails."

Although Edith's father praised her for her boyish ways, L. J.'s upwardly mobile parents sensed that the way L. J. wanted to gender herself might affect her chances of getting ahead. L. J. made an astute choice when she adopted the veterinarian's wife as her hero in the fight to cut her hair. The vet's wife offered living, breathing proof that short hair could coexist with heterosexuality, white skin, *and* class respectability.

Setting up "the tomboy" as a precursor to "the dyke" can make things difficult for women of color who want to project themselves as lesbians, especially to white audiences. Not that it would be impossible for a black or brown girl to portray herself as a tomboy who had graduated to adult gay life. After years of working in the fields, Rose laid claim to all the requisite tomboy attributes: baby muscles, constant motion, a preference for the outdoors. But white people sometimes read those attributes in African-American girls as par for the course rather than the sort of gender rebellion imagined to lead to "other things."

According to Patricia Hill Collins, the most prevalent images of African-American women either desexualize them (the mammy) or hypersexualize them (the welfare mother, the whore). A person who buys into these representations will not picture African-American women as young ladies who need to be sheltered, courted, and protected. So a girl like Rose who violates prescriptions for white, middle-class femininity may come as no great surprise. Many Anglos fail to recognize differently raced and classed styles of gendering, in which a girl can be physical, assertive, street-smart, athletic, but still and all, not mannish.

Asian-American women often find themselves in a different kind of double bind. As JeeYuen Lee has noted, they face an uphill battle if they want to be taken as butch, given the feminized stereotypes applied to Asians. The distorted view of Asian Americans as a thoroughly middle-class "model minority" doesn't help. But let a Korean-American girl adopt an appearance that translates into "femininity" in the dominant parlance, and white people are liable to mistake her for straight. So will at least some African Americans and Latinas, although there has been much less discussion of the ways that race/class/gender-typing comes into play when women of color relate to one another *across* colors.

Does childhood gender-bending imply lesbian identity if a person is not Anglo, "American," and middle-class? No wonder Teresa speculated about what it would have been like to live out her sexuality in Cuba. Would "it" even have been the same sexuality? Although playing a "male" part on stage might have signaled a mild form of gender rebellion back on the island, would such childhood episodes have signified "queer"? Looking at gender through the prism of race and class and nation opens up the whole question of what counts as gender inversion, gender transgression, or "cross-gendering."

And just whose prescriptions were these young girls supposed to be defying? The tomboy as gender rebel and the lesbian as tomboy survivor challenge a certain conception of middle-class white womanhood. But L. J.'s struggle for short hair would probably not have played itself out the same way in an

American Indian context. For some Native American groups, long hair marks a young girl (or boy) as "traditional," signifying a particular kind of "Indianness." Clamoring for short hair can register as cultural rebellion rather than a predictor of homosexuality down the road.

It's not that class and color and gender and sexuality operate independently. They're just not always intertwined in the ways that people tend to assume. Teresa constantly encountered Anglos who took one look at her complexion and defined her right out of "Latina." Or pitied her for a poverty she had never experienced. The end of the day left her bone-weary from ricocheting back and forth between the ignorant and the exotic in the eyes of these beholders. Finding a Chicana lover allowed Teresa to "find identity" and, with it, a peaceful resolution to her immigrant saga. Or so the story goes. But maybe that's a bit romanticized, as happy endings tend to be. Presumably not just any Latina lesbian would do, or Teresa could have ended up locked in conflict with a whitewashed version of her younger self.

Rose lost her son to the court of law that declared her an unfit parent. Did this young African-American woman, tomboy or no, look too much like a bulldagger for the judge's taste? Or did he gaze right past her emerging sexuality to see another "welfare mother" without the steady job required by the standard of white, middle-class "fitness" built into the system?

Yvonne was in no danger of being taken for a bulldagger. But like other African-American lesbians perceived as femme, she had to fend off unwanted attention from people who treated her as God's special gift to them. Growing up middle-class did not deliver her from racist representations that confused African-American femininity with sexual availability.

Ballet was just one kind of lesson Yvonne carried with her out of childhood. "If you're a middle-class black, you learn to be white," she declared. "Or at least in certain circumstances." This is a complicated statement, because it recognizes the racing of class at the same time as it cedes "genuine" black experience to poor African Americans. Dance lessons could signify as a "white thing," as well as an index of girly refinement and a luxury only money could buy. Yet Yvonne's color kept her from slipping effortlessly into whiteness. In a world without racially segregated neighborhoods, Yvonne's mother would have been spared the long drives to take her daughter to the ballet lessons that were supposed to train her to assume her proper station.

From a working-class perspective, Rose wondered about all those middle-class lesbians in their raggedy jeans. How could they ever go out for a fancy dinner? Class granted them the privilege not to *have* to dress "up" to make the scene. But Rose's comments also move discussions of gender beyond simplistic contrasts. At some point it occurred to her that dressing up didn't necessarily mean going white or going African-American femme. "I dress nice," Rose said, "but I dress nice *different*." Race and class relations guarantee that there are as many versions of lesbian gendering as there are versions of childhood stories.

Contrary to what you might expect, women who marshaled tomboy stories to "explain" *sexual* identity often denied that childhood experiences had anything to do with *gendered* identities. ("I used to play with trucks, so there's no doubt that I'm a lesbian, but that doesn't make me butch.") Despite her youthful passion for short hair, L. J. did not consider herself a stud. Yvonne and Connie thought others perceived them as femme, but neither identified as such. Rose said she disliked "roles," preferring to think of herself as more not-femme than butch. In private moments with her lover, Edith saw herself developing a more flexible approach to gender. Teresa believed in masculine and feminine "sides" but refused to locate herself squarely in either.

The thing about childhood stories is that people always formulate them in retrospect. Women construct the past as they construct the narrative. If depicting yourself as a tomboy is the easiest way to claim a lesbian identity, you can, as Connie put it, "emphasize the more physical aspects of your story." Might as well focus on tree-climbing instead of little details like pregnancy or that collection of Barbie dolls. Edith went to great lengths to portray herself as her "father's son" when she could just as well have cast herself as a "teenage mother." Rose downplayed childbirth as an outcome of growing up in a part of the country where she couldn't find "nobody else gay." Inconsistencies with the tomboy survivor narrative can be edited out, and consistency manufactured in the telling.

Rose suspected as much. "I wonder were they like that all their lives?" she asked of the women who showed up at the bar in boots and leather, dressed to kill. If they could "butch up" their presentation so drastically over the few years Rose had frequented the club, they seemed perfectly capable of modifying stories from childhood.

Knowing what you know today can also change what you see when you look back over your shoulder. If Edith had gone on to remain unhappily heterosexual, she might have remembered her habit of giving flowers to girlfriends as part of the intimacy associated with friendship. Teresa could have characterized those behind-the-bookshelf kisses as a passing grade school fancy with no real bearing on her adult life. It's often a matter of interpretation, not fabrication.

Memory falters in the absence of a story. But what about the conditions in which people grew up? Did early childhood experiences encourage lesbians to re-vision themselves as tomboys, or tomboy-nots? Or were these women, as

Connie believed, picking and choosing from the debris of time to come up with tales that would "support the whole myth" of the lesbian as tomboy survivor?

However you answer that question, it is clear that families do not have the power to set a gender agenda for life. For one thing, families are not the only sites for socialization. Edith may have been raised as a son, but she also learned about gender through organized sports, not to mention "girl training" courtesy of the Roman Catholic church. While Rose's public school teacher was lending her books on sexuality, Yvonne was coming to terms with the specter of "Miss K," the headmistress at her private girls' school. Miss K's studly manner proved as frightening to the young Yvonne as *la marimacha* Pat had been to Marta Rosales. But the gendered differences Yvonne discovered at school, Marta studied at work.

Shifts in the political and economic winds can bring the sites of socialization full circle, from education to religion to employment and back again to families. If Teresa's father had not traveled the globe in search of a job as a refugee from the Cuban revolution, Teresa might never have ended up playing "boy games" with her brother. Moving so often threw the siblings back upon their own resources and gave Teresa another story about an unconventionally gendered childhood.

To complicate things, "the family" is not one entity, a single site for learning about gender. Rose's family looked nothing like the nuclear family of *Father Knows Best*, or even the blended family of *The Brady Bunch*. After working in the fields as a child, she never once aspired to "lay at home and let some man take care of me." Uncles shared Rose's household; other relatives lived down the road, including a grandmother who sheltered Rose when things got rough.

Even within families, childrearing can be at odds with cultural prescriptions for "proper" behavior. Rose's stepfather molested her. How much farther can you get from the way family relations are supposed to be? Not that childhood sexual abuse makes you queer. If she had been rich, Rose figured, she could "just run away, fly away" from the abuse and "probably came out sooner."

As any parent knows, even the best-intentioned attempts to teach children do not always bring about the desired effects. Ballet lessons worked to feminize Yvonne in a way that L. J.'s sewing lessons did not. Like many self-described tomboys, L. J. envied boy-boys their perceived freedoms. Left to her own devices, she headed outdoors. Because some gender lessons "take" while others do not, socialization alone cannot explain gendered differences. In a case such as L. J.'s, gender instruction ran headlong into gendered insurrection.

If tomboy stories have a moral, it's that there's more to childhood gender rebellion than "crossing" between two fixed positions (boy/girl, masculine/feminine). Edith, the consummate tomboy, didn't want to grow up because she thought adulthood would entail becoming a man. Tomboy turns out to be one thing, man another, butch another, transgender yet another. (Unless you avail yourself of hormones and surgery, Rose insisted, "You still a woman, right?") And if you recognize the racing and classing of a term such as "tomboy," it makes even less sense to talk about gender inversion. How can you switch from girl to boy, or boy to girl, if these terms have no set meaning? Working-class African-American girl to middle-class African-American butch, maybe. Get specific, though, and you end up with more than two positions.

Then there's the practice of out-boying the boys. Edith didn't mimic her childhood companions. Instead, she hit the ball farther than any of the guys in the neighborhood. As an adult, she worked an eight-hour shift with a broken finger that would have sent most male coworkers to the emergency room. When people like Edith haul out the storytelling equivalents of childhood photos, they are surely up to something. But the name of the game isn't inversion.

Chapter 4   Copycat

Scratch a lesbian couple, and you'll find a couple of heterosexuals. Or, more precisely, heterosexual wannabes. After all, somebody must be "the man." For the better part of a century, that's been the prevailing wisdom about lesbian relationships. The best efforts of the "women-loving-women" of the 1970s to eliminate gendered differences from their relationships through the look-alike, act-alike stance of androgyny didn't do much to shake this misconception. Too often, ambiguity just paved the way for harassment and interrogation. The bottle thrown from a passing car sailed toward its target on the back of a question: "Who's the guy?"

The belief that gay relationships mirror straight relationships is the stuff of fantasy, fiction, and stereotype. Almost to a person, lesbians say it's not that way. Some fight back against this simple-minded claim with the argument that same-sex relationships are about shared gender, not gendered differences. Women-loving-women, right? Of course, that leaves the little matter of so-called "roles."

When it comes to femme and butch, charges of imitation reappear, this time in the mouths of gay women. Perhaps, some speculate, butch/femme is just another form of male/female worming its way into gay relationships.

Like many lesbian-feminists of the 1970s, they see butch/femme as a practice that takes heterosexuality as the standard for measuring all things queer.

The second-hand clothes of a borrowed gender are almost sure to come up second-best, given the premium placed on originality in the United States. Where's the pride in mimicking someone else? But imitation is itself a vexed subject. Exactly who, or what, are lesbians supposed to be imitating? Individual heterosexuals? People who may be as deviant as your mother, as law-abiding as your Uncle Frank (who never did get around to applying for that green card), as fun-loving as the family down the hall, as quiet as the couple with the cement deer on the lawn before the police arrived to arrest the man of the house and carry his wife's shattered body away?

If imitation does not set its sights on individuals, then what? Too many *I Love Lucy* reruns? How about something more abstract, like gender roles? But what are roles, anyway? A white, middle-class model for gendering? Then wouldn't your relationship to imitation differ, depending upon whether you yourself are white or well-off? Could there be as many ways of gendering heterosexuality as homosexuality? Does it even make sense to talk about a prepackaged "woman's role" or "man's role" (much less femininity and masculinity) apart from race and class?

The flip side of the imitation argument contends that gay women have created relationships without the benefit of models. Their partnerships represent forays into uncharted territory, completely set apart from heterosexuality. So what if one partner always takes out the garbage? Why does that have to have anything do with heterosexuality, much less gender? In this interpretation, butch/femme appears to carry forward a uniquely lesbian "tradition."

Some of the women in this chapter think imitation whenever they think butch/femme. They wonder why anyone would bother incorporating gendered contrasts into lesbian relationships. Isn't the point of being queer to get away from all that mess? Yet they voice questions and desires that testify to a lingering ambivalence, even attraction, to forms of gendering they associate with heterosexuality.

Later chapters feature women who argue just as strongly that it is possible to have gendered differences in a lesbian relationship without casting that relationship in a straight image. These women are more inclined to ask why people so easily equate femme with femininity, or butch with masculinity. Isn't there anything distinctive that sets lesbian gendering apart from heterosexual relationships?

Cynthia Murray: "The Dads Always Drive the Boat"

"It's something that I never did quite understand: the why. Why women are extremely butch, or why women are extremely femme. My perception of it has always been, if I wanted to go out with a guy I'd go out with a guy. I wouldn't go out with a butch woman. And I can't understand the mountains of makeup. But I can understand the feeling glamorous part of it.

"I lived in Los Angeles before I moved up here, for eleven years, and I met a lot of older women that were gay. I saw photographs of them when they were young and one of them looked like Rory Calhoun. He was an actor. He did a lot of Westerns in the 1950s and early 1960s. Really dark hair and really blue eyes; quite the ladies' man. This one woman [who] showed me the pictures of her looking like Rory Calhoun—she looked so femme when she was in her fifties! She just died a couple of years ago. She was telling me that she went through so much inner turmoil because that was the only way she could get to go out with the women she wanted. Because the femme women liked butch women.

"A lot of the women that I met in L.A. that were butch were like that: in one way or another, they all acted like my dad. And some of them dressed like my dad. He was a hunter, a kind of rednecked street kind of guy. He was a party guy. So he was fun but he was very macho and had his opinions. He had my mother on this pedestal; that's where she should be. He installed swimming pools, so [he wore] everything from coveralls to Levis to man-pants and man-shoes. Shoes made out of petroleum products!

"My initial thought, I suppose, when I was a kid was that I wanted to be a man, not that I wanted to be gay. I wasn't content being a woman. I waterskied and liked driving the boat. The dads always drive the boat—the mom never got to drive the boat. I did things that women just didn't do when I was really young. Like most girls wouldn't walk into a bar by themselves. I would walk into a bar anywhere. I never cared. If I wanted a cocktail, I'd go into a bar! And that was unheard of. Things that it was okay for men to do but it wasn't okay for women to do.

"[Then those things] became more socially acceptable among people in general, among the masses. You saw women going to the moon and they weren't gay. You saw women driving cars and there wasn't someone in Arkansas saying, 'Oh my god, she's queer!' That's one of the good things I think the women's organizations have done. And I'm not on the feminist band-wagon, either.

"A lot of the so-called feminists, they've come a long way, they've accom-plished a lot for women, but they've also made it very difficult for women, especially in the corporate atmosphere. Because a lot of times now men will automatically think, 'She's an executive, so she's a bitch. It just goes hand in hand, because she had to fight twice as hard to get where she is.' And that's not true, so it's harder to deal in business now.

"Being gay has never been a major thing for me. No, the butch/femme thing is what confused me. I was fine with being gay; it seemed very natural to me. My parents were very good about it, very understanding, and it didn't break their hearts or anything. But before I knew what gay was, I thought, 'Why do I want to sleep with women? I must want to be a man.' I used to fantasize about being butch and actually about being male. So I took that and ran with it, and that was what made it hard.

"But then when I got older and became more aware of my sexuality, I was really glad that I was a woman. I became more confident with myself. So that is what led me to be more femme than butch. I'm getting a little too old to be active enough to be that butch! As far as being the truck-driving type mama, I don't know! Since I'm calmer now it doesn't make me so aggressive. When I think of butch I think aggressive."

Given what Cynthia described as a change from butch to femme over the course of her 34 years, I was curious about how she thought others perceived her. "First impressions mean a lot. That's why I think how I'm dressed would have a lot to do with it. If it's on one of those days where I just climbed off of a motorcycle, I think I'm going to look more butch than femme! But women that know me think of me as more femme than butch.

"I used to hate it, when I was a little kid, being called a boy. It still pisses me off on the telephone if someone calls me 'sir.' But I think it's for different reasons now. Now it's because I like my voice and I'm comfortable with my voice and I don't feel that it sounds like a man's voice. I feel that they're not paying attention to what they're doing. (You'll listen to this [on tape] and go, 'She *did* sound like a man'!) But when I was a little kid it was because I was afraid of my thoughts, of what I was thinking about wanting to be a boy. And so when they called me that by mistake, I would feel that they knew my deepest, darkest secret. So it was much more sensitive for me then.

"I don't think the butch women are going femme because of their careers. I just think that many more feminine women are coming out of the closet. Especially on the West Coast, because it's so much more socially acceptable here. When I was in a job position that I had to dress up every day, I really resented wearing skirts and femme clothes and lace. I really resented it, because I dressed up every day, so it wasn't special. But now I don't have to and it's more fun to dress up and go out. I get more looks when I'm dressed like that than when I'm dressed more butch. From men *and* women.

"When I flew to New Orleans [on business] recently, I had a layover in Texas. All the guys in Texas were like, 'Oh, let me get your bag! Let me get the door!' They were such gentlemen in that respect. It was real different, because I wasn't accustomed to that in L.A. And I do that for men, too. I don't think that courtesy should stop at whether you're butch or femme or male or female. It's just common courtesy.

"I've always thought people should capitalize on their talents. So I feel I should accentuate being a woman. Not trying to change it but trying to accentuate it and make it better."

Charlyne Harris: "You Act Like a White Girl"

"A lot of black males, they don't know that I'm a lesbian. I have a good relationship with them. And it's how I treat them, too. I'm not real aggressive with them. I think men in general have a real strong ego, but black men, especially, their egos need to be acknowledged. You know: 'I am the man and you are the woman.' So it's very few black men that I have a good relationship with that *know* I'm a lesbian. I can't think of one.

"Right now I'm pretty much involved in the black community. But they don't know that I'm a lesbian, too, see. It would dampen our relationship. There would be less trust. Most of them are Muslim, and they *really* believe that homosexuality is bad. Who I sleep with would change their whole ideas about me, when yet and still, my personality is the exact same with them. But just saying that I was a lesbian, I'd be a degenerate! I'd be a degenerate, that's what I would be. And they would try to change my mind.

"When I moved to the Bay Area [as a child], it was really something different for me. I had never lived where it was all blacks, or a majority of blacks. I had a little trouble there. Because my slang was a little different, and just my whole character was different. And you know they noticed it right away. They said, 'Aw, you talk like a white girl. You act like a white girl.' Because the schools I went to [before] was majority white. There was not a lot of racial problems. Kids played together and you never tripped. Well, you know you're black and you know they're white, you know the skin color's different, but mentally you don't really know. It was never like, 'Oh, you're different than I am.' None of that ever came up until I got older.

"[Growing up, we] never really suffered, as far as financially. We always had. My mom made her way. And my grandmother had a little money. I mean, not too many black kids take tap dance. [My mom] always made a little bit of money go a long ways." As an adult, Charlyne made her living in the trades.

She was amused to discover that "some women find that real romantic. I don't. It's money. The money's good, and I like what I'm doing, working with my hands.

"I had a boyfriend tell me that I would end up sleeping with women. I don't know what made him think that I will. I know I was real aggressive with him. He couldn't tell me what to do. It was always, 'We are equal!' And I was always making that known. 'There's nothing a woman can do for me.' I remember telling him that.

"I was messing with older men, and they would want to be the aggressor. You know, 'Do what I say.' I started coming out of that shit—I couldn't take that. Then the real me started coming out: 'Uh-uh, buddy, wait a minute! No, no, no.' And then we started clashing. My relationships with men changed, became bad relationships. I remember with my ex-boyfriend, he wanted me to be home at a certain time, wear certain clothes. I couldn't wear this, I can't wear that. 'You're not my father! Shit!' We'd get into arguments like that. I couldn't take that 'I'm the man, you're the woman.' This kind of a relationship [where] you're down here.

"I go to church. Baptist churches are real, real dramatic. They leave a heavy impression on you. When they preach, it's kind of scary. People start shouting. I don't know who said it, but it stuck in my head that if you're bad you go to hell. You know, God is watching you! At all times! I had to come to believe that God, as I understood God, is a loving God. It doesn't matter who you sleep with, just as long as your heart's good.

"If I'd have stayed in my neighborhood, I probably would have never came out. Never. But here there's so much support to be who you are, not to deny yourself. [My mother and I] talk about men. I'd say, 'Well, you know, I *am* attracted to men physically, just not emotionally.' And I said, 'Well, I could get married and see women on the side.' And she's saying, 'No, you got to make up your mind. You can't go back and forth. You got to make up your mind.' She thinks it would affect my relationships, and it would. It would. So I just decided for right now that I enjoy being with women and that's who I'm going to be with.

"I think, being a woman, I'm a woman, and women have certain moods. I don't think that I should put myself in a category and say, 'Well, I'm butch,' and deny myself to feel certain things. I like wearing dresses sometimes. Sometimes I like wearing makeup. I couldn't do it every day—I wouldn't want to do it every day. But yeah, sometimes I get in real feminine moods. Some of [the men at work] might not even believe me [if I told them I was gay]. Because they have such stereotyped ideas about how lesbians are supposed to be. Real aggressive at all times, and real, real butch."

When she first moved to San Francisco, Charlyne had tried to change her style. "A certain [butch] way of talking, a certain walk and dress. Until I learned that, no, I'll just be myself. [It helped] seeing different, other lesbians. Experience." In the beginning, though, "the [racial] prejudice thing threw me off guard. I didn't think I would have to deal with that [in the gay community]. Prejudice is something that no one has to say to you. You *feel* it. You would think that, because being gay you know what that feels like to be discriminated against, that you would not want to make anybody else feel that.

"And this butch female thing, I stereotyped that to the max, [until] I found out different. Just because a woman seem like she's real feminine doesn't mean she doesn't have butch qualities. And that doesn't mean that they don't come out. I'd rather come up to a female than for them to come up to me. It makes me nervous or uncomfortable when a woman approaches me. When women do come up to me, I find that I'll switch it around real fast where I'm the aggressor. I think that's my part in being butch! I like being the aggressor. Not in bed, though, all the time.

"You pick up male-orientated things from being around males, and I try to watch it that I don't have male-orientated ideas. Like I went to a strip show once, a female strip show. That's male-orientated, and I had to really check out why, why was I going?" "So why were you going?" I asked Charlyne. "Women were taking off their clothes," she replied. "Women were taking off their clothes, that's why I was going! I had to let that be okay, and not really trip off [by telling myself], 'Well, this is male-orientated.'"

Paula Nevins: "I Never Knew There Were Feminine Lesbians"

"I didn't give a shit about being a lesbian. I wanted to sleep with Stephanie. If that meant that I was a lesbian, fine. So one day when we were having lunch — we were having a tunafish sandwich in Union Square — I told her that I was interested in having a relationship with her, and I wasn't real picky about what it looked like. It could look like friends if she wanted it to look like that, but it felt like more.

"Stephanie was really the first woman that I knew [who] was up front and gay. [The first] that I had an opportunity to be with and talk to and not be afraid. Because the only lesbians that I really knew were the — how can I say? — the obvious, very butch type. I never knew there were feminine lesbians. Stephanie was a prom queen." Ironically, Stephanie had always assumed that Paula, as the veteran of a heterosexual marriage, was straight. The two women embarked upon what turned out to be a five-year relationship.

Although Paula considered butch/femme "role-playing" and "a trap," she thought she could understand its attractions. "The roles have sort of been cast, so you don't have to worry about who's butch and who isn't, who should do the asking and who should wait to be asked, who should make the first move. You know, all of the 'shoulds' that go on with women that make women kind of crazy."

As a small business owner with a large lesbian clientele, Paula said, "I've talked to a lot of women and [butch/femme] comes up consistently around this whole dating/sexual issue. They have a hard time with it. Also, it's not easy to find women who are very interested in being casual and not wanting to bond to you. I mean, you can talk about 'I just would like to be sexual or see you once in a while.' Most women don't want to go for that. They really don't. It may be just a three-month period of time, but they basically want to eat, drink, and sleep you. I don't want to do that, and so what I want may be difficult for me to have at this point. I'm going to try and have it, though.

"I'm not sure that the only way to have a casual affair in the lesbian community isn't to get somebody who has a primary relationship but wants to sleep around. So then you're safe. But I think that with women, the bonding issue comes up much stronger than with men. I have very close, intimate relationships with men that are not sexual, but I have never had the real intense, intimate relationship with a man that I have with women.

"Although I've been very, very sexual in my life with men, I was never into it. It was always like paint-by-numbers. I never did anything from an emotional place; I was always absolutely detached from the person. I always felt there was something wrong with me, because I never liked to go to the drive-in and make out. And the interesting thing is, men never had any trouble getting into it. I always wondered, well, can't they sense that I'm not really into this? But I don't think they could, because I think their own needs were primary."

Sometimes Paula wondered if she were moving into bisexuality. "There are times when I don't feel like a lesbian at all. There are times when I do. Certainly relationships with men are a lot simpler. Men are very simple beings." A few months earlier Paula had met a teenage boy while hiking at Yosemite. She described him as "this very beautiful, innocent being. I can't really consider him a man." Contrasting him to "a street-smart nineteen-year-old from San Francisco," Paula found him "lovely, small-town, virginal," with hair to his shoulders. After the two made love on a rock with the river waters swirling around them, Paula decided that "in a sense it wasn't really about sex for me. [It was about] opening up to a very innocent, masculine, young part of myself."

Since she was a child, Paula said she had always "identified with the

Superman archetype, or the Mighty Mouse archetype, or the young boy that slays the dragon and saves the princess. I feel that I'm really kind of androgynous. [Yet] I'm definitely more on the masculine side of the scale. There's no doubt about it, because I'm very attracted to the other side of the scale: blonde, blue-eyed Renaissance maidens."

Jeanne Riley: "All These Women Were Throwing Themselves at Me"

"I was a very awkward, gawky straight woman. Somebody said, 'Yes, sir,' to me once when I was wearing a dress! I didn't walk right, I didn't talk right. I was never very comfortable in the classic female role. And I went from a very awkward straight woman to realizing at a certain point, when I was younger, that I was a gorgeous dyke. I used to be able to walk into a social scene or a bar or whatever and women would be immediately interested in me. I was very used to being looked at, and sought after. So I became conscious of feeling that I was quite nice looking and quite attractive. [Coming out] really did change my sense of self-esteem."

On the other side of the room Jeanne's young children played with a block set, thoroughly engrossed in the construction of towers, ramps, and bridges. Over what Jeanne called "leftover kid food"—macaroni and cheese and hot dogs—we sat talking about the process that had led to Jeanne's self-definition as a lesbian and her distaste for the categories "butch" and "femme." She had grown up white in an area of the Western United States with a predominantly American Indian population. "When I was twelve, we started working in the fields. Then, any money we made went to the family, so we worked *for* the family.

"All of my friends were Indians. There was a real different orientation towards money. You get your Indian money, go down to the city and blow it. And you wear it. You drive it. People were very conscious about clothes and dressing. So I think by the time I went to high school, wearing my mother's clothes cut down to fit me was not exactly socially acceptable. I was very conscious of being poor. Now everyone [in that area] was poor, so it was relative. But there were people that spent money and people that didn't. Like my parents felt that it was wasteful to spend money on things like glasses. So I was blind when I was a very small kid. Probably the most phenomenal experience I've ever had in my life is the first time I was able to see. To look at a tree and know that it has leaves on it."

Jeanne began dating after she left home, over her parents' strenuous objections, to attend college on a scholarship. "Southern Baptism does not lend itself to romance," she smiled ruefully. "The rule was there about [not] dating, but I went to an Indian high school. So it was mixed up with racism."

Unlike many women who first defined themselves as lesbians during the 1970s, Jeanne did not come out in the context of the women's movement. "The community's gone through different phases. I think at one time, to be a real lesbian, you had to wear a vest and write poetry. And it helped if you worked as a printer, too." Speaking of her own employment history, she added, "I think that a lot of the women who have gone into the trades have been seen as butch. Not all of them are, in a classic sense. But because it is definitely a woman doing a *man's* job, then you sort of take on the clothes, the attitude. You're around men a lot. It's hard for women who are separatist to be in the trades, because you have to survive with men.

"Some people say, 'Oh, you're going into the trades. You just want to be a man.' I think that there are some women that do that. But that isn't why *I* do it. I like the work. But in that you're doing what's considered man's work, you're seen more in terms of those masculine kinds of things. If you say you can fix a car, people are like, 'Oh, well, that's a male thing.' You get some, 'What do you do?' 'Oh, I'm an accountant.' Or, 'Oh, I'm a nurse.' 'Oh, I'm a teacher.' All of those have sex roles that are attached to them. So when you say, 'Oh, I'm in the trades'—you *have* to be butch! There's nothing left.

"In my teaching [vocational education classes] I really try to get people to not feel they have to do that. In fact, it's *easier* if you don't act on all that stuff. I have a woman in my class right now who's into wearing leather. She went on an interview for UPS in a leather vest, a leather tie, and leather pants, and wondered why she didn't get the job. I says, 'Eh, uh, let me tell ya! Next time you're gonna go looking like a Catholic schoolgirl!'

"I think the most awkward time I ever had was [when] there was a James Dean party. I love James Dean! We all had to go in fifties things, so of course I went as James Dean, with the engineer boots and the rolled-up pants. Put Dixie Peach in my hair. What was really interesting that evening was [how] all of these women were throwing themselves at me. I really became conscious of there are women in the lesbian community that want a woman to look like a man. And so it bothered me, the whole butch/femme thing.

"I like women who are strong and independent and very much who they are. But they don't have to look like a man or a femme fatale. I went through a period where I had girlfriends who were like Miss Arizona. They were all classically gorgeous. After going through that, I really got more of a sense of looking at people for who they are, rather than for what they look like.

"At that James Dean party, where people were interested in me, we went out and we toured all the bars, of course, because that's what you were supposed to do in those days [c. 1975]. And because I looked like a man, it was interesting. I really became sensitive to that: people *wanting* me to be butch, or wanting me to be this male person. That *that's* what was attractive.

"People consider Diana, who I've been with for the past twelve years, to be very butch. And so it's real confusing to people, because people that know *me* consider *me* to be very butch. We've played on ball teams before, where we've both been on the team. We played for this one black team in Oakland. There were three white women on the team: me, the pitcher, and Diana. And the role of girlfriend on that team, which was much more segregated into butch/femme kinds of roles, was to sit on the bench and yell! It was real confusing that we were *both* playing and that we were *both* good players.

"Diana had a better social context with them, because I'm sort of country. In the black community, being sort of rural, I don't make the urban connection that Diana does. I'm too polite or something. So they decided, all right, Diana's the *real* butch. And they started treating me like I should be on the bench! Like, 'What's your problem? Don't you know your role? You're not supporting your woman,' and all this. Including me with the girls.

"I've been in contexts where people have wanted me to be the femme and people have wanted me to be the butch. When you go into the trades, it's considered to be not exactly feminine stuff. And I've never been considered feminine, when I was straight or a lesbian. I was always the person asking people to dance. I think that some people would characterize me as butch, but that in my own sense, I see myself as more androgynous. I enjoy confusing people."

Copycat: Double Takes

What is it about fluff and stud—but particularly stud—that bothers people like Jeanne Riley? Above all, they wonder why anyone would go to great lengths to live as something she's not. If you're so enamored of "boy" things, why not become a man? Improved surgical techniques, hormones, and the support of a growing transgender movement make the female-to-male move an increasingly viable option. A related objection, directed toward women who choose butches as partners, asks why they don't get themselves a "real one" if that manly swagger turns them on. Wouldn't it make more sense to "stay straight" (much less hassle) than go through life as a femme?

These commonplace reactions make few, if any, distinctions between man and mannish, between regendering your style and transgendering your body, between masculine and stud, between feminine and femme, between wholesale replication and playful impersonation, between becoming male and passing for male, between passing for male and presenting as butch. "If I wanted to go out with a guy I'd go out with a guy," insisted Cynthia Murray, momentarily collapsing "butch" into "man." Yet Cynthia didn't reject butch/femme out of hand. Only its "extremes."

Jeanne tended to use "butch" interchangeably with "masculine." Shocked by the number of women attracted to her gelled, jeaned, and booted character at a James Dean party, Jeanne concluded that some lesbians want a woman who looks like a man. Melissa Simpson, in contrast, claimed she had never known a butch who had actually wanted to *be* a man: "In fact, most of them didn't *like* men very much."

Raye Porter had spent years controlling anger and shame when people mistakenly called her "sir." For Raye, this kind of oversight produced a gendered invisibility compounded by the invisibility she often experienced as a woman of color. Neither Raye nor Melissa considered transgender a logical extension of butch. Reconstructing anatomy was something else, although women who went the transgender route may once have thought of themselves as studs.

Then there was Cynthia, who said she used to "want to be a man." What did those words mean to her? As a child, she thought being a man would give her the freedom to walk into a bar by herself, the authority to pilot a boat. In retrospect, she described her youthful longing to "switch sexes" as the product of a particular time and place. By 1990 it had become more acceptable for white women of her class to frequent clubs and other public spaces without a male escort. As social conditions changed, what Cynthia wanted and her reasons for wanting it changed. Her desire to go boy disappeared, having had as much to do with power and the historical moment as with anatomy. Over the years and the changes from aspiring male to butch to femme-loving-femme, Cynthia's deep voice remained untouched. In her current reincarnation as femme, did those bass tones make her sound "like a man" or, rather, "sultry"?

"Like a man" occupies a key position in the meager vocabulary available for talking about gender and power. It is a phrase thrown around all too lightly, never designed to bear the weight of complex negotiations or to cover such a multitude of situations. What is this notion of "like a man," if not that old bugaboo, imitation?

When Charlyne Harris entered the trades, she did it for money, not because she thought she could attract women by looking "like a man" or because of any romanticized notions about joining the working class. Growing up with enough, but not much, had made her very pragmatic about the importance of a steady income. Jeanne first applied for a blue-collar job because she thought she would like the work. Even though she acknowledged that she had gradually assumed the clothes and "the attitude" that came with a "man's job," Jeanne maintained that her work boots had nothing to do with imitation, transgender, butch identity, or aspirations toward anything male.

Jeanne resisted the idea that crafting things from wood or metal made her "like a man," just as she resisted people's attempts to label her butch on the basis of occupation. Yet Jeanne herself could not completely separate the embodied effects of working in the trades from matters of gender. Remember, this is the same woman who once got called "sir" in a dress.

Problems begin when you try to reduce elaborately gendered effects to terms such as "male-identified." ("What was all that 'male-identified' stuff about?" younger women who had missed the heyday of lesbian-feminism repeatedly asked me.) Charlyne discovered the inadequacy of this particular concept at a strip show. The performance, which some of her friends dubbed "male-orientated" by definition, did not reproduce heterosexual relations in any simple sense. Charlyne attended the show as a woman fully conscious of her desire for other woman. ("Women were taking off their clothes, that's why I was going!") Her gaze lingered on performers who gendered themselves butch on stage, as well as more "traditional" acts in feathers and lace. Did stripping by women for women set the venerable heterosexual institution of striptease on its head? The infamous dildo debates that rocked coastal lesbian communities several years later posed a similar set of questions. Must a dildo necessarily signify as a "penis substitute," or can it be, when harnessed by a lesbian, an erotic experience in its own right?

Butch-identified or not, most gay women in the Bay Area had no intention of passing for a man, much less becoming one. Faking out the boys for laughs as a twentysomething baby dyke was one thing; carrying through with the impersonation day after day was another. On the rare occasions when women had tried to pass in a serious way, they explained passing as a response to restricted economic opportunities or dangerous city streets. If passing was what it took to get a decent job at certain points in history, especially for a mannish woman, so be it.

The figure of "the butch" haunts discussions of passing, just as she does tomboy stories. Paula swore she had never suspected that lesbians could be femme, much less dazzling like the women in Jeanne's tales of her younger years. In fantasy the male-identified copycat stands in for all lesbians by taking "the" heterosexual male as her object of imitation.

Does this make the topics of passing and imitation irrelevant to feminized lesbians? Hardly. Women perceived as femme had to deal with gays and straights alike who treated them as forever on the verge of passing over into heterosexuality. This reading of femmes as a threat to "authentic" lesbianism collapses gender into sexuality in some remarkable ways. Why would anyone regard them as likely to turn bisexual or straight? Because femmes are not marked as gender rebels in the same way as butches, or even androgynous dykes. But femmes do not necessarily imitate heterosexual women, any more than butches imitate heterosexual men. Femmes can wear their gender(ing) very differently than straight girls. And they often make highly conscious decisions about how to handle the privilege that comes with passing (for white, for heterosexual, for male). Witness Cynthia, who hated to dress in frills when her job required it but rushed to don those heels for weekend wear.

The train of associations that leaves passing to the boy-girls never stops to consider what it costs a femme to go out with women who are regularly, or even erratically, slid into "male," whether or not they wannabe. And it ignores the potentially disruptive effects of gender fuck. Put that dildo on a woman with Scarlet Sunset on her lips, and who's imitating whom?

Butch/femme derives much of its appeal from an erotics of juxtaposition. Sweet-talking with silence, muscles with breasts, tenderness with bravado, a rock-hard clit under brushed cotton denim. What makes a stud is the boyish figure who remains recognizable *as* a woman. Ah, there's the excitement, and there's the rub. To anticipate a later interview with Sarah Voss: "You're presenting as a man to the most naive heterosexual from Indiana, maybe, but in the city where you probably live, you're presenting as butch. You're a slap in the face of heterosexuality. You're putting yourself in a position where you may at any time be killed by the nearest man, and his woman would probably applaud, if she doesn't go home with you."

But there's something else besides mimicry that alternately puzzles and annoys detractors of butch/femme. Many are disturbed by the apparent rigidity of "roles." They say gendered contrasts incarcerate you, hedge you in, narrow down the possibilities for what two people can build together under the auspices of a relationship. They depict butch/femme as light on creativity, heavy on prescriptions for how to behave. Studs do thus-and-such, femmes do the other. Set aside for a moment the many ways in which the practice of butch/femme has changed over the years. What sense does it make to put two women together in a household, only to legislate who orders from the menu, who paints the apartment, who asks the other out on a date, or who makes the overtures in bed? Why not celebrate instead the flexibility of an arrangement with the potential to bridge any and every gendered divide?

Paula disdained butch/femme as "a prison" and "a trap." What exactly were femmes and butches supposed to be trapped inside? The same thing they were supposed to be imitating: a "role." Accordingly, Paula emphasized sexuality over gendering in her account of coming out lesbian. In place of a tomboy story, listeners got a narrative about a woman who merely "wanted to sleep with Stephanie." Paula believed that femmes and butches had passed up a unique opportunity to break with straight ways of doing things. Sure, roles fixed the "problem" of who would make the first move. They told partners who should take responsibility for what. But they also seemed to limit the options available to women who chose other women as partners.

If jail is the dominant metaphor in discussions that fix butch/femme as a copycat maneuver, its flip side is escape. Attempts to rescue the prisoner of gender don't always target butch/femme. Sometimes they seek to purge gender from the familiar and the mundane. When Cynthia argued that holding open a door for someone is only common courtesy, she emptied an everyday gesture of gendered significance. No power relations here! (Then why are the guys in the story still the ones getting the door?)

Role theory never did much to illuminate the straight relationships it was invented to explain. Why should it be anything but a disaster when applied to same-sex relationships? The concept of "roles" freezes time and paves right over differences with homogenized terms such as "manhood" or "womanhood." If role theory is to be believed, people have little choice but to shoehorn themselves—more or less successfully—into boxes of prescribed behaviors marked "woman" and "man." Too cut-and-dried, say its critics.

Fitting all the complexities of gender into a couple of boxes requires you to ignore most of life's ambiguities and contradictions. Forget the cultural differences that made sports peripheral to Jewish conceptions of masculinity. Forget the historical changes that saw middle-class lesbians of the 1980s adopt and modify gendered styles developed in working-class neighborhoods. Forget the oversimplification entailed in reducing gender to a glittering array of two—mark that, two—choices (femme qua woman, butch qua man). For role theory to work, you need lots of consistency, no troubling glitches like the compounding of gender with race or class, and an implicit theory of motivation (the assumption that most people wannabe, or at least wannamodel, these mass-produced parts).

People tend to imagine roles as things outside the individual that tolerate no sudden deviations and brook no unannounced departures. The very idea of a role feels confining because it demands conformity to a scarcely changing script. A person has to hold the object of imitation steady in order to go about the process of reproduction, right? But is this how gendering works? How many heterosexuals would be happy with Paula's facile dismissal of their sex lives as a picture out of a paint-by-number set?

"Just because a woman seem like she's real feminine," Charlyne remarked, "doesn't mean she doesn't have butch qualities." The one who waits for another woman to ask her to dance may prefer to lead in bed. Likewise, it doesn't take an appearance in a skirt for a butch to rattle the prison bars of gender. Every butch who remains recognizable as a woman—however streetwise her posture, however close-cropped her hair—highlights inconsistency, not consistency. And inconsistency is anathema to roles.

When people talked about butch/femme as roleplaying, they often had in mind a "daddy goes to work while mommy plays house" scenario derived from reruns of 1950s television shows. Cynthia tended to view gay history through the prism of family: older gay women "all acted like my dad." But in her story of the woman who changed from butch to femme to get the stud she wanted, the reference point for "femme" may well have been an ex-lover or the femmes from the bars, rather than heterosexual relatives. Even imitating relatives could have produced queerness. If a femme's straight mother can ride and shoot with the best of them, you have to wonder which particular form of heterosexuality her daughter is presumed to be copying.

To castigate butch/femme for confining people to inflexible "roles" is to set ablaze a straw woman. Why? Because there is no single idealized, timeless, shrink-wrapped "woman's role" or "man's role." No color- and class-blind prescription for the way (gendered) things are supposed to be. Not even for heterosexuals. Jeanne grew up working in the fields for wages. Why should she ever have expected to assume the stay-at-home position of TV's Donna Reed? Charlyne's boyfriend once predicted that Charlyne would end up sleeping with women because she was aggressive. Yet "aggressive" is not a stand-alone trait. "Aggressive" is the way a have-not tends to look if she reaches for something.

When Charlyne moved to a predominantly African-American neighborhood, she faced accusations that threatened to turn her white. First there was her speech ("You talk like a white girl!"). Then there were after-school activities. Her new neighbors may have perceived tap dance lessons as a middle-class luxury with a complicated history in which black entertainers often performed for whites. For Charlyne charges of imitation were as raced and classed as they were gendered.

As an adult Charlyne tended to socialize primarily with other African Americans, and more specifically with black Muslims. She was quick to deride African-American men for getting stuck in an "I am the man and you are the woman" position. Does her statement simply apply two universal gender roles (man + woman) across racial lines? Not in light of the repeated attempts to emasculate African-American men. Not in light of the lynchings, both literal and metaphorical, that brought the defense of "African-American manhood" to the forefront of black nationalist politics. There's no doubt that "I am the man and you are the woman" had spelled oppression to Charlyne and many African-American women before her. Even so, "I am the man" means something different in response to a racist demand to bow and scrape and shuffle than if Cynthia's Euro-American father had voiced the same sentiment as he took over the wheel of the boat.

Jeanne was the rare white girl who actually talked about having a racial identity. Nevertheless, she tended to perceive herself as white in relation to people constructed as Other: classmates who spent their "Indian money" on fine clothes when her own parents would not buy her glasses; Native Americans her parents had forbidden her to date; African-American teammates who searched for gendered contrasts in order to divide Jeanne and her partner into butch and femme.

Embedded in Jeanne's narrative about the softball team are intricacies of gender and race, class and place that exceed the simplistic concepts of roles or imitation. Although Jeanne played a mean game of softball and worked in the trades, African-American women on the team eventually dubbed her partner "the butch." This calculation seemed to have involved a series of associations of (black) masculinity with street smarts, urban location, verbal repartee, and the skill to "play" at things other than sport. Where did that leave Jeanne, with her hard-shell white Baptist country roots? "Too polite or something." And, for once in her life, pegged as femme.

In a complex world, no one creates relationships, much less "traditions," in a vacuum. Because gay people pursue their relationships within a larger world, you can pretty much expect things to be mutually affected and connected. Call it the "lesbians have TV, too" theory of cultural innovation. So maybe what's at stake when lesbians gender themselves is neither mimicry of a mythical heterosexual standard nor a uniquely lesbian way of doing relationships, but something else. Could it be that queers have borrowed from heterosexuality to gender themselves in ways that are of it without being contained within it? Even—perhaps especially—in the case of butch/femme, the form most often dismissed as imitation?

Besides, there's no way to tell a copy from a model unless the copy is somehow different in its own right. Imitation is as much about divergence and distortion as a faithful, point-by-point reproduction of whatever you have in your sights. Add to this the endless possibilities raised by working with "found" materials to create something new that plays off the old. Rumor has it, writes Debbie Bender, that butch women of the 1960s used Kotex to create that unseemly bulge in their jeans. Appropriating and transforming as they went, they took the ultimate piece of "woman's" gear to fashion the genital signifier of "man." In the process, they ended up spoofing biological explanations for gender well before the era that officially gave butch/femme over to playfulness and irony.

If there is no such thing as "mere" imitation, then who knows where transformation may lead. A number of things set lesbian couples apart from the most prevalent kinds of straight relationships. Perhaps the most famous example is that of stone butches: untouchable women who derive their own satisfaction from the satisfaction of their partners. Stone butches constitute only a small segment of the women who identify as studs. But when was the last time you saw a representation of heterosexual masculinity in which a man got his pleasure by getting his partner off? Period?

There were also less dramatic contrasts, evident in Louise Romero's sense that gay women, however butch, are more likely than straight men to take "no" for an answer. If Carolyn Fisher had been interested in men, she probably would have had less difficulty finding someone older to date. Relatively few gay women in the United States support their partners financially. Femme/femme relationships such as Cynthia's tend to unsettle the whole idea of butch/femme as a heterosexuality manqué. Likewise when butches pair up with other butches.

Are there other ways to think about gendering than as a glorified color Xerox of straight relationships? Cynthia thought so. Arguing that "people should capitalize on their talents," she used a concept of accentuation to explain her decision to play up "the feminine." In an interesting way, Cynthia also ended up putting gender into motion. Her shift from butch to femme raised the possibility of regendering over the course of a lifetime. And the looks she garnered from both men and women after she styled herself femme cut right across the lines drawn by sexual identity.

The movement in Jeanne's chronicle of gender didn't even require a new wardrobe. By changing the way she saw herself in the process of changing her sexual identity, Jeanne transformed herself from an "awkward, gawky straight woman" into "a gorgeous dyke." Fluidity was something Jeanne cultivated on an everyday basis. The joy she took in "confusing people" made gender over into an expandable resource. Buy it, sell it, play with it, get lost in it, decorate and defend yourself with it. Gender for pleasure, gender for hire, gender for self-protection . . . what next?

Chapter 5   Chameleon

You can't catch me. Maybe you can't even see me. So don't try to pin me down when it comes to gender. That's the message put out by women who go chameleon. Sometimes they move back and forth between categories. Sometimes they're more concerned with blurring, blending, or pulling up gendered distinctions by the putative roots. They may take occasional refuge in a label such as "androgynous" or "queer," so long as they believe that the label itself permits a range of motion.

Chameleons like their gender fluid rather than fixed. One person's words can encompass many contradictory formulas for breaking through the monotony of "a woman is a woman is a woman." At the beginning of the interview she may proclaim the irrelevance of gender to her daily life ("I like to think I'm beyond all that"). By the end she may embrace a term like "swish" for camouflage or cover. One minute she switches between gendered positions like a lane change on a superhighway; the next she sets about balancing feminine and masculine "sides." She may delight in the discrepancies produced by playing gender mix 'n' match, or she may celebrate movement as empowering in its own right. This mobile approach to gendering contrasts sharply with Raye Porter's conviction that taking a stand as "a femme" or "a stud" offers your best defense against a world given over to injustice and to rage.

What's to be gained by following a strategy that places you here, there, everywhere? Safety? Survival? Power and pleasure, in some measured combination? Why knowingly risk the dangers of changing horses in midstream? Do the hazards and attractions of putting gender in motion depend, in part, on your location in race and class relations? Is there anything that women who articulate the chameleon position tend to share . . . say, another kind of mobility, like the one Jeanne Riley experienced when she became the first in her family to attend college?

How much shelter does constant motion give you from violence or forced dislocation? Does a little wildness, a dash of ambiguity, add up to freedom? What about the concept of gender as a resource, packaged and available for individuals to manage? Is "playing with gender" just a fancy phrase for indecisive? Are gender chameleons as different from copycats as they would like to think? Or are they equally unreflective about the categories they propose to abolish, or move between?

Is it even possible to arrive at a place beyond gender? What happens if you mix together all the categories of the gendered palette? Do you end up with a rainbow or with a color that has all the radiance of mud? What about the uncertainties that class and culture introduce when people try to move between gendered positions? You may think you're momentarily playing in the fields of femme, but what if other people read you differently? Without some context, you can never know whether that package of Lee press-on nails will be enough to do the trick.

Lourdes Alcantara: "I Spit in His Face"

"It's so hard to find out in Latin America, because women touch each other, touch hands. They kiss each other, hug a lot. They sleep together, like friends. So it's hard to tell. And besides, do you wear makeup? You can't be a lesbian. That's their minds, how they think: 'Oh, no, no, she can't be a lesbian, she wears makeup. No, no, she can't be a lesbian, she has a kid. No, no, she's married, she's not a lesbian.' So you should see a picture of myself. A *lot* of makeup!

"One thing that I wanted to remember [to say] is that I used to be like a man. Not in my behavior. Act like a man on the street, no. In bed. But it's kind of weird to think this is like a man, because men are kind of selfish. They like to get sexual satisfaction. But I didn't. I was making love to them, but they never made love to me back. Her satisfaction was my satisfaction. I never knew what an orgasm was like. So I never had sex in my life until I met this [current] lover, Lauren.

"[In Latin America] it is *supposed* to be that way, okay? Because I come to you, because I am the lesbian, you are the straight woman. In this case, it makes sense to compare it like men, because men go to women, right? And they make sex to women. They don't know if women get satisfaction or not, but they have the initiative, right? So I used to do that. I would go to them, take them out, flowers, chocolate. And then finally, let's go to bed."

When Lourdes first arrived in the United States, she lived with heterosexual immigrants from Latin America. "Aagh! I wasn't out to them! I was still wearing makeup, wearing dresses, high heels. Ah, it was terrible! I thought, 'I didn't come to this country to be the same. To keep hiding!' I said, 'Where are the homosexuals?' I didn't know 'gay,' the word 'gay.' 'Lesbian' I knew." Finally Lourdes found out about the Duchess, a lesbian bar in Greenwich Village, where she began to meet other gay women.

"Coming here, I'm finding a whole material world. I would say, 'Let's go out for lunch.' And I would pay, because that's the custom [where I grew up]. You offered, you pay. But here, no. 'Let's go' is an expression. It means you pay [yours], I pay mine. So I was really kind in New York. I went to a bar for the first time in my life, a gay bar. And I spent $120, $150, just buying everybody drinks. Taking this woman for dinner, the other woman for dinner, the other woman for pizza. Because that's the way I was! But they thought I was [a] sucker. Huh! It was so hurtful to me when I found that out.

"Because you take care of your lovers in Latin America. It's like a man, okay? Women stay home, and men go and work. So I met this woman. I was so in love with her! And the first thing she did was: 'I don't have any money for my rent.' So I said, 'Don't worry, I'll pay your rent.' I was working in the factory. Her rent was $800 a month. So I was paying her rent, and she wasn't even my lover! 'Let's go here, let's go there.' And I would be paying. I didn't care! But then I realized that she was *using* me. And another lover, again, this same shit. My friend, my best friend, she would be using me. Qué disgusting!"

At this point Jo, Lourdes's cat, interrupted the conversation by overturning the tape recorder in a bid for a seat on the couch. Although Lourdes and Lauren had given the cat an (admittedly ambiguous) "girl's name," Lourdes insisted that Jo was "really a male. But now he's neutered. So I guess he's androgynous!" Stroking his fur, she continued. "They say two butches don't get along. I mean, like lovers. I doubt that, because all my ex-lovers there were butch! Right? And I copied their behavior. I walked like them, I started talking like them. Acting like them. Because I *liked* it all. And people called me butch so I believed that I was butch."

Of all the women I interviewed, Lourdes was one of only two whose partners supported them financially. Careful planning allowed the couple to stretch Lauren's paycheck to cover not only the necessities of life but also a modest monthly remittance to Lourdes's mother back in Latin America. Lourdes considered this a temporary arrangement that would end once she secured the green card that would make her a permanent, legal resident in the United States.

I asked Lourdes how it felt, after so many years of being a provider, to rely on Lauren for an income. "Well, in the beginning it was hard. I wouldn't even touch one penny. And I'm the [money] manager. So Lauren would say, 'This is your money.' I'd say, 'No, it's not my money. It's *your* money.' We would fight days and days and months and months for that. Then I finally realized that it is okay. Lauren made me understand that, first of all, *why* does it have to be only for straight people? It's all right for men to bring money to the house, and their wives take care of the kids, take care of the house. They cook, clean. Laundry. So I do the same. Why not? 'This is a job, too,' she said. 'You are doing a job.' All the shopping, taking care of her food, taking care of her meals, bringing the bags. It's heavy. It's a job!

"I don't believe in butch or femme. I had a long, long discussion with my friends, some butches and some femmes. We realized that it's *disgusting* to consider a lesbian like that. Because it's like competing with each other. Because always femmes are looking down [looked down upon]. It's like straight women. And butches are like men. Oh yeah, they are macho, they are strong, so they are good. I think we are androgynous. We have both sides. Because nobody can be butch 100 percent, nobody can be femme 100 percent, being gay. Otherwise you wouldn't be gay."

"What do you mean," I asked, "'otherwise you wouldn't be gay'?" "If you are gay, you cannot be either one," Lourdes replied. "You have to be both. That's *why* you are gay! Because it doesn't make sense [otherwise]. Then be straight and play roles. Because in the gay community we play roles, but we are supposed to play both roles to be ourselves. Otherwise you just follow the straight examples. The straight models.

"I really believe, in myself, I'm really tender, I'm really gentle, I'm really sweet inside. But in your culture, I think there are a lot of things that make you *act* different ways. More aggressive, more defensive, you see? More paranoid. Because I walk around this community [San Francisco's Mission District]. There is a lot of Latin people, at least, [to] who[m] I'm really *sure* I look like butch, really butch. They will call me names, and I have to fight with them, you see. Because I won't let anybody try to put me down. Like, 'Hey, *marimacha*,' in Spanish. So I'm *marimacha*, but I'm so proud of that. So what?

"One day a man slapped me in my face, because I was with a gay man. He treated me like a piece of shit. I said, 'Well, who do you think you are?' Just buying a record. 'You shut up! I don't even know if you're a man or woman.' 'I'm a woman. He's the man, but he's gay. So am I, so what?' And see, he slapped me in my face. He called the police. I spit in his face. Latin men! So you see, they will call you names. You have to be more aggressive, just in the way you walk. You have to. 'Hey, don't even fool around with me.' *That's* when you have to be butch. Because otherwise, forget it! They put you down, or they try to put you down.

"Before, I used to have a lot of problems. I'd say, 'No, I'm butch, period. One hundred percent. I don't show my feelings. I don't do women's work.' But I was bullshitting myself! I cook! I clean the house! That's considered femme work! But a straight femme, not a lesbian femme. That's another change in my life, too. Before I used to consider myself so femme, because I was pretending to be straight. Then I went to the *other* extreme, being butch. It wasn't me. So now I'm both."

Elaine Scavone: "Half-Man Half-Woman"

"I have this painting that I did when I was seven years old. I went to a Picasso exhibit and I decided that I was going to try to be a Cubist. So I went home and I painted this picture, right? What it is, is a combination of things. I did this picture of a half-man half-woman. I made a triangle into a square, a triangular square. I put a happy face on the woman and a sad face on the man. I gave them different hats. The man, of course, had a pant leg, and the woman had a dress. She was happy because she had just bought a new purse and he was sad—this is really funny; are you ready for this?—he was sad because he had gotten his middle finger stuck in the door and it was swollen. So he's standing there in the picture with his middle finger stuck out."

Yoli Torres: "When I Say 'Sex,' I Don't Just Mean the Coming"

"Some people fall in love with anybody. Some women fall in love with men. And I fall in love with women. It's not even the sexual thing. I mean, I *love* sex, and I enjoy it. But technically there's not all that much that's all that different. Right? You know, there's the oral stuff, and there's different forms of penetration. I mean, there's only so much technical difference between making love to a man and making love to a woman. But it's not that. It's that other stuff: the intimacy, the degree of closeness that I can feel with a woman. That crazy kind of feeling of can't-stand-to-be-without-her has never happened with a man.

And I doubt that it will. It just is not there. So why am I going to have such a hard time for that?

"Ever since I was little, [my mother] wanted and encouraged independence. She said, 'There's no such thing as being independent unless you can be economically independent.' For her the major emphasis was on let's keep this kid off the streets, off drugs, in school, and serious about getting an education. Doing the migrant or immigrant dream. Getting out of poverty and living in the mainstream. That was much more a concern to her than whatever I was doing sexually.

"Because I am a Puerto Rican, because I come from a working-class, very poor background, I don't have the same kind of delusions that a lot of my sisters and brothers who are white and upper-middle-class have, about what the society can do for their liberation as lesbians and gay men. Fact is that this society does give them privilege as white people and as middle-class people or upper-class people. But it's privilege that will go out the window in a second if we turn to fascism. Who cares, you're white or you're middle-class? If you're a faggot, you're a faggot.

"Once having made that choice to be out, I wasn't going to go back. It scared me to death. Because I said, 'Well, now what? You opened your big mouth, but now what? Now how you gonna get a job?' The world definitely would look at me differently, and *treat* me differently, than it would anybody else. I was just heartbroken. The sentiment is very clear to me: one of heartbreak, not guilt. Heartbreak because of what it would mean in the future, and how much time and energy I'd put into getting the goddamn degree, and the fact that there were people out there who didn't have to deal with this.

"There's a lot of pressure that racial minorities feel in this country to assimilate. For obvious reasons, right? Because that will get us ahead. So therefore, in the process of assimilating, you don't want to admit to the thing that the standard or the model group rejects. So no, there's no lesbians in Latino society, right? There's no gay men in black society. Which is not true. And I know for a fact that Latin people, black people, and Asian people who say those things *know* it's not true. But it's more like, 'No, we're not going to take public issues around this stuff. It's too much already, all right!' Politically I think that that's a mistake. But I understand where the hesitancy to deal with the issue up front comes from.

"The reason I say I know that they know it's untrue, is my experience in my own family. I do have a couple of cousins who are gay. Everybody knows they're gay, and nobody has thrown them out of the family or denied them love. But you ask those same people anything gay and they act totally dumb. They don't know nothing about gay. 'What gay? Lesbian? Hmmm. . . .'

"My parents migrated to New York City when I was six years old. I lived in the mountains in Puerto Rico, so it was all an absolute wonder to me, and tremendously traumatic because it was also so huge and concrete and fast and impersonal. And it *smelled* bad. I have a very distinct memory of how awful bus fumes, for example, smell. What it smelled like to go into an elevator crammed with people. All those different perfumes and hair sprays. I had never experienced that. My family was poor, but most of the time that I was awake I was outside. I never had to be jammed up with anybody.

"I could go on. There's a million things. I remember blowing at ice cream because I thought it was hot. You know, the steam from the cold? And I had a terrible time figuring out how to control my bowels and my bladder movements, because I never had to do that. Before I would just go, and all of a sudden I was being told I had to wait until I could go into this closetlike thing and sit on the toilet bowl. It was totally bizarre to me. It took nine months or something like that before my body would physically learn to do it. So that was awful, because I'd embarrass myself and my family, and then they'd yell at me.

"There was also a strangeness around . . . I guess people call it personal space. Because even though I had spent the first six years of my life in an environment where I had a lot of space around me, it was very easy and natural and comfortable for me to be close to people. You know: to touch, to embrace, hug, kiss. And that's another memory that I have that's very distinct about coming to the United States, is a sense that people were distant from each other. Physically. They'd shake hands and like that, but that they wouldn't hug hello just was very bizarre to me.

"I think that there is, within Latin culture, an incredible degree of nurturance within the family setting. Like I was saying before, encouraging physical contact and closeness to people and affection. And although there are a lot of strict distinctions that are sexist in character, when you really look at it, it doesn't play itself out that way. The sexist stuff is more for show. At home I never got a sense that my mother was the weak one, or anything like that. Not just in my family, but in lots of families, there was a respect and an authority in the woman in the family that was very strong, and still is.

"So for me, making the jump between being close to women emotionally, and then the sexual, was very easy. I wasn't traumatized by it. Because I had spent most of my childhood playing in bed with my cousins or my sisters, romping around and wrestling. Whereas I've experienced in relationships — either friendships or sexual kinds of things—with white women, that there's a lot of ambivalence about the physical stuff. So there might be emotional closeness, and friendship, and intellectual mutual stuff, but a lot of problems sexually. A lot of ambivalence around allowing sexuality to be okay. And a lot of rigidity about . . . you know, only certain kinds of sex, or it's more important to work than it is to [have sex]. Sort of like sex can wait. Or even just the physical can wait. So sometimes, when I say 'sex,' I don't just mean the coming but the holding and the affection and the playing around kind of stuff. That, in my experience with white women, has been different.

"As I'm saying this, I'm catching myself, because it's not just white women: it's white middle-class women. I just had a discussion along these lines with my lover now, who I've been with for two years, who is a white woman, who comes from an Italian working-class background, though. Culturally, there's not a whole lot of difference. And there is a lot of shared kind of craziness, buoyancy, excitement, warmth, affection. Passion.

"'Feminine/masculine' or 'butch/femme' are social terms that are *loaded*. Right? They're loaded with value, because one's supposed to be good and the other's supposed to be less or inferior. But if we can get rid of all that value stuff, I think it's just that we're both. Most human beings carry within themselves the potential for aggressive, calculating kind of behavior, and more passive, take-care-of-me, intuitive kind of behavior.

"I engage in both. I mean, there's a public persona that is definitely more butch. Tough, cool, ties, aggressive. More in charge. And then there's another part of me that does *want* to be more passive. Not in the negative sense, but I want to be taken care of. I want somebody else to decide what I'm going to wear today. Or what I'm going to eat. I want a break from making decisions, leading and pushing people, and thinking."

Rona Bren: "Little Did I Know She Was a Black Leather Motorcycle Queen"

"By the time I could really speak [English] and get into things [in the United States], it was 1964 and the Beatles and everything was starting. I felt so unconnected to that. I could care less if John, Paul, or Ringo dropped dead or walked into my house. The things that everybody took for granted, like baseball or Mickey Mouse or the Civil War or slavery, I would just sit and stare. Even if I understood the words, I didn't have any idea what anybody was talking about. So I think I withdrew, feeling that I better not open my mouth because I'll sound really stupid.

"I left Israel when I was ten. If you go to Israel, if you've been born in Israel, you are always a citizen of Israel. Always, always, and forever. With all the rights and responsibilities of being a citizen of Israel. And so, when I went back, not knowing the rules very clearly, I got to the airport with my little American passport and they said, 'Well, that's very nice. Where's your Israeli passport?' I said, 'What?' And they said, 'Well, you need it to get out of the country,' because once I'm in Israel I'm 100 percent an Israeli citizen, as if I'd never set foot in the U.S. I got real upset because not only did they want me to have a passport but they said I had to serve in the army, which I wasn't prepared to do at the time.

"I don't think that Jews have a real permanent place anywhere. They're not really accepted. And so I don't feel that I can ever really belong 100 percent to any country. Even if I chose to. In other words, I can choose, just as the German Jews chose to be Germans. That didn't make any difference. They weren't, really. I would hesitate to even say in what order, but part of my identity is an American. If I go to Europe and people look at me, I'm sure they look at me as an American. I think I've picked up the mannerisms and the dress and the language and all of that. [But] that's only a small part of how to define myself. Israelis always told me I'm not an Israeli, but I totally think I am.

"[Home] is a certain kind of belonging to a place. Whether you've lived there or not. Whether you're an army brat and you've moved twenty times in your life or whatever, there's still a place for you if you want it. I think Jews never feel that. They never have, through the centuries. Home is a goal, it is a utopia, it is an ideal. It's someplace where I would really feel comfortable. I'm tired of moving around, so make this a place where I could stay and put down roots. Where I can grow in the place and it can grow with me, as opposed to feeling like I'm always transient and always slightly refugee status, running from one place to another. A place where the past, present, and future is.

"It's like if I'm standing in front of the room and I know I'm supposed to talk to people, I'm not shy. If I'm standing at a party and I'm not sure what I'm supposed to do, then suddenly I get shy. [With lesbian-feminism] I had this more clearly defined place in my life, so it made me feel much better. My hair [now] is a lot longer than it ever used to be. Back in 1973 I cut it. It was about an eighth of an inch all the way around! We were all doing a lot of very drastic stuff, and part of it was for some kind of solidarity. I think we wanted to stick out. It was one way to learn what oppression was about. Cut all your hair off and wear suspenders and you'll see what it's all about!

"I'm not in a relationship right now and I don't know where I would be [in terms of gendering] if I was. Physically I've always considered myself a butch because I've always felt that this certain feminine quality in walk and talk and carriage, I never had. Like my aunt, when I was first smoking, used to say, 'That's disgusting! Women don't hold their cigarettes like that.' But you know, I'm also not flat-chested. I have round tits for a woman. I also really like to cook and love to take care of the house and love to take care of the kid, and well, maybe that's femme. I love making love to, but I also like being made love to.

And I like to play the game. I could definitely see playing butch for a whole year. But then I can definitely see switching. I think that's what androgynous is: having both parts being very clearly there and being able to draw on them.

"Sheila, who I've been involved with for the past number of years, she has *very* feminine qualities about her. And yet before she and I got involved, she only considered herself a butch. I mean *only*. It was like, 'Nobody makes love to me.' And when I first looked at her, I immediately reacted butch to her. Because I took one look at her. The way she dressed and the way she carried herself, to me she was the epitome of femme. Little did I know that she was a black leather motorcycle queen. I've never seen her in those terms. And that wasn't the relationship we had. In our relationship she was definitely the femme and she definitely wanted to explore that. But nobody else has seen her that way, and I do, so both things have to be a part of it. I think that we kid ourselves if we think it can be any one way.

"She's the first out-and-out what I considered femme, the first relationship where I really played it in that way. And I had a great time. I don't have to have feminist love-making all the time: you know, you don't penetrate, I make love to you for five minutes and then you make love to me, it's equal and we both count how many orgasms we have. No, I've never fucked that way! Within the evening, both parts don't have to [come into play]. But within the whole relationship I think that both parts have to be there. That's really what it's about."

Chameleon: Double Takes

Elaine Scavone's sketch of a half-man half-woman illustrates the conviction that people are double-gendered. To create the half-and-half impression, Elaine drew upon symbolic contrasts of the sort that tend to arise when people play guessing games. Who's who? Predictably, clothes carry much of the burden of identification. "He" gets a pant leg, "she" a neo-Cubist fragment of a dress. In the gendered activities department, shopping for a new handbag puts a smile on "her" face, not "his." And what would a portrait of gender be without a little phallic symbolism? Maybe "he" should be the one smiling with relief, having narrowly avoided castration of that middle finger by a slamming door.

"We have both sides," Lourdes Alcantara insisted. Still, what Lourdes meant by "both" was far from clear. Femme and butch? Masculine and feminine? Androgynous and ungendered? In any event, according to Lourdes, no one can live in a single consistently gendered dimension, at least not if she's queer. Like the figure in Elaine's drawing, everyone wears two hats. Here Lourdes joined a legion of street philosophers whose notion of going chameleon was to balance what they conceived as opposing aspects of a unified self.

As Yoli Torres saw it, "Most human beings carry within themselves the potential for aggressive, calculating kind of behavior, and more passive, take-care-of-me, intuitive kind of behavior." Like a two-party political system, these sides can divide into warring camps. One side may subordinate itself to the other, usually with disastrous effects. At best, "feminine" and "masculine" (or whatever) qualities coexist in a fifty/fifty split; at worst, one "side" lies fallow, allowing the other to hold sway. When Lourdes described herself as "tender, really sweet inside," she staked out a gendered territory that she hoped would restore balance by complementing her "tough guy" response to harassment on the street.

Balancing "sides" represents just one of several modes of going chameleon. An equally elusive approach had players moving from one gendered position to another. Looking back, Rona Bren concluded that she had navigated her way in and out of "butch." Although she claimed to occupy only one position at a time, she shared Lourdes's notion of differently gendered worlds within. A person had only to draw upon one or another of these worlds in order to make a move. Like Rona, many women saw nothing restrictive about settling down into a gendered category for a longer or shorter stretch. So long as they believed they could switch.

By caricaturing "feminist love-making," Rona tried to highlight the absurdity of demanding equal time for "opposing sides." Imagine counting orgasms to ensure perfect balance! Not that Rona eschewed balance. She just believed in taking stock over a longer interval, such as a relationship, rather than moment to moment. In her view, the most restrictively gendered covenant of all is the one produced by a constant tally.

So much for gender du jour. The concept of moving between defined positions leaves unexplored a third possibility for going chameleon: the pursuit of ambiguity. Gender blend finds its exemplar in Lourdes's neutered cat, Jo. Lourdes and her friends had turned the cat into a flag-bearer for the charms of innuendo and contradiction. In Jo they saw a creature with a biological substrate (s/he's "really" a male) that contradicted a surgically altered surface. Jo's fugitive body seemed to challenge any clear-cut guidelines for assigning gender by fusing the concepts of gender neutral and sexually neuter. S/he also mixed, as people often do, markers of ostensibly discrete genders: size, genitals, designation, stance. Small wonder that the owners of this mistress of double entendre gave her a name that could go "either way." Gendering doesn't get much more indefinite than this.

If gender blend doesn't do it for you, maybe gender's end will. Some women didn't want to locate themselves, even for a minute. They refused to make peace with the term "lesbian" or described themselves as lesbians without a community. Name tags just paper over all the subtleties. Why restrict yourself to being "either that way or just the opposite way" if you can dodge gender and sexuality altogether? These women tended to dedicate a portion of every conversation to extricating themselves from categories that never seemed to fit. A world without classification would have suited them just fine.

One of the striking things about going chameleon is that it sets gender in motion twice. People imagine they can shift between presumably fixed gendered positions: today you see me androgynous, yesterday you saw me femme, by Friday I may be back as butch. But chameleons also move back and forth among these four different modes of indeterminate gendering. In the course of a two-hour interview, Lourdes traveled from balance ("you have to be both") to gender du jour (makeup for Peru, chinos for the North American streets) to gender blend (meet my "androgynous" cat) to gender's end ("I don't believe in butch or femme").

Whatever the mode, Lourdes was in the business of unsettling gender. Hadn't she stopped producing false consistencies? She no longer lied to herself about refusing women's work when she knew very well she did household chores. Hadn't she also challenged conventional wisdom by leaving "roles" to the heterosexuals? By arguing that without masculine and feminine sides, "you wouldn't be gay"?

Paradoxically, chameleons often stumble over the very categories they're working so hard to evade. Whether people like Lourdes talk about balancing sides, moving between butch and femme, becoming androgynous, or leaving gender behind, they tend to take it for granted that everybody knows what these terms signify. Otherwise what would you be balancing, or moving between? This forces them to hold steady the meaning of gendered terms when each is more mobile than the next. "Androgyny" can represent a jail break to the woman who considers herself a prisoner of gender, untold riches for the firm that markets a rock star, or a mandala of fifty differently gendered interior worlds. One person's gender blend is another's world without gender.

When people assume the meaning of terms like "swish" and "stud," they end up fixing gender in the very act of reaching for fluidity. Each pigment in Elaine's sketch of the half-man half-woman naturalizes "he" and "she": first, by presenting these as the only possible gender categories, and second, by portraying gender through the innocence of a child's eyes. Isn't this the way all people are made? Part masculine, part feminine? At such a moment, the copycat lies down with the chameleon. A half-man half-woman combines aspects of gender s/he cannot afford to question.

Does this mean that, as long as you traffic in gendered categories, you're stuck? Can you ever hope to budge if you hitch your desire for change to immovable categories? But how viable was the genderless position that some chameleons suggested as an alternative? Individual efforts to dissolve gender always occur in a larger context. Can you keep other people from reading gender into the things you say and do? Can you exit masculine and feminine if social institutions distribute gender-tinted glasses right outside the door? Even if you succeed, won't evasive maneuvers locate you at the center of an age that celebrates novelty and constant change, in gender as in all things that can be marketed, updated, and acquired . . . for a price? How much is even the gender outlaw the product of her time?

If you can't get away from gender, maybe you can start by asking what you're doing when you move with it. Yoli was more interested in teasing apart the meanings of terms like "sex" than ricocheting back and forth between unexamined categories. Her expansive definition of lesbian sexuality included just about everything straight people do. Why should Lourdes have to say, "I never had sex in my life," after years of sleeping with women? Orgasm isn't everything. Why label penetration a heterosexual act, when tongues and fingers can serve as well? No point in calling up a straight/gay split that obscures as it divides.

If it ain't the meat, it's got to be the motion. Top and bottom, butch and femme . . . Yoli's approach opened sex and gender to perpetual reinterpretation. Anyone could play with those categories. Yet interpretation would be incomplete without considering the ways that affection, for Yoli, carried over into other aspects of living working-class Puerto Rican. Wrestling, romping around in bed, and skin-to-skin comfort never belonged to a separate realm marked "sexuality."

To hold the meaning of gendered terms steady, you have to hold them apart from class and ethnicity and nation. An impossible task, really, since there is no feminine and masculine, no androgynous or butch or femme, that is not already race- and class-specific. Remember homegirls, church ladies, class tourists, traditional elders, WASPs on holiday? The implicit white middle-classing of female passivity? Cutting these "complications" out of the picture is especially ironic, because race and class and nation have everything to do with why many women go chameleon in the first place.

Chameleons do not change color randomly. They change in relation to environment, to conditions, to circumstance. Regendering allows people to disappear, reappear, rise to the occasion, and run for cover. So it's worth noting the particular kinds of situations in which (some) lesbians are likely to play with gender. Women show their moves to attract partners, to improve their chances of physical survival, to establish spaces of guardedness or belonging, and to negotiate the intricacies of class, race, and immigration. All of these scenarios set gender in motion, but with very different consequences.

Changing partners supplies one common occasion for going chameleon. When Rona first saw Sheila, she claimed she had "immediately reacted butch." After the two struck up Rona's only "serious" butch/femme relationship, Rona switched from vaguely androgynous to stud and Sheila from butch to fluff. Regendering can become an erotic game, and women like Rona its seasoned players. Also an entry in the fuck-and-flirt division of gender-bend: the Saturday night femme and the weekend stud. Dresses to kill for an evening at the clubs but sheds those boots and mascara come Monday morning. The class relations at work here belie the playfulness with which these dilettantes appear to approach butch/femme. Many employers won't tolerate the attitude or the look.

Sometimes observers mistook erotic play for the sole purpose of going chameleon. Many were dismayed by the apparent ease with which younger women moved from one gendered position to another. (Those whippersnappers just don't appreciate the struggles of femmes and butches in days of yore. They ought to pick an identity and stick to it. Their elders knew what they were doing when they coined the term "ki-ki" to disparage women who couldn't decide between butch and femme.) Was the so-called butch/femme revival the product of a post-gay generation that regarded the world as its oyster? Is there anything to stud and fluff *but* fluff?

In San Francisco the lighter side to going chameleon often had little to do with privilege or disrespect. Women regendered themselves as a respite from dead-end jobs, no jobs, and the day-to-day grind. Gender play extended its pleasures to the lesbian who was dirt-poor as surely as to the sheltered preppy or to the independently wealthy few. At the same time, regendering was not all fun and games and trivial pursuits. Plenty of women turned to shape-shifting for survival. Lourdes regendered at the slightest threat of violence. Although she no longer wanted to move into butch mode, in the United States she had repeatedly encountered situations that made gender mobility difficult to avoid. Take the stranger who slapped her and called her *marimacha*. *"That's* when you have to be butch."

Whether and how a woman shifts depends upon where she begins. A lesbian who already presents as a stud wouldn't need to go butch to ward off an attacker. On the other hand, she might reserve the option of moving toward femme to become a less identifiable target for antigay violence. Or she might consider femme-inflected modes of countering harassment. Handbags can make quite a weapon.

Migration through gendered differences can establish temporary spaces of danger, security, protection, belonging, alliance, and circumspection. Yoli described Puerto Rican men gendering themselves according to whether or not they were among *familia*: "The sexist stuff is more for show." When Yoli returned home from her own job, she wanted "a break from making decisions, leading and pushing people, and thinking," activities she tended to view as butch. Behind closed doors, she gravitated toward behavior she considered femme. (Of course, you could make a good case that Yoli's dream of having someone else pick out her clothes just extended butch into the realm of the domestic. "Which tie should I wear, honey?")

No matter how Rona gendered herself, she was convinced that she would always feel betwixt and between. At home or at work she remained a Jew to Americans, an American to the Israelis with whom she had grown up. Betwixt and between may be a permanent condition, but it does not describe a permanent place. Maybe it's no coincidence that three of the four women in this chapter had relocated across borders at some point in their lives. As migrants they were already in motion. They had no single home, at least not in Rona's sense of home as a "place where the past, present, and future is." Why should they claim a single gendered identity? Each had spent many years learning to shift back and forth between cultural contexts. Such transitions were bound to challenge preconceived notions about gender. If anything had become home, it was movement.

Border crossings add another dimension to the negotiation of class, race, age, and nation that is already an integral part of regendering. When Yoli was not wrinkling her nose at the stench of bus fumes, she was acclimating to a land where people scarcely seemed to touch. Lourdes had to get used to the idea that putting her arm around a girlfriend could imply a sexual connection, the farthest thing from most people's minds when women expressed affection in the country of her youth. "Let's go" turned out to mean "let's split the bill," upsetting the delicate calculations that governed the exchange of money when one person asked out another in Latin America. Who would have thought that paying a lover's rent on a factory worker's salary could translate into "being used" rather than signifying the expected generosity of lover for lover?

Like many children whose parents had embarked for New York with fantasies of a better life, Yoli had received lessons on the importance of blending in for cover. After coming out, she worried that a lesbian identity might destroy her chances for upward mobility. People get fired for that, don't they? Rona was only too well aware of the hazards that gender play could pose for an immigrant already coping with displacement. She had arrived in the United States unversed in the most basic tenets of its history and popular culture. Bad enough not to know about slavery or the Beatles. Why add gender transgression to the list? "Cut all your hair off and wear suspenders and you'll see what [oppression] is all about!" Or did gender conformity hold out the same illusory promise of security that beckons immigrants to assimilate in other aspects of their lives?

As a lesbian of color from a working-class background, Yoli had serious doubts about the effectiveness of an assimilation strategy. First of all, assimilate to what? In a highly diverse society there is no "mainstream" outside the one in your head. Light skin color or a high income might give you the impression of being here to stay, but if push comes to shove, those "assets" will not save you. In the eyes of white supremacists and their ilk, "If you're a faggot, you're a faggot." And not even the best chameleon can hide forever.

Yoli still preferred her gender fluid, but her politics combined with a scene-by-scene regendering that made her more, not less, visible. At seven o'clock she could be speaking out at a community meeting, fighting the myth that gayness is a white thing. Two hours later she would be recovering at home, asking her girlfriend to take the lead.

Chameleons celebrate the freedom associated with regendering for very different reasons. There are rich girls with credit lines who have the luxury to buy whatever mismatched outfits they please and call it gender blend. There are white girls who use the language of primitivism to talk about gendered "sides" running rampant. ("It's the femme in me that seduced you."/"I hate losing my temper, it's so male.") There are immigrants who think they can assimilate via gender mobility and immigrants who embrace gender du jour as the only practice that allows them to cross back over the borders.

Gender play can ally itself with the kind of privilege that catapults you into the naive belief that you are the undisputed master of your circumstances. If I don't want gender, I don't have to have gender, right? But even women who consider themselves infinitely flexible sometimes refuse to bend. If gender doesn't mean so much, why does the girl draw a line when it comes to sleeping with men? Gender play can also open up options in circumstances that are anything but privileged. Without a green card, Lourdes couldn't legally work for wages. She had decided to accept financial support from her lover, but that meant dealing with the implications of femme in a way that those mountains of makeup back in Latin America had never required. With so many versions of going chameleon, even the meaning of movement won't stay put.

Chapter 6 On and Off the Scale

So gender turns out to involve a little bit more than a division of humanity into symmetrical halves. So it's not enough to talk about femme and butch, male and female, or an androgynous balance between masculine and feminine "sides." People are out there regendering their memories, moving like chameleons, inventing themselves in stories, chanting gender in a lesbian key, introducing terms such as "swish" or "ki-ki," trying to escape from gender altogether, racing it and classing it until they end up with so much more than two. That old grade school trick of lining up the class single file, girls on this side of the room, boys over against the wall, looks pretty feeble going into the twenty-first century.

For as long as there have been people, there have been people who are "intersexed" (hermaphrodites). According to the biological research of Anne Fausto-Sterling, it makes no sense to speak about two discrete sexes, much less "the opposite sex," when people born intersexed combine genitals, chromosomes, and/or secondary sex characteristics (breasts, body hair) in ways that defy classification as male or female. Far from being the odd folks out, they testify that there is nothing natural about imagining men and women as members of two clearly bounded groups.

Medical science often (too often?) provides intersexed people with the consistently gendered bodies "nature" never gave them. The transgender community has made creative use of the same technologies. But what's commonly called a "sex change" is not always a journey from Sex Number One to Sex Number Two, with a short detour through the operating room. Although many transgendered people speak of themselves as "male to female" (MTF) or "female to male" (FTM), there are all sorts of possibilities that don't fall neatly into these categories. Years of certain hormones can yield a once-female body with dense muscle tissue and very little in the way of breasts. But without surgery, that body still packs a clit. Genitals can signify one thing, body contours another. Take them together, as they come, and what do you have?

You could think about gendering as a never-ending process that engages the hermaphrodite in all of us. Is there a woman in the United States who can afford to go through life ignoring everything that her peers associate with "masculinity"? Regardless of her own convictions, at every twist and turn, she bumps up against the social certainty that gender matters. But what is she to make of this "thing" called gender?

On the street, people have come up with their own ideas about how to handle the complexity that a two-bit system of gender can't manage. One way to break through dichotomies such as "man versus woman" is to bridge them. A continuum is a device that bridges two seemingly exclusive categories—say, femme and butch—by placing them at opposite ends of a number line. People can occupy positions along that line anywhere from one to ten, with "one" customarily representing the most femme and "ten" the most butch. It doesn't matter whether individuals picture themselves scrambling up and down the scale like a chameleon or assuming a fixed position as "an eight." What matters is that a continuum allows for gradation, and gradation means more nuance than you'll ever get using rough classifications such as "feminine" or "androgynous."

Almost everyone who's spent time among gay women knows about the butch/femme scale. It's standard issue equipment for playing the guessing games in which lesbians try to locate one another with respect to gender. You say she's femme, but how femme is she? A one? A three? A playful directive to "check out the shoes!" can get you pegged as a four. Taking the stairs instead of using the elevator may move you up a couple of notches.

The butch/femme scale is popular because it offers a handy tool for grasping subtleties that fall between the either/or alternatives of butch versus femme. You can use it to explain shifts in gendering over the course of an hour, a week, or a lifetime. If you convert the continuum into a sliding scale, it permits gender mobility for women who want it. Androgyny becomes an imaginary space somewhere along the line between femme and butch rather than a practice that challenges the very notion of "roles." A scale fine-tunes the usual ways of thinking about gendered differences. A butch is not a butch is not a butch, nor every femme interchangeable with another femme.

But does a continuum do anything to clarify the ways that gender is raced and classed, or does it just obscure those connections? How well does the practice of assigning people to numbered positions work? Is anything lost in the tabulation? Why don't women tend to locate themselves at the extremes: one, ten, or smack dab in the middle? Do people ever formulate gender in ways that force them off the scale? Does a scale mark the death of either/or thinking? And what about attraction? Can a continuum really allow you to have your gender and eat it too?

Rachel Tessler: "I Feel Most Femme When I'm Wearing No Clothes"

"There's a certain violent edge to some stone butches, I think. I'm talking about the real leather-and-motorcycle kind, and I'm thinking of a more 1980s or 1990s stone butch, not a 1950s one. A woman that can almost pass as a man. I think there's something intriguing about it. I mean, some stone butches are almost beyond butch. They're almost in a kind of territory between genders, beyond being women. I think some stone butches aren't really women, in the way that they think about people. I also feel like there's something lost in relating to them, in that, in that case, one would almost be relating to a man. Which could be interesting, but then you wouldn't be a lesbian, I suppose.

"Maybe some femmes are attracted to men. Maybe some butches are, too. There can be chemistry with anybody, if you don't have barriers there. But probably it's true that the social codes are strong. We don't really know what our sexualities would look like in a different kind of society. I think most people are attracted to a lot of different people. Whether they're going to act on it or not is something else. I know a lot of lesbian-feminists who shaved their heads in 1978 and they're now straight, so that's how far that gets it.

"I've still been very attracted to men. I've acted on it occasionally. For a long time I couldn't deal with that. I [also] thought there was something wrong with [the fact] that I was attracted to butch women because, well, did this mean I really wanted to be with men? Now I've just accepted the fact that there's people that I'm attracted to. I want to be involved with women, and I'm attracted to butch women. I also have attraction to some men, and they also tend to be butch men. It is what it is.

"The times that I've gone out with women that I would consider femme, I have not felt right. I'm thinking of one situation in particular in college. I remember feeling embarrassed, almost, because the woman was reacting to me as though I were butch, and I didn't like that. We were making love one time, and I just remember a way that she looked that made me feel really uncomfortable. It was an expression on her face that was sort of expectant. Girlish, in a petulant way. Fluttering eyelashes or something. I can't explain any more than that.

"I probably would not be seen as a femme by a lot of people, but that's how I feel. I've softened a lot. When I came out, I didn't have as strong a sense of self as I do now and was much more insecure. It would have been hard for me to identify as a femme. Because I would have associated that with weakness, probably. I also think it would have been confusing for me to think that I could be a lesbian and still have some of the same feelings I'd had when I'd been involved with men. A lot of those femme qualities were things that I associated with [a] threat to my lesbianism. So part of [beginning to identify as femme] was accepting my sexuality in general, with all the contradictions and complexities of it.

"I grew up in a classic liberal, white, Jewish middle-class family, not religious. Middle-class people seem to invent themselves, or have the illusion that they do, [more] than working-class people. Not that I was encouraged to think about my sexuality, but I was encouraged to think about other things. So when [sexuality] came along as something to think about, it was typical for me to be questioning it and talking about it. My perception from working-class friends is that it's just that much harder [for them] to be given the space to look at [sexuality]. It's considered a luxury and not something you have to do in life. The kind of thing you have to do in life is get ahead. Hopefully do better than your parents did. You don't want to be worrying about foolishness like your identity.

"Working-class butch/femme images are borrowed or stolen for use by a lot of people. Or perversions of those images: taking what is perceived to be who those people are, and making a virtue or a fetish out of it. Like a slut image. I think that's probably conceived of as a working-class woman, femme. And if you look at *On Our Backs* or other lesbian sex magazines, those images are all over the place: the butch motorcycle or construction worker look, or the cop. Given that working-class people are sort of shit on, I think it's really interesting that those images are considered so exciting erotically. A lot of lesbian sex magazines and films do what the straight media does in eroticizing exotic black and Asian women, continuing the same stereotypes that exist in the regular straight society about women.

"The femme would tend to be the one who seduces the butch, tends to be the one that draws the butch out emotionally. I think of being seductive as being able to pull someone in. It sounds like manipulation, and in a way it is manipulation, but it could also be manipulation that's not negative or damaging or unhealthy. More like a game. It's a subtle thing with me, because I don't wear lace teddies and seven-inch spiked heels and lick my lips or something. I'm not that kind of seductress. But I feel that the role that I play and the way that I feel comfortable is to entice another woman.

"There's a coolness about butches, for sure, which can sometimes be maddening. Maybe parodying what they understand to be male. But I find it very attractive. It's something masculine, but it's not masculine—it's butch. There's a self-possessed stance that they have, and they seem to be kind of in charge. But there's also this soft side, that you have to really work to get to, but that's a real gift when you do.

"Sex for some reason makes me feel very young. It brings out this little girl feeling. I associate that very much with being femme. That's probably why I feel the most that way in a sexual situation. Or it doesn't even have to be sex: it can just be an intimate situation with someone. I feel most femme when I'm wearing no clothes. I guess I would feel less femme if I was involved in something like sports because it's more [to] show off, strut a little bit.

"It's complex to me. Am I a femme all the time in my life, or am I femme in these [particular] relationships, or what is it? In the larger world, forget [about] butch or femme. Being a lesbian, that's already something that's a problem. It's not okay to be a lesbian. It's about justifying your life, really. And possibly defending your life.

"The unfortunate thing [is] that people want to know who everybody is, and they want to feel like they have 100 percent guarantees of everything. That's just not the way things are. I'm in a position that's pretty envious because I can probably pass all over the place for whatever I want to pass on. Or maybe I'm lying to myself.

"I don't feel I'm ever going to fit into any kind of box in a perfect way. I like the idea that people probably think of me one way and I feel of myself in another. I like to keep people wondering. I don't know why. Maybe I like to keep myself wondering, too."

Helen Garcia: "Who I Think She Wants Me to Be"

"I'm a five. Right in the middle. Who I am by myself, I guess. Not relating to any particular person." In her relationship, however, Helen characterized herself as "a one or two. Depending on how I feel, what we're doing, whether we're being sexual. I don't think that I'm being a different *person* because I'm relating to my lover. But I think that I allow myself to be more on this side of the continuum of who I am. It would be a lie to say that my identity isn't involved. My relationship is part of who I am.

"[Being more femme] is something that I want, too. *Sometimes* it's who I think she wants me to be. I mean, I don't always think that there have to be two sides, but I think *she* sees it that way." Helen Garcia knew that her partner identified strongly as butch. But, she said, "I don't see her as very strongly butch! I mean, I respect how she sees herself. But if there's something *she* doesn't see herself being or doing, that doesn't mean that *I* couldn't see her taking it on." Especially when they made love, Helen believed that she could touch "the femme" in her partner. "Sometimes I wish that she could see herself in a variety of ways. That maybe she could allow herself that.

"It's easier for me to talk about my last girlfriend, since you don't know her. I would always buy her lingerie. It was fun, and I used to love it when she'd put on (or put out!) for me. That was *great*. So I can play the other side. Except in that relationship, it never went the other way. *That* was a problem for me. I was always put in that [butch] role.

"It's easier for me to play the femmy role. That femme side is more flexible and fluid, whereas butch seems to be more defined by polarity. Whereas femme, or feminine, is not always being defined by polarity, but being defined by . . . I don't know what!" In a sarcastic tone, Helen ventured answers whose obvious inadequacy sent both of us into laughter: "Softness! Intuitiveness!"

Did Helen think all women could regender? "Only if you're in the middle anyway. Initially my response would be no. I think a big part of that question is whether they have the *desire* to be the other thing. Like if you're just saying they want to do it for this specific occasion, then they still see themselves as butch, and the desire doesn't come from wanting to explore a different part of themselves but more from wanting to pass for a particular thing—I think that can't be hidden. But if they themselves are changing who they are on the inside, yeah. Like [my lover], she could be a different person if she *thought* of herself as a different person. Clothes are just the dressing on top."

When Helen thought of butches in generic terms, she pictured them as working-class; femmes she imagined as "middle- and upper-class. Although, no, not necessarily. When I think of the *Latina* femmes, I think of Latina working-class femmes and white working-class butches." Latina butches she also presented as working-class. "There's not that many Latinas that I know that are upper-class."

"Sometimes it seems like, how can I say any of this? I don't even know any lesbians! I know some, but it's really hard to make generalizations without having talked to people. I feel at a big disadvantage [coming out in my thirties]."

Because I don't really feel like I'm part of any community. That's a broader issue for me: finding out more about who lesbians are and who they think of themselves as. [Butch/femme] is a way of starting to think about identity in general.

"I was reading this Judy Grahn book. I'm trying to think what I got from the book. [Butch/femme], it's kind of outside masculine and feminine. It's more a third alternative or a fourth alternative."

Paulette Ducharme: "More Butch and More Femme Than Most"

"I would always defend homosexuals before I ever came out, even when I was in high school. I don't know why, exactly. I think maybe that connects to my father showing us the lesbians in the car wash. My sister got totally sick to her stomach, realizing that these women, who were dressed in black pants and men's work shoes and T-shirts, with acne on their faces, and crew cuts like they just got out of basic training, horn-rimmed glasses, et cetera [were gay].

"They were not very attractive women, in your typical sense of the word 'attractive.' And they were poor. They were definitely very poor. So maybe it started then. Because in general my father showed me all of these people with problems with money and poverty, right? He took me to all of these bars and things. It made me very defensive and protective of these people, because he always expressed some concern for them.

"I wasn't going to be a lesbian, because everybody *told* me I was. Because I was a tomboy. And if I wasn't going to go into the convent, forget it; that's all there was. Even if I would have gotten married, probably people would have made up stories about my relationships with women, and maybe they would have been true! But I suspect I would have been killed before my husband would have been cuckolded by another woman. And it would be justified in the eyes of the world. I couldn't see myself getting into that kind of a dilemma. And so I just refused to get married.

"As much as I was attracted to women, I was totally terrified of them. Because my mother was an incredibly violent woman. Even the very first girl-friends that my brother used to try to set up for me, like other tomgirls, tomboys, right? As soon as they looked at me and smiled, I would run away. I would just run, bolt. They would chase me until I gave up, and they would never hang out with me again.

"I always knew that I couldn't trust men, because they would ultimately have to have all this power. Whether they wanted it or didn't want it, they would have to have it, because that's the rule of the game. At least that's how all the guys I went out with were. You know, they could make a lot of different agreements, but any time anything public was going to come up, it was like a show of force all of the time. It was ridiculous. And I knew that I wasn't going to spend my whole life mad and fighting with somebody, trying to convince them of something that they didn't need to be convinced of, about sharing power. They weren't going to change. They didn't need to change. There was nothing compelling them to change. The world wasn't changing.

"I have to say that I have been always attracted to women. Course, I was always attracted to penises, too. Breasts and penises. Well, I had penises for seven or eight years. It wasn't *me*. It was all me spending myself for somebody else. Men! My fantasies of sex with men have always been much better than my actual relationships with men."

In her mid-twenties, Paulette got up the courage to ask a woman out on a date. "But if anything sexual was going to happen, it was going to have to come from her, because I had absolutely no idea of how to go about it. And so we stopped at this bar at the beach. We had a beer and then we had to go piss, so we went back to the ladies room. She put her hand on the door so I couldn't open it. Then when I turned around, she kissed me. Oh my god! It was great! I loved everything about it. I just *melted*.

"But then we were trying to find a place to have sex. Who knows where to go, you know? I didn't have money to rent a room or something like that. So we took all these small streets, and finally we found this place where we could pull off into this pasture with all these cows. Anyways, we were just in the front seat of my car, and she went down on me, but I wasn't that into it. I was really excited about kissing and being fondled and fondling and touching and stuff, but I just wasn't that into oral sex.

"The second or third time I went out with this woman, I found out that she was on probation, she was 16 years old, and that I could be in big trouble for being involved with her because of my work, because of my age, because of the racism. I was a white woman taking advantage of this poor black girl. Plus I worked in community services, and so I could also be taking advantage of her because she could think that I could be helping her out in some kind of way that had to do with her situation, being on probation.

"She was on probation because she was truant. She just didn't go to school because she liked working the streets. She flipped me out, really. My relationship to her was really shocking. Her brother was a transvestite. I met him at the house, and then when she introduced him to me on the street I didn't even recognize him. I was old—I was in my twenties—and I was totally naive. Not intellectually, but emotionally, being up close to this whole world."

Shortly afterward, Paulette became involved with one of her housemates.

"She walked across the room and she climbed onto the bed and was over me. She just came down over my face so slowly, and then she hovered right above my lips. She kissed me, practically not even touching my lips, for seconds that seemed like forever. Then she said, 'How was that?'" It did not take long for Paulette to discover that sexual compatibility with someone of the "same" gender did not guarantee harmony in a relationship. "I talked to the women that I worked with about my relationship and how frustrating it was. Edie was there and she says, 'God, it sounds just like my relationship with my husband!' All of the ways that I talked about it sounded so typical to the women that I was working with in terms of the issues that they struggled with, with their husbands. They couldn't understand why I would want to bother, then. Why be with women, then? I said, 'I like it.'

"I always hung onto the oddest little pieces of education. Like a banner in my English class when I was in high school that said, 'Nothing here below profane for those with eyes to see.' And I always thought that I had eyes to see. I always wanted to be that person who could see something that was underneath all of the garbage. That is more of how I know myself, who I know myself to be, than any social label or role or thing that gets put on top of a person.

"Sometimes when I'm femme and I'm being dramatic, I feel like a faggot. Because I played with boys all of my life and I feel like I have a certain male mentality or something. And so when I act feminine, it feels like I'm acting. It doesn't feel exactly like this is what I'm really feeling. I expect other people, too, to see it as though it was acting, and so therefore to seem more like a faggot.

"I think I was much more butch before I ever came out. Coming out has been a process of getting in touch with the feminine in me. It gave me the courage to do it and it gave me support to do it by giving me a community that allegedly respects women. When I'm femme, I'm really femme, and when I'm butch, I'm pretty butch. I'd say I'm more butch and more femme than most!"

Jerri Miller: "They're Feminine, but They're Not Femmes"

"I was going to a class the other night, and a friend said to me, 'Oh, are there many lesbians in the class?' And I couldn't answer, because the answer would be based on how people looked. There were like four women that I would have thought were lesbians, or I would have said that at least a couple were pretty butch, and they all turned out to have husbands or boyfriends. I guess there were a couple who I would say, 'Yeah, I guess they're lesbians,' but that really discounts who I am. Because what about those women who look more like I do?

"Last semester I came out in front of a [community college] class. It was one of the straightest groups of people I've ever come out to. You could hear a pin drop, it was so quiet in there. People were so shocked because I didn't look like they thought. It was like the whole mythology of what a lesbian was, was just blown."

When Jerri Miller came out in her late teens, "It was in the 1970s. I just wanted to fit in and I wanted to be a lesbian and I didn't really know how to do it. So I started to consciously try and look like what looked like a lesbian. No makeup. Of course there were no dresses, but not even flowered shirts. It took a couple years of me being uncomfortable, feeling really bad. Not bad about being a lesbian, but really missing my makeup and feeling like I had to give all this up to be a lesbian. Even at one point I started having doubts about my being a lesbian because I wanted these things."

By the early 1980s Jerri was "starting to develop more outward signs of femininity that I had repressed, starting to wear dresses and skirts and high heels and jewelry. All those things that I hadn't done since I was a teenager. And it was almost like *violence*. I mean, people were *very* hostile. (Not everybody.) The thing that used to make me really angry was that people would not take me seriously as a lesbian. People would come up and look at you like they didn't know if you were a lesbian now or maybe a bisexual or maybe you just came out last year and you hadn't really gotten around to cutting your hair.

"Now the only time anybody harasses me for being a lesbian is when I'm with my lover and we're being physical. But what most people don't understand—which really pisses me off—is, it's not that harassment stops. There's just a different kind of harassment, because then you don't get harassed for being a lesbian, but you get the same kind of harassment other women get, which is men trying to pick you up more. In that way, I almost felt less safe, because men would come onto me a lot more, or make remarks more on the street. I've had a couple men follow me home in their cars. So it's not like you pass over into safety or something.

"And also, people would act as if women who were femme could pass and women who were butch could not, and that's not true. I mean, some women who are butch cannot pass and everybody's always going to know they're a lesbian, *but* there are also women who may look totally different on Saturday night than on Monday. [On Monday] they put on a dress, or maybe they put on their slacks outfit, and they're 'so butch,' and they go to work and they pass. Maybe not as much as somebody who's very outwardly feminine, the kind who's got hair down their back, but they're still looking femme.

"Middle-class women can pass easier, usually. The only reason I say this," explained Jerri, whose mother had raised her children on a clerical worker's salary, "is because I think I'm a more middle-class woman for the past two years, and I've noticed this. I don't want to pass. I feel like it's real important to be out. I'm more out than my lover is, who's a butch. She's in a more conservative job than I am.

"The way I get to be feminine, which is probably different than a straight woman gets to be feminine, is that I get to do it and be appreciated for it, and not exploited. See, there's a big difference between femmes and straight women. I don't feel really good about straight women or have straight women friends in my life, with the exception of my sister. They buy [into] everything. They're just passive, like inert. And they're not self-defined.

"Also, it's context. If I'm sleeping with my girlfriend and I'm putting on lingerie, or if I'm going out in a miniskirt, which I've been known to do, I don't ever feel exploited by her. Never, ever. But if I was a straight woman doing that with a man, I don't think I could *ever* do that. I don't think they're finding some guy out there who's so cool that she can go out there in this little, tight dress, and she doesn't feel like some sort of object to him.

"If you're talking about women who are straight, and they're feminine, they can be feminine but they're not femmes. I don't know how they can deal with that big of a contrast [between partners]. It would seem like dolls or something, like mannequins. I mean, the only men that I can even hardly see relating to at all are gay men who are more femme than straight women. Most [heterosexuals] are such extremes. There's this woman that my lover's friends with and she's straight. Her boyfriend is such a *boy*. He's just like this *man*, like a regular man, and I don't understand how she could possibly see him. Very unemotional and really affected and extremely aggressive. It's like [heterosexual men] have no femininity at all.

"If I define myself as femme, I don't think passivity. I don't feel like, oh, I'm the kind of person who goes out and doesn't know what to order for dinner because I need somebody else to help me decide! Because I feel very strong-minded and opinionated. I know what I think and I'm able to say what I think and feel about something. So those negative images where somebody defers to their lover, I didn't start to do any of that. Although I did have that problem for a while before, where I would get involved with women who were butch and have to defer to them and give them too much power and give them too much control. At that time, when I was younger, I thought that that was their fault. That they were too aggressive or something. But I think it was probably both people's control over the relationship.

"I've heard women who are femme complain about how butches are: they're too aggressive, and they try and control the relationship, and they do *x*, *y*, and *z*. After a while I just felt like those were the choices that [a person] made.

Those were the particular women she went after. I mean, she would find people who are really controlling and see it as being butch, where you could find just as many women who were femme who are controlling in their own way.

"Like I've seen women get in relationships with other women who are living with their lovers. Being real self-concerned, like it doesn't matter about anybody else's feelings. Then you're in this triangle, and on and on with this soap-opera-like thing that we all do. It's very embarrassing. I don't think [butches] go around saying catty things or being haughty the way that I've seen femme women be. There's been an issue of jealousy between women who are femmes and in the lesbian community as a whole.

"For example—this is like a play—I'm always with my lover, going out with her, and this woman would come up and flirt with her all the time in my face. In a femmy, flirty way, because she was interested in her. And she knew that she was going out with me, and we're in a monogamous relationship, and also that we're living together. I got into this argument with her and started to get into a fight, this nasty thing. My lover was just standing there, having no idea what to do or say. I just wanted to put the cards on the table and say, 'I know what you're doing. Don't do this around me. Fuck you! Cut that out, it's just ridiculous.' I don't know if I handled it the best way. But it's a big problem. And people act like it doesn't go on, so it makes everybody so nuts.

"Femmes probably push for commitment more. Like I think femmes might be the first ones to say, 'Well, we should really be in a monogamous relationship.' I think butches are more afraid of that. And I think femmes generally have a tendency to take care of the emotional part of the relationship. Butches can get really nervous in the beginning, trying to be tough in that way. It's attractive and it's nice to be strong and to talk like that, but you've got to accept the other part of yourself, too. Maybe you're trying to get close to somebody or fall in love with somebody and you feel vulnerable.

"In my present relationship, I felt very comfortable saying 'getting married.' She'd say, 'You can't say "getting married." We can have a commitment ceremony,' or some nonsense like that. I'm going, 'Fine, I'll call it a commitment ceremony.' That is a commitment that made her very nervous, but she's willing to do it. Mostly she's willing to do it because I want it so much, and she's in love with me. She didn't want me to go completely overboard. I mean, I could start going to bridal fairs and really get carried away.

"Some of her awkwardness was that she feels like I'm so femme, but she's not as butch as I am femme. Do you know what I'm saying? In terms of extremes. So it's kind of like, 'Well, what am I supposed to be?' I mean, it's not like she'd think, 'Oh, I'm going to wear a wedding dress, too,' but she's not going to wear a tuxedo. This is 'going too far,' even to the point of my wedding dress, which I will probably not have.

"We've talked about having children in the future. Anybody who knows us, they assume that it would be me who would physically have the baby, which is not my idea at all. It didn't seem logical to me. I would rather have [my lover] do it, because I want the baby to look like her, and she's physically stronger than I am. I mean, she does all this athletic stuff. It seems to me like she should do it! Well, that gets me out of that, but I would probably end up staying at home at least part of the time with the baby. I think I would probably be more like the mommy type in the family."

How did Jerri's lover feel about the prospect of bearing a child? "Oh, embarrassed. She feels like she wants to do it, but she also feels like the whole idea of her walking around pregnant and everything and being butch is very strange. I can understand her feeling that way. I think that it's unusual.

"Speaking about stereotypes, I think it's very unfair for people to say that butches are like men. It's just saying, 'Stay in your place. You're not in your place.' It's like the flip side of saying to somebody who's really femme, 'You're a bisexual or straight woman.' See, butches are the women that women are not supposed to be, and I think they're very threatening to people. I'm not talking about lesbians, but to straight people. They're just the opposite of what women are supposed to be like, so for a woman to be butch is very defiant even in itself. Even if she doesn't do anything else. Just wearing her leather jacket around or riding her motorcycle. They take chances that I wouldn't take.

"You know, I've had femme lovers. Maybe 5 percent. I don't really know that many women who are as femme as I am. Who are all-out. And I feel kind of badly about that. I miss that. [I have] my sister, who understands lesbians as much as anybody who's straight can. She's gone to the bars with me. She's not at all homophobic, and she really gets it. She's very feminine also, but not any more so than I am. I get to connect in that way and share about stuff. I don't always get to do that with other lesbians.

"I don't know why I feel so silly talking about it, but it's like I want somebody to talk about clothes with me, and go shopping with me, and talk about hairstyles, or even just talk about relationships from the kind of perspective that I come to it with. 'Oh, I was the perfect wife. I'm okay now, but in the beginning I was really good! I was really trying to take care of her. You know, making sure the house was clean. Gourmet meals every night. Then I got tired, and I stopped doing it as much.' But who can you talk to about that? [Heterosexuals] would laugh and think, 'Well, she isn't straight!' Make a few jokes. But I wasn't really joking. That's the thing: I was serious."

On and Off the Scale: Double Takes

Remember Paula Nevins, the hair stylist who considered butch/femme a trap? Paula described herself gravitating toward "prom queens" and "blonde, blue-eyed Renaissance maidens." Despite Paula's disdain for "roles," her attractions were thoroughly gendered. "Maiden" conjures up images of utmost femininity, while a "prom queen" can hardly be mistaken for a tomboy survivor.

As a white woman who believed that "people are people," Paula would probably have said that her attractions had little to do with race or class. But Paula's maiden was not just the ultrafemme of European legend; she was also a highly condensed version of white. Put race on a continuum, and the blonde-haired/blue-eyed combo symbolizes one extreme. The high school prom queen is also a figure with an implicit nation and a location in either the middle class or the "respectable" working class. How much more all-American can you get?

In the lesbian pulp novels of the 1950s, the fair-haired, light-skinned femme's partner was often brunette. Just like Paula. Was this another case of "tall, dark, and handsome"? Or did that chocolate-haired butch at the other end of the continuum say something about fears of interracial sex displaced onto mannish white women?

Paula's inventory of attractions raises questions about how race, class, and nation help to define the poles of gendered scales. Although these aspects of the poles usually remain implicit, they play havoc with the notion of a single continuum. A second-generation Filipina's version of ultrafemme might be very different from Paula's, though no less raced and classed. Ultrafemme might bring back memories of Barbie dolls, or the aquamarine eyes of an old flame. Or it could mean her honey-colored, brown-eyed self, and no blonde about it. Put her conceptions together with Paula's, and what do you end up with? Many differently gendered scales, rather than one supermodel of a continuum for all people, or even all lesbians.

Rachel Tessler used degrees of impenetrability to position the untouchable butch at one end of a continuum. Studs ran the gamut from hard ("hard-core," "stone," "the really hard women") to soft ("a soft butch"). And who was the stone butch's complement at the other end of Rachel's scale? Another version of the ultrafemme, this time construed as a bimbo or slut. Where Paula's notion of the prom queen incorporated middle-class respectability, Rachel's femme remains determinedly working-class, when she is working at all. Likewise with representations of the stone butch, who, as a street butch, is about as far away from briefcases and expense accounts as you can get.

Casting the slut as the epitome of femme resurrects a tired old stereotype of women of color and working-class white women: the sexpot. But the untouchable butch exudes magnetism in a way that bends the definitions of "sexual," since in theory a stone butch derives her pleasure not from touch but from satisfying her partner. Not exactly most folks' idea of heterosexual male prowess, at least in the United States. Rachel had to hold this knowledge at bay to characterize stolen kisses with an untouchable butch as "almost . . . relating to a man."

Jerri Miller hated the throwaway line that equates butches with men. "Butches are the women that women are not supposed to be," Jerri explained. Calling a butch the equivalent of a man is just another way of saying, "Get back. You're not in your place." But the copycat move that collapses "butch" into "man" does something else much more interesting: it sets up a separate male/female scale alongside butch/femme.

If "butch" and "he-man" occupy the same position on the same gendered scale, one should substitute for the other. There should be little difference between falling for the macho hero of 1990s action movies, Wesley Snipes, or the butch heroine of 1950s pulp fiction, Beebo Brinker. But for most people, these two representations are not interchangeable. Maybe there's more than one continuum operating here.

Why else would Rachel puzzle over whether the partner of a stone butch should be considered a lesbian? Her confusion on this point alludes to at least three scales: butch/femme, man/woman, and gay/straight. Either a stone butch is another variety of man, making "her" lover heterosexual, she reasoned, or to be stone is already to be lesbian. In either formulation, butch/femme has as much to do with sexuality as gender.

Rachel's own attractions cut across sexual identity. Unlike many women who call themselves lesbian, she did not reserve the term "butch" for the gay-identified. Studs turned her on, whether they came packaged as male or female. Where did she locate herself in the midst of this whirl of categories? In Rachel you have a woman who identified as lesbian and femme, whose friends saw her as butch, who displayed gendered consistency in her attraction to butches but no consistency at all with regard to the sex of the people she found tantalizing. Ah, the limits of linearity.

As if this weren't complex enough, Rachel assigned stone butches to "a kind of territory between genders, beyond being women." In this passage butches move from the extreme end of a continuum to the middle, but this time the scale stretches between male and female rather than butch and femme or masculine and feminine. Not quite a third gender, butches occupy a space "between" and "beyond." What then to do with "androgyny," another gendered term customarily assigned to the "middle ground" between male and female? As the epitome of lesbian *machisma* the stone butch seems nothing like the androgynous woman who tries to blend or balance masculine and feminine "sides." How can they both occupy "the middle"?

Just when you start thinking that a knowledge of masculinity and femininity might help you understand, Rachel pipes up to insist that a butch's way of carrying herself is "not masculine—it's butch." Helen Garcia agreed. Maybe, she speculated, butch/femme posed a third or fourth alternative, "outside masculine and feminine." So masculine/feminine occupies yet another scale, playing off others like butch/femme, but positioned slightly to the side.

Notice how an account of gender that begins with a single continuum ends up producing multiple scales to "explain" even the simplest gendered differences. People tend to speak as though they're operating with a one-scale model. But their explanations do something more complicated. In practice they slide back and forth from one scale to another, pretending that these separate scales correspond perfectly, even when they don't. Rachel begins by depicting butch/femme as a continuum that maps neatly onto man/woman. If butch equals man, then femme must equal woman. All the poles line up. But a few minutes later Rachel identifies butch as the magical mystical ingredient that attracts her to both males and females. This time butch can apply to either men *or* women and so, presumably, can femme. Now the scales fail to line up. And no one's even broached the question of transgender.

Sometimes false correspondences get people into trouble. Consider women who use a butch/femme scale to measure "how lesbian" someone is. Usually a butch "ten" stands in as the most authentic lesbian of all. Jerri knew from personal experience that femmes who logged in at "one" or "two" had to field doubts about the "realness" of their lesbian identity.

Even today a woman in skirt and heels can have her lesbian credentials questioned. ("What do you mean, am I queer?" replied a woman with cascades of brown hair, when challenged about her sexuality in a lesbian club. "Aren't I a woman, and didn't I just ask you to dance? Or," she added, looking down at her erstwhile partner's crotch, "is there something about you I should know?") Why did women located at the femme end of a scale encounter so much mistrust? What made some heterosexuals and "butchier" lesbians identify them as good candidates for going straight? Why should a dash of eyeliner stack the odds against a woman in the game of "more lesbian than thou"?

For this logic to work, you have to construct and then confound two scales: butch/femme and gay/straight. Start by assuming that ultrabutch corresponds to ultragay, which leaves ultrafemme paired with straight. The result? Feminine lesbians stand accused of trying to pass for straight and betraying "pure" lesbian sexuality. Bisexuality becomes a less than authentic choice.

Little do the women who denounce femmes realize that, as the years go by, some (butch) "nines" and "tens" end up married to men. And while "obvious" butches may draw more antigay violence, Jerri had to fend off unwanted attention from men who mistook her for heterosexual. Between the suspicions of other lesbians and the threat of violence on the street, "It's not like [femmes] pass over into safety or something."

All this mismatching of scales, and these women haven't even figured in class and race and nation yet. Or have they? When people do not imagine race and class as factors that compound or lines that "intersect" gender, they tend to incorporate these terms implicitly into whatever gendered scales they have already assembled. Paula Nevins's preference for blonde-haired, blue-eyed prom queens is an example of implicit incorporation. So is Rachel's characterization of a "one" on the butch/femme scale as a (working-class) slut.

When Jerri wanted to explain what she meant by calling herself an "all-out" femme, she talked about being the kind of girl who could spend weeks attending bridal fairs. Her desire for a commitment ceremony might go either way, classwise, since neither the working class nor the middle class has a corner on marriage. But when Jerri, as a femme from a working-class background, plans her wedding, she also stakes a claim to the title of "good woman" rather than whore.

In Paulette Ducharme's story about the car wash, lesbians appear not as knights in black leather but as victims of dead-end jobs and urban squalor. Paulette's little sister threw up at the thought that these car wash attendants were homosexuals. All too easy to slip from lesbian to butch, butch to ugly, and hard-core butch to physically repulsive. Historically butch/femme *had* emerged from the American working class. But working-class butches often displayed more charm, self-respect, and fighting spirit than this portrait born of fear would indicate.

By the 1980s Rachel had observed even middle-class lesbians adopting a "motorcycle or construction worker look." Did women have to appeal to working-class imagery to make femme and butch visible as gendered locations? Although Rachel said she felt femme, she admitted that many other queers would peg her as a "seven" before they accepted her as a "four." She nudged herself toward the femme end of the scale with the boast that she could entice a woman in a femme manner without the benefit of lace teddies or seven-inch heels.

Conjuring up these stock symbols of the hooker and the slut, only to dismiss them, allowed Rachel to begin to define a distinctive (middle-class) approach to femme. But Rachel still wasn't sure whether middle-class femmes and butches had appropriated working-class styles, or whether they were recycling stereotyped ideas of what working-class women are all about. Not all working-class girls hit the streets in "watch me" haircuts, underwear that doubles as outerwear, the latest in athletic gear, or stilettos. Where in the butch/femme "revival" were their sisters in their well-laundered T-shirts, polyester blends, and Sunday best?

Class and race infuse gender and sexuality in ways that are not easily grasped in terms of a continuum. Paulette had her first sexual experience with a woman in a car because she lacked the money to rent a hotel room. A trip to the country brought temporary freedom from human scrutiny, even if it meant sharing their hard-won privacy with a pasture full of cows. Who was the "most butch" in this scenario? Paulette did ask the girl out, but the girl was the one to make the first move by blocking Paulette's exit from the rest room. So much for quantifying gender.

Paulette's involvement with this young woman led her to a new awareness of differences among people at the bottom of the economic heap. Although she herself had grown up working-class, through her lover Paulette gained access to a world where families did not even try to play by white middle-class rules. After she discovered that her lover was a minor on probation, she stopped seeing her for fear that people would gossip about "a white woman taking advantage of this poor black girl." But in the name of liberal politics and professional responsibility, Paulette ironically ended up taking advantage after all. She found the gay experience she had been seeking, then left her lover to pick up the pieces.

As a child Paulette had imagined gender in terms of discrete categories ("tomboy," "nun," "married woman") rather than a continuum. As an adult she preferred to highlight and accentuate gender rather than stick to one consistently gendered position. "When I'm femme, I'm really femme," she proclaimed, "and when I'm butch, I'm pretty butch." You could say that Paulette liked the poles. Superfeminine, hypermasculine, very butch, outrageously femme: any extreme form of gender would do.

But were all extremes created equal for Paulette? Was a "ten" really equivalent to a "one"? Paulette sometimes spoke of femme as an overlay upon a "male mentality" carried over from childhood. Coming out supplied an opportunity to experiment with something called "femininity" instead of moving directly from tomboy into butch. But the times that Paulette went into "high femme" left her feeling "like a faggot." Not like a lady or a slut, not even feminine, but like the kind of boy whose womanish ways are taken as a sign of homosexuality. By equating high femme with faggot, Paulette jumped right off any butch/femme continuum. Where would you locate "faggot" on a butch/femme scale, especially if you've already tagged yourself (for the moment) as femme? A butch "ten" didn't afford Paulette the same sense of drama, or dislocation.

Jerri departed from the butch/femme scale at a different point. Her notion of femme was active, egalitarian, distinctively lesbian, and certainly not to be confused with femininity or faggotry. A femme could be feminine, but the two were hardly the same. To Jerri's knowledge there had never been a recognizably lesbian version of femininity equivalent to the stylized masculinity of gay male clones in the 1970s. Jerri wondered why. Not that she envied the mustachioed kings of Castro street their look-alike fashions. Turning urban chic into a dress code would have taken all the fun out of it. But Jerri wished that "feminine" lesbians were not so easily mistaken for heterosexual, especially since she had no interest in passing for straight. Besides, she continued, femmes had the most to gain from femininity.

As Jerri saw it, femmes had a better shot at self-definition than heterosexual women because they didn't encounter the same social pressures to defer to their partners. In contrast, femininity made straight women vulnerable to mandates and extremes. By "extreme," Jerri did not mean the far end of a gendered scale. Straight women who bought into extremes gendered themselves "like dolls . . . like mannequins." Jerri considered herself an "all-out femme," though not "extreme" in this sense. The idea that donning bangles could transform you into someone's plaything horrified her. It would probably horrify many heterosexual women as well. But Jerri's point was that, like it or not, straight women were in more danger of getting tangled up in representations of what an appropriately feminized woman should be.

Not all queers would agree with the way Jerri divided up "feminine" and "femme." But many femme lesbians and bisexuals shared her discomfort with using femininity, of whatever sort, as a tool to separate the gays from the straights. Even Jerri occasionally had to stop herself from setting up multiple scales only to conflate them. After speaking to a college class, she found herself on the verge of doing to the female students what she despised others for doing to her: using a "masculine" appearance to infer homosexuality and a "feminine" appearance to infer heterosexuality. Locating a person on one scale can't predict her position on another, because there is no regular relationship between butch/femme, masculine/feminine, and gay/straight. How can there be, when people define the poles of the scales they invent so differently?

Jerri went a step further when she contended that location on a butch/femme scale cannot predict a woman's ability to pass for heterosexual. Some middle-class "eights" pass more easily than some working-class "threes." An African-American woman and a white woman, however femme, can be outed in a minute on their way to the movies in a racially segregated neighborhood. Why else, passers-by may speculate, would they be spending the evening together? Let each accompany a woman of the "same" color to the show in an "appropriately raced" neighborhood, and the issue of sexuality may never arise. Where is the gendered scale that can account for these differences?

Meanwhile evaluations often conflict, for reasons that may or may not involve ethnicity, class, and color. "People . . . think of me one way," Rachel explained, "and I feel of myself in another." Mannerisms that other people found "dykey," Paulette interpreted as having "a certain aesthetic flair." Helen assigned her lover a different number on the butch/femme scale than she thought her lover would assign herself. Although Helen's partner resolutely maintained a butch identity, Helen didn't always see her as particularly butch. But no matter. What turned Helen on was the gendering she saw in her lover, not the gendering her lover saw in herself.

Helen admitted that she was never sure how others saw her. While she called herself "a five," she reserved the option to shift in relation to a lover. "Who I am" on my own might not be the same as "who I think she wants me to be." When her partner had a strong butch identity, Helen slid all the way down an imagined continuum to "one" or "two." But she believed that movement came easier to a person who established a home base somewhere in "the middle." For Helen to move toward the butch end of a scale required not only mobility but a certain give and take. Helen had no problems dressing a girl-friend in lingerie, so long as the girlfriend switched occasionally back to butch. On the other hand, Helen claimed that she didn't care whether she unpacked her own bags at "two" or never ever came back to femme. Helen might be a chameleon, but not for all seasons.

But for all her reservations about scales, Helen could picture only a limited repertoire of sites where gender comes together with race, class, and sexuality. When she thought in combination, who appeared in her mind's eye? Only working-class Latina femmes, (upper-)middle-class white femmes, and white or Latina working-class butches. Femmes ended up class- and race-segregated in particular ways, with butches confined to the working class and no room for women of many colors in her Latina-Anglo model of race relations. And Helen hadn't even gotten around to eroticism, which many women described with a new set of scales, including top to bottom and vanilla to s/m.

Helen, Rachel, Jerri, and Paulette each produced different scales in the course of trying to explain gender. And each periodically abandoned those scales when the concept of a continuum proved inadequate to the tasks of description. Why do people who begin with a butch/femme scale end up either producing multiple scales or discarding the very notion of a continuum?

Sometimes they're trying to account for discrepancies. Other times things get too hot for a scale to handle.

Whenever you use a continuum, you make the assumption that gender can be quantified. Does the girl belong two or three inches over on the number chart? Who has the longest, the biggest, the most? But your location on a scale is only as valid as the traits cited as "evidence" for placing you there. And, as the chapter on guessing games showed, there's not much validity to the practice of describing people in terms of gendered traits. Take the common association of butch with "cool, reserved" and femme with "emotional." What gets coded as shyness in someone marked femme may pass as reserve in a stud. And what are butch tears and butch rage, if not emotions? Jerri, who could be extremely sophisticated in thinking about gender, also claimed that femmes "push for commitment more." (I suppose that includes femmes fatales?) Most sweeping generalizations have their counterexamples. Women toward the femme end of the scale can't wait to bear kids, right? Not Jerri, who wanted her partner with the hardy constitution to get pregnant. Not the many femmes who have no interest in raising children.

A scale might seem as if it's composed of identical numerical divisions, but look again. Partners do not always distribute themselves symmetrically along a number line. Jerri, for example, described a lover who's "not as butch as I am femme." The girl just couldn't picture herself standing there in a tux next to Jerri in a bridal gown. And Helen wondered whether there might be more "flexibility" toward the femme end of the continuum. She thought most femmes would have an easier time going butch than vice versa. Is the distance as far from one to six as it is from ten to four?

When all is said and done, a continuum is just an abstract model. As a model it does some things well, and others not at all. When you picture gender as a scale, you go beyond the either/or alternatives of "androgyny versus roles" or "butch versus femme." Drawing a line between the stone butch and the ultrafemme certainly allows for more nuance. But any continuum, no matter how finely graded, is still defined by its poles. It's only as useful as the butch-versus-femme opposition that frames it. In the end it doesn't get you *much* beyond binaries.

Adding scales until you end up with two or ten or twenty doesn't get you out of this mess. At best, multiple scales become unwieldy. At worst, they obscure what they're trying to describe. A continuum still applies a single measuring rod, one universal all-purpose scale, to some very different people.

How can any continuum account for Paulette's attraction to breasts *and* penises, much less the affinity she felt for gay men? Simplistic dualities—masculine/feminine, Anglo/Latina, male/female, gay/straight, middle-class/working-class, butch/femme—cannot grasp the processes of gendering described in even a single story. As scales multiply, it becomes less and less clear how they come together in one body, one life. As this thing shades into that, something is lost. Whatever the continuum, however many the scales, there are still ways that you can't bring gender into line.

Chapter 7   Me, Myself, and I

Gender is about race is about class is about sexuality is about age is about nationality is about an entire range of social relations. Why should it be otherwise? In a society where these terms matter, people cannot check identities at the door. In a society where standing on the "wrong" side of one of these terms can get your head bashed in, people ignore identities at their peril. You carry them with you, or at least other folks think that you do. If you don't proclaim them, somebody else will be sure to do it for you. You can try not to linger in the fields of identity, but you cannot escape these terms altogether. And it's a package deal.

When Teresa Cruz first came to the United States, she thought that becoming North American might subsume the many other ways that she thought of herself. But no: "It was all at the same time, all these different things." She had journeyed thousands of miles to become a young brown middle-class queer Cuban-by-way-of-Latin-America-American girl. How to understand this coming-together, in all its specificity and mind-numbing glory?

One popular way to try to grasp this complexity is with the concept of "intersections." Think of an intersection as a way to organize those multiple scales discussed in the previous chapter. Then think back to geometry class, when an intersection named the point where two or more lines meet. Each line is called an axis, a sort of modified scale. When people talk about intersections of identities, one line represents race, another gender, a third sexuality, a fourth class, a fifth ability, a sixth age, a seventh religion, and so on. Except that this time the drawing isn't done on graph paper. This time your body occupies the point where all those lines meet.

Intersections have the great advantage of allowing you to look at more than one aspect of identity at a time. In the olden days (a few decades ago) people who studied gender tended to examine it in isolation. Or at least the white folks who studied gender did. They used only one axis, a single scale extending from woman to man, which led them to treat other identities as add-ons or after-thoughts. But suppose you are Teresa Cruz. Can you say that you are more queer than Cubana, more middle-class than lapsed Catholic, more woman than American, more Latina than light-skinned? Who's to say which is most important? In practice they're impossible to separate.

Without some notion like "intersections," Anglos end up encoding white-ness into the world around them. Blonde-haired blue-eyed prom queens become the picture of ultrafemme. And people of color can pretend that race does not crosscut other identities. There are no queers in brown and black communities, right? Oops, didn't notice that axis labeled "sexuality."

As any motorist knows, intersections can be dangerous places. Route a slew of identities to the same point and see what happens. Don't be surprised if you get a twenty-car pileup. In a country where billboards shout BEAUTY IS WHITE! and the infrared sensors that turn on faucets in public rest rooms don't pick up darker skin, it would be strange if millions of women didn't struggle with what it means to be a brown American girl.

Sure, identities may be inseparable, but don't specific identities come to the fore at specific times? What happens when they're in tension with one another? When people are more articulate about some identities than others? Can intersections explain the gut-wrenching feeling that ushers in conflicts of identity? What happens when people do not formulate every axis *as* an iden-tity? ("Yes, I'm a third-generation Polish-American woman, but I don't really think of myself as having a class.") So much for a nice, neat meeting point of all those lines.

The intersections model has a hard time with contradictions or hard-nosed questions. It portrays all axes as equivalent, all lines coming together, all of the time. Could it be that stories do a better job than geometric models of con-veying how race, class, gender, sexuality, and the like come alive? Embedded in stories are particular *renditions* of gender that are already raced and classed, renditions that show people in action, chasing down the curve balls that identity throws their way. The moral of the stories? Gender may assume a million shapes, but it is never just gender.

Eriko Yoshikawa: "Shifting Gears All the Time"

"When I go out by myself and people come to ask me if I want to dance with them, it's always clear to them that I'm a femme. It's *so* clear to them that it almost offends me. I almost want to say, 'Well, I'm not!,' you know, just in principle. It's the way they put their arm around you, the way they talk to you.

"And I think it's different being Japanese, I really do. In some ways you attract the worst kind. I have had one woman who I met at a bar in L. A. We danced, and she bought me a beer, and we were talking, and she said how she really loved Japanese girls. I wanted to pour the beer over her head. I said, 'Oh, you do? Well, you should find one. I hope you do a good job of it. Good-bye.' I just don't want to attract the kind of people who say, 'Oh, I want a Japanese girl.' That, to me, is very offensive, in a way that I want to kill them.

"The other thing was that nobody assumed that I was a lesbian. Maybe it's because I'm Japanese, or maybe it's because I have long hair, or the way I dress, or whatever. I just didn't do the right things. It was really hard for me to find somebody that I could hang out with. I used to be the only nonwhite woman who would go in a certain [lesbian] bar. They used to harass me in ways that I never did really understand. They were always worried that I was picking up somebody or I was being picked up or something. I never drank very much because I can't drink. I fall asleep. And yet they would be hesitant to sell me a second beer.

"I started to be involved with this woman, and [she] only had her arms around me. We certainly weren't doing anything out of the ordinary at all. They came over and they said something like, 'That's enough, don't you think?' I just looked at [the bartender] and I said, 'Beg your pardon.' Because there were other people there clearly kissing, or [doing] something that we probably weren't even doing. I complained about it, and for a while we had a boycott."

When Eriko Yoshikawa discussed racism with her lover, a white woman who identified as butch, it always made her "feel how different we are, and it creates a certain kind of distance. There's only been a few times it's come up between us. She was driving and she saw this truck with a sticker on the back. There was this circle with a slash, with this Oriental-looking face with one of those hats—you know, those grass hats that people wear—and very Oriental-looking eyes. She saw it with her friend, and they took down the license number. She asked me what I thought she should do about it, and I said, well, I thought it would be really difficult for her to get any response from the company [that owned the truck]. But I thought that what she should probably do is call JACL [Japanese-American Citizens League] and they can take it on, because they have a lot more resources and they know how to go about dealing with that.

"We were talking about it and I said, 'What's so funny to me is that our reactions are so different.' And she said, 'What do you mean?' And I said, 'Well, my immediate reaction is a sense of panic.' I always feel panic, I always feel threatened by that kind of situation. There's not a lot of anger. Only when I have some distance can I react with anger. I feel like, oh, if I cut in front of him, he might shoot me.

"This is a fear, I think, also coming from a country in which we have very little firearms available. So it scares me if I have to walk by a policeman. He's got that gun right next to him. I used to be frightened as a child, and I never wanted to go near them. I still have that sense whenever I see a police car with the gun sticking up. I just panic. Like, you know, what if there's a mistake and he shoots me?

"The other thing is, I've been in situations where people would say things to me, nasty things, and I'm sure that if it was somebody who was white they would say, 'Fuck you,' or something, but they would say to me, 'Why don't you go back to wherever you come from.' Or say something about being a Chink or a Jap or whatever. It's that difference: that I can't intellectualize the problem. At first she felt like I was accusing her of intellectualizing the problem. I said, no, I didn't expect her to react that way. There's no reason for *her* to respond that way. But I wanted her to be able to understand that difference.

"I had some contact with Asian lesbian groups in which they felt that, well, somehow you were not really facing your own ethnic identity by always being involved with white women. I felt like, oh great, we've gone through this already. The lesbians in the Asian-American community have basically been blacklisted because we're sleeping with the wrong people, meaning women rather than men. Because you know we're supposed to always stand by our brothers. Stand by them or sleep by them or whatever! I expected Asian lesbians to go beyond that, since we've already done something wrong in the community. So I was very intolerant that they can excuse themselves with this kind of political rigidness. I think it's extremely important to deal with race; I think that it's very difficult in personal relationships."

Eriko described herself as leading a "split life," moving between two countries. "Since my mother wasn't communicating with me for a while, I thought if I got sick and couldn't go in to work, what would happen? I can't even collect unemployment." Her decision to try to stay in the United States derived from "a clear sense that I want to be in *relationships*." Although Eriko often despaired of getting the kind of job that would allow her to qualify for permanent resident status in the U.S., she felt that in the Japan of the 1980s it would have been difficult to set up housekeeping with another woman.

"[In Japan] nobody really thought of one as being gay or lesbian. Those are foreign terms. They didn't think in terms of that kind of *identity*. I think there is really a lack of identity, still, in Japan. It's very common for young girls to have crushes on older girls. There was a student who was two years younger than me, who had a crush on me. She would send me letters and all that. When I was leaving Japan she was really sad. She came to see me at the airport. I mean, my family knew about it, because she called and she asked to talk to me. Somebody else would answer and they'd say, 'Oh, it's her again!' I never wrote letters; I thought that was a little too mushy. But I remember she knew that I was really attracted to her. Everybody knew about exchanging letters and gifts.

"We had uniforms at that school, and it's funny, because most of the kids were middle-class or wealthier. We would call up one of the students who had already graduated and you'd pass on uniforms to other students, even though they're not relatives. I got a uniform from my older sister's friend who was a basketball star. Everybody wanted to touch the uniform that I was going to wear! 'Oh god, you're going to get her uniform!' 'Oh, can I see it?' So I wore it every day. And they would say, 'Oh, you're *so* lucky,' and, 'I have So-and-So's. So-and-So isn't quite as interesting or quite as exciting.'

"Being in Japan at that time, we used to go away on trips and we would take baths together and check everybody out and see who has a nice body. And I think that's when I *really* became aware of what it meant to be physically attracted to other people. Because in junior high you kissed boys, but it's not real attraction. It's the excitement of doing that. You're supposed to do it and this is new. It's not like, 'Oh, he's so beautiful,' and you really want his body.

"We went away to this tennis camp from school. We took baths in groups, but we couldn't wash our hair at bath because it would take too long, so we had to wash our hair in the sink. I had really long hair then. So I was trying to wash my hair, and one of the senior girls came over. This wasn't the one I was attracted to, but my best friend had a crush on her. So she came over, and she just, without saying anything, started to help me wash my hair. I said, 'Ooh, this is really weird!' Every night she came and washed my hair. It never occurred to me that she was attracted, but it made my girlfriend just jealous. [My girlfriend] had terribly short hair—I mean, there was nothing to do with her hair. All she could do was pour water over it! It would really be awful to come and help her wash her hair!

"I've had a lot of friends who had difficulty coming out as a lesbian, calling themselves lesbian. I was so ready to have all this trauma, and I never had them. I thought about it and thought about it. Why was it not difficult? And I decided that perhaps it was [that] I've always had so much ambiguities about my identity in terms of being caught between Japan and the United States. That was never really resolved. I just sort of decided that I was not going to be either. If I went to Japan I became more Japanese. If I was here, I was more comfortable in certain ways, but in certain situations I knew I had to shift into something else. It's like shifting gears all the time. And so the whole question of being a lesbian was just so much easier, compared with what I had to grow up with.

"Ethnic identity is always difficult to deal with in my case, because in some ways being Asian-American is very different from being Japanese. And yet I spend my life here, and so much of my experience of being Japanese is being Japanese in the United States. That part is very close to being Asian-American. But the fact that it wasn't until I was ten or eleven [when I moved here the first time] that I realized that I would be an outsider makes it different from other people who grew up here as an outsider. I don't feel very Japanese in other Japanese's eyes. I don't have the roots to be American. Being a lesbian is the only identity that I feel as though I don't really have to make qualifications for.

"I'm very logical in the way I argue, so when I argue with somebody, I end up being dominant. With men it's a real problem, having a fight with them. And at the same time, I am *hardly* the butch type. Being contradictory in many ways as to how you're supposed to be, it's a lot easier with a woman. I mean, it's not easy with *any* woman, because some women have these strict ideas about what roles are supposed to be. Either roles are terrible, or if you are into being a femme you have to be [one particular] way. I have been with a woman where she thought that, being a femme, I should be dressed this [certain] way. It was clearly wrong, because, first of all, I hated aqua. An aqua nightgown was just not me. With my skin, it made me look green and sick! It was too long. I didn't want to hem it. I would trip over it. You know, that kind of thing. Something so wrong is just *wrong!*"

The first woman Eriko slept with was an older lesbian who refused to allow Eriko to touch her sexually. Later Eriko became involved with a woman she considered femme. The relationship made her feel more butch, "but I just couldn't live up to it! I was very good in the mechanical part, in terms of sex and being able to fix things. It's just that she had these expectations.

"My mistake was that I screamed when I saw this huge lizard. That just made her furious. It's one thing if she's disgusted with me because I am an adult and I can't deal with lizards, but she was mad at me because I wasn't supposed to behave that way. I thought that was ridiculous. I made it very clear to her that, sure, I can play games, and I can be in certain roles, but I didn't see myself as being a butch.

"Butch/femme is fun. It's exciting. I take it seriously sexually; I don't take it seriously in terms of roles. I don't mind somebody being dependent on me emotionally, but not because they're femme and I'm butch. I thought, 'Oh, if you want that, you can go and find a father or a mother.' I have always found it very fascinating for me, that somebody would have such strong ideas about what that meant, being butch and femme."

Judith Mayer: "In the Days of the Big Orgasm"

"One of the benefits of getting older, and one of the disadvantages, is *nothing* is clearer," explained Judith Mayer as she looked ahead to her fiftieth birthday. "There aren't any simple solutions. It seems to me that every solution I can look at creates another problem. I mean, it may be better than the problem that's there, but it creates other problems. And it's murkier. It seems harder. So no, I don't feel grown up. I still have the illusion that to be grown up means you understand what's going on and things are clearer.

"My father had a store in Greenwich Village, so I was aware [of gay people as a child]. I lived in New York. I knew where the bars were. At that point, if you could recognize someone, especially a woman, as being gay, it was usually a woman who was dressing like a man or looking very much like a man but you knew wasn't a man. People really were stereotyped. And the butch and the femme was not just a few people dressing up that way. That was the majority, the *vast* majority, of people. You wouldn't have the range of clothes styles that you have now. It's a different world.

"In the 1950s in the Village, interracial couples could get beaten up by the Italian kids. Gay men could get beaten up by the Italian kids if they were either too obvious or they were walking hand in hand. There may still have been some sense of code that you didn't do that with women. You might whistle at them, you might give catcalls, but you wouldn't use dirty names at them and you wouldn't do anything physical. And that's changed so that women, also, in that sense are targets.

"It really did look to me like the model for being gay was alcoholic. Being in roles. I wasn't femme—that was real clear—and I wasn't attracted to very masculine women. So I didn't see any possibility for being gay. I was going to live alone and write the Great American Novel, and probably commit suicide before I was twenty-one. The mental image I had for myself was of someone sitting up there in her room typing and occasionally having sexual flings. What I wanted was to be all that stuff that you were proud of: 'Oh, you write like a man' or, 'You think like a man.'

"The first gay couple that I ever met, one of them had just gotten out of an institution where she'd been four, six months, and was violent. Somehow I didn't think this might be unusual—[that] this might be a strange couple. I thought, 'Yep. This is what being gay is! And this is scary!' I mean, this was the 1950s. It was the McCarthy era.

"Have you read the 1950s lesbian novels? Well, a lot of them have the theme of the older woman who really is gay, and the younger woman falls in love with her because she's had this unhappy sexual relationship with a man. Then she has this very volatile relationship with a woman, and then she meets the perfect man and lives happily ever after. So there was some kind of, I guess, fantasy that I was going to have a successful, quote, 'normal' sexual relationship. And a 'normal' relationship would be with a man. This was in the days of the big orgasm, and we used to get together to find out if anyone had had it. And since *nobody* was having it, there obviously was hope!

"When I met Nadine I was a published, active writer. I assumed that most of the people we met through business knew we were lovers. But it was never said, so it always felt awkward to me. Nadine also had this thing about coming out. That we were different from all the other lesbians, and therefore there was no reason to identify ourselves as lesbians. Lesbians were only interested in playing cards, going to bars, watching TV. Whereas *we* socialized with writers and poets and publishers.

"When Nadine and I came to San Francisco [in the 1960s], the woman below us was gay. I remember she was just so paranoid I couldn't believe it. Never take your ID when you go to a bar; never give anyone your right name. I don't think things will ever go back that far, but what I see [is] a lot of the more professional, the BACW [Bay Area Career Women] lesbians as being more concerned with making money, being comfortable with professional careers. I don't know that they're being closeted again. I think it's the difference of not being up front. Being quieter about being gay. You're not going to introduce someone as your lover. You might introduce them as your roommate. But you're more likely to introduce them as your friend.

"What I've felt mostly from the older lesbians in roughly my age circle is more conservative. Ten or fifteen years ago, when everybody was dressing in khaki drag, that bothered me. There was something about too rigidly down-dressing. That felt like a real age difference. I still have difficulty around the issues of—in this society—status and money and what one is supposed to do with one's life based on one's background. Et cetera. I was saying to someone,

'I can't stand people I know whose major form of conversation is the next building they're buying.' At the same time, I'm not comfortable with people who don't seem to have a career and are just filling in jobs."

Once, at a Halloween party where everyone came in costume and was supposed to stay in character, "After half an hour I said, 'Okay, we can start being who we are!'" Although Judith found "roles" of any kind restrictive, she believed other lesbians were much more likely to see her as butch than femme. "On the most absolute, silly level, because I don't have grown-up clothes. This is always a problem. My cousin, who's gay, is in town, and he has a very, very well-paying job. Whenever he can't get another person to go out with him, he'll call me up and take me out to dinner, which is nice. So I get to eat at these places. And I notice I don't have the clothes to go to the place I could suggest to him that we go to eat dinner. That's partly what I mean. Grown-up people don't dress the way I do.

"I used to think that Greta Garbo was the way women were. If I could walk into a room like Greta Garbo, I'd be grown up. And I'd be a woman."

Chris Parker: "The Power of Boots"

"I've got to be one of the mildest, most timidest butches in the world. It feels like sort of being a tomboy, sort of, but being grown up. But always having that little bit of a tomboy in me that likes to strut around, put a lot of stuff in my pockets. I don't feel like a man. I mean, there might be someone who would be able to think of themselves that way and pull it off, but [with me] it would be a joke. I wouldn't believe it and neither would anybody else.

"I had this friend once who told me that if you're going to be butch, if you're going to be a boy, you have to decide what class boy you're going to be. That's what she told me. So I thought about it, and I thought, well, I'm sure I know how to be a middle-class boy. My father's a perfect model. But that kind of bores me, because he's wonderful in a lot of ways, but he's kind of useless in a lot of other ways, because he doesn't know how to do a lot of things for himself. I thought, well, I'd be a working-class boy, but I don't know exactly what that is. I don't have much experience with it.

"I kept going around and around in my head, and I finally decided what I really wanted to be was a cowboy. It was one of those things where I thought about it and thought about it and thought about it, and couldn't really figure it out, so finally I just threw up my hands and said, 'I want to be a cowboy!' It had something to do with the power of boots. Clearly it has to do with my love of the West and just a way of feeling about being in nature and being able to fend for oneself. And something to do with a way of walking that really I can't even get. You have to have really long legs, and then a really small ass, none of which I have."

Misha Ben Nun: "Good for Their Egos and Nothing for Me"

"I've always felt like the teenage girl in the house. We had a teenage girl who lived here, too, and it was great. We got together like *that*. Because she was just turning thirteen, and she was into all this stuff that I was getting into, too! She had started wearing makeup, and she wanted to put makeup on me all the time. She was just starting to wear nylons and tiny little pumps. She got so much criticism from my other housemates. I loved it! I was really encouraging her.

"This friend of mine that moved in was saying that there's this special kind of femme-femme relationship you can have that doesn't happen between butches. There's that ease of relating and getting really intimate, but still being able to remain on a friendship level. [Though] I definitely have seen femmes who are together [as a couple]. So they must be attracted to each other. But at first I was really confused when I would see them: two femmes together. If they identify with butch/femme, then they probably wouldn't come together as a unit.

"I don't really see things in terms of opposites. Like, I can only look at my relationship with my [butch-identified] lover and see all these similarities. The way we perceive ourselves in the world, though, is pretty different. And I think that maybe that's what is the main thing behind your identity as butch and femme: how you see yourself in the world, in relation to your lover. Your self in relation to other people. But it's not opposite, because to me, opposite means that everything that I do, my lover would be opposite to me. Which is not true at all.

"I was a very femmy hippie girl. I never had button-down Levis, or a jacket, and I *really* wanted a pair. I bought them all in one day: jeans and a jeans jacket. I remember my housemates saying, 'Oh, Misha! You don't have to do that to be a dyke!' This twenty-one-year-old kid. I wanted other more straight people to know that I wasn't available to them.

"Both my class stuff and gender stuff is really confused. Not confused, but it's been really changing. And part of it's being Jewish. Because my mother was this really strong, strong woman. And that was my image of a woman. Totally dominant, but holding it all together, and working. Really resisting any kind of putting her in a role. Like she would not be femme. Clearly would not identify as femme!

"And then classwise, my parents came to this country basically with $500 in their pockets, but with an education. My father grew up in a very poor family, and my mother's parents actually were poor, too. So growing up, we didn't have a lot of excess. I don't even know what class we were in. We saved for education; everything was for education. So there was some level of deprivation. I got really class confused, and I moved into this new neighborhood, where we moved but we didn't have anything to put in the house. It brought up a lot of insecurities for me, living in this community where people were going skiing every weekend. Never heard of that!

"Culturally, there's a lot of identification [with being Jewish]. There's a sense that there's another country [Israel], and then you celebrate the holidays as a cultural activity. Hebrew was spoken at home and we weren't allowed to speak it, or learn it, or anything. Also, though, my parents sort of used us, my sister and I, to bring in the culture—what we were learning [about] American culture—into the home. I remember being asked a lot of questions: When you go to a friend's house, what do they do? What are their parents like, and what do they eat? Just feeling that constantly I had to teach them what it was to be American.

"I guess it was after junior high, I had this revelation that you are whatever you want to be, and you don't have to be put into these roles. But I went on this really weird extreme. My role was being this very serious kid, and keeping myself on the outside, and always seeing how I was different. And that's how I was until I decided to check it out, what it'd be like to be totally mainstream. I got into high school and I became a cheerleader, and I hung out with the football team. Did that for about three years, then got really disgusted and dropped out. I got a lot of encouragement from my parents. They were always pushing me to be more of what I wasn't.

"I think those were some of my most unhealthy years, when I was getting mainstreamed. I was getting drunk all the time at age fourteen, and high, and getting really fucked over by boys. But I was really popular. I was really right there, the American high school girl. I look back on it, and it was really a sick, sick time for me. But that's when I got most of my praise and acceptance.

"Being the daughter of a [Holocaust] survivor, and parents from another country, and being Jewish in the community that I grew up in (very Catholic and very blonde), I was never really part of the mainstream anyway. And I think that once you break out of that image that you're trying to be, then you start realizing you have choices in your life. Something about feeling really strong and powerful is what was happening when I was coming out. Like I can cope with anything now, because I can see all around me, as opposed to seeing in front of me. Knowing that there was a whole life that was all planned out for me, and that I did not go, just sit on the train, and ride through it.

"When I realized the impact of what it meant to be a daughter of a survivor, and what I had gone through in keeping that hidden when I was growing up, it was like my whole past came out through my heart. None of us would really believe that [our relatives] were dead. We just believed that they were lost, and we had to find them. And so there was a lot of stuff around wanting to meet foreigners not from this country, thinking that I would be led to my father's family. Always searching for that."

When Misha told her parents she was involved with another woman, "It went back to that they were victims in their lives, and that they brought us to this country to have freedom and not to be a victim. And by being a lesbian I'm putting myself in a victim role." Far from seeing herself as trapped in a role—as a lesbian or a femme—Misha believed that "the majority of heterosexual people are really repressed into a role, and are very fearful people, and cannot leave that role. We're just freer, in a lot of ways.

"I really think butch/femme has *nothing* to do with heterosexual roles. It's a whole new realm that we're only beginning to understand. Maybe it's something to do with aesthetics: what we think is beautiful inside ourselves. I don't know how to describe it, but I know that beauty to me is a real different sense than beauty to my lover. There's this real beauty to me about the way she'll pick something up, or the way she'll move her body, or hold me. It's this sense that I can't imitate. I just see it. And I know that she has that same sense of me. The way I walk, or move, or touch.

"This other woman who moved in [to my household], who very much identifies as butch, she's also a carpenter. So I immediately allowed her to do a lot of stuff in the house which I always did before they moved in. It's weird, because when I was straight and a femme, I allowed whatever man I was with to do a lot of that stuff. I hated [doing] it. Then once I came out, I did everything myself. I would get great satisfaction out of doing electrical things, and painting, and constructing anything, chopping wood. And now I *know* I can do everything myself if I want to! But I really enjoy going back to some of those roles. [The butches] get off on it; I don't. It feels good for their egos, and nothing for me."

Diane Kunin: "Downtown on Main Street"

"I find that I'm having what I speak of as a midlife butch crisis. It's not your average midlife crisis, but a lot of things I never really wanted suddenly seem appealing to me. I actually have entertained the thought: What if I just chucked it all and went and found a man and got married and had some babies? A lot of my desire for a baby is to bring it home to my parents. And I just don't think they could cope with having a lesbian father to my baby! I think it's as upsetting to me to have feelings like this as it's upsetting for the average straight male to suddenly think about going to the men's room and sucking cock.

"Partly it's just that I'm tired of fighting all the time. These are the kinds of things that come up for me when I feel real depressed and defeated. These are my nightmares. Other people have World Communist Takeover; the Right Wing goes bananas. When our defenses are down and we're not feeling good, all kinds of things can come up. Even fantasies of getting married to boys.

"Basically, I have an identity as a butch lesbian. And sadomasochist. It's really funny, because my identity is really very strongly gay, but I sometimes, even within that identity, have some sexual impulse toward men. It's not very often. But it is there, so. . . . I think sex and gender are more fluid than most of us tend to think. And part of why it's not so fluid is that we have to make lives. We have to be adults, one way or the other. You make choices, and then you're embedded in an institutional structure, whether it's straight or gay. The institutional structures of homosexuality can be as threatened by occasional heterosexuality as heterosexual institutions are threatened by homosexual flings.

"A lot of how I used to fulfill my 2 percent heterosexual quotient was with gay men. And with AIDS, that's not possible anymore. So they're not the kinds of sex objects to me that they had been, off and on, for a while. AIDS combined with age. I just feel mortality all around me, and I never used to. I think that's another reason why so many of us are depressed these days. Our friends and comrades are all engaged in it.

"Butch means a lot of things to a lot of people. I'm not a macho butch. I'm a sissy butch, but still, basically, I'm much more comfortable feeling maleness in me than femaleness. And there is a lot of femaleness. I mean, I'm not a screaming butch about it.

"I was the first person in my town who was not a working-class male to ever show up in Levis anywhere. Except for horseback riding. Well, I shouldn't say that, but in places where women, especially middle-class women, didn't do it. Like downtown on Main Street. We had very strict codes at school. Girls did not wear pants to school. We *had* to wear skirts. I'd run home and I'd get into my jeans. You know, people who lived on farms were allowed to do this. But not people of my class background in the city. I'd get in jeans and my mother would just have fits. It was okay in the house, and it was okay if I was out with my friends at the drive-in or something. But it wasn't okay if I wanted to go downtown. And it wasn't okay if I was being sent to visit someone who was in the hospital. I mean, these were sort of public events.

"I remember, to get those jeans, I had to go to this store that was mainly patronized by working-class men. They were quite astounded to see me, as well. I was violating gender expectations and class expectations by shopping there. We'd have *screaming* fights about it, me and my mom. My mother is very proper. She has this almost nineteenth-century, early twentieth-century sense of correct behavior. This was before the 1960s. It was the South. And she wasn't the only one. There was a sense of formality, and the higher up you were in class, the more that was enforced. So I think there was a lot of fear that my mother had around my determination to look like a working-class male.

"And then we also had real fights about glasses. I was nearsighted and always wore glasses, and she and my father wanted me to wear contacts. I put them in, and I hated them. They hurt. I wouldn't wear them. And my mother would say things to me like, 'You'd look so *attractive* if you just didn't wear those disfiguring glasses!' I also felt like that was sex discrimination, because I look a lot, in fact, like my father. He wears glasses, and everyone calls him handsome and distinguished.

"We also had fights about religion. I decided I was an atheist and I didn't want to go to synagogue anymore, because it felt like it was hypocrisy. My mother said, 'What will I say to people when they ask me where you are?' I said, 'I don't know. Tell them I'm an atheist! Tell them I'm sick. I don't care what you tell them. I don't care what they think.' A lot of the conflict between my mother and me was that she was very concerned about social control and what people thought. And I always felt like she would side with other people against me even when they were exercising illegitimate authority. Because she was worried about, quote, 'scandal.' And what people would say.

"My mother didn't think I looked good in clothes, and gave me a real hard time about how I should lose weight. So I always felt fat, even when I was quite thin. When I was about fifteen, I just suddenly started putting on a lot of weight. It's sort of like, 'You want a fat daughter? I'll show you a fat daughter.' I also was upset about my emergent sexuality. I think I put on weight to protect me from that. I was pretty driven by the tides of teenage lust, and I just didn't know what to do with it."

At college in the 1970s, Diane was "a one-woman lesbian hit squad there for a while, until there were more of us. I made an ass out of myself the first couple of times I tried to proposition anybody. I *still* make an ass out of myself when I try to proposition someone! But I was peculiarly graceless in the first couple of rounds. I was definitely a dyke. You know, I wore boots. I had big tits. I got a motorcycle after a while! I was very feminist, and 'dyke' was a female term, and it was an aggressive term, and it was kind of an 'up yours' term. Now, 'dyke' seems like one of those 1960s terms that doesn't have the same content, so I don't use it as much.

"There hasn't been an Orthodox person in my family for a long time, but there was this sort of Talmudic attitude about argument and discussion. That if something was right, it was right! That you would look at things and you would consider every side. You didn't have to be sucked into the prejudices of the moment. Also, my class background gave me a sense of entitlement. If this was who I was, then, goddamn it, I was entitled.

"I define as a butch bottom. My lover at one time [was] this wonderful woman, who's very strong and very athletic. The muscles of death! I mean, this woman had shoulders! And we were playing, fucking, one night, and for a variety of reasons she'd gotten jealous of me that day, and she turned me over and fucked me in my ass. With a finger. And I came all over the place! It wasn't so much the . . . well, some of it was the anality of it, but some of it was that I was being held down and overpowered, and that I knew she was a little bit angry with me. And the next morning she said, 'Oh, I'm so sorry! I'll never do it again!' Because she's really a sweet, gentle person, and it just appalled her. And I said, 'Uh . . . wait a minute! I kind of liked it. I was sort of hoping maybe we could do it again.'

"The other thing that happened was that I was at a conference, and there was a panel of some gay men on s/m. I just suddenly had this revelation that there was a *community* out there, of real people. And if there was a community of real people, they had to survive from one sexual encounter to the next. You know, people get up in the morning, and they put their clothes on, and they even go to work, and they come home at night. It's a different image altogether. I went back home and I thought about it and I realized that they were real sadomasochists, and that sadomasochism wasn't this wild-eyed fantasy that was only practiced by psychopaths. That it really was doable. But no one in the town wanted to do it, so it was very isolating. It was a much more painful coming out.

"The routes of access into other worlds, other sexual worlds, are much more difficult than even the gay world. They're much more hidden. People are much more secretive. They have to be. And it's just much harder to find your way in. It was part of why I moved out here, was to find my way in. It took about two years to find other people I really could do [s/m] with.

"I have several types. I like them smart. I like them butch. I like them top. Top is very important. I'll take a femme top long over a butch who's not a top. Most of my lovers have been non-Jewish, but on a few rare occasions, I've had real intense connections with women who are Jewish. Muscles don't hurt, but they're not a requirement.

"There are all possible combinations. There are butch tops and butch bottoms and femme tops and femme bottoms. They do interact in terms of scenes that I'll do. Like when I do scenes in girl clothes, to me it's marked as forcible crossdressing. It gets very convoluted. But I don't know that being butch and being bottom have any sort of intrinsic connection. I mean, they're connected in *me*, but. . . .

"I think butch/femme is really very lesbian. I wonder where the terms came from? I bet you they came from lesbian into gay male culture, rather than the other way around. I don't think 'butch' was a gay male term in the 1950s; it was a lesbian term. [Among gay men] it's more often, I think, that there are queens with queens and butches with butches. Although there *are* some crossovers. I think there are some couples, gay male couples, that are butch and femme in our sense, but I don't think that's as common. A lot of the leather scene is based on male-male, butch-butch connection. I've always wondered what someone who's an effeminate man who's into s/m, and likes to wear dresses and stockings, where he's going to find partners. Because you don't see him in the men's leather bars.

"For me, a lot of discovering butch/femme was being able to acknowledge things about the gender identity of me and the people around me. Like why all these short-haired people kept getting involved with women with earrings! But I have the feeling that all good ideas become overused, and beaten into the ground, and can be used as cudgels. Sooner or later people take them too seriously. If you talked to me about lesbian-feminism in 1972, I would have just been ecstatic about it! By 1974 I was ready to nuke the women's movement. It wasn't that the ideas were bad. It's that they became overapplied and used in contexts that they really weren't designed to be used in. It's like canonizing some words and making them holy scripture and forgetting what it originally meant.

"I think the same thing might be happening, actually, with butch/femme now. It's gotten to the point now where it's a fad, and pretty soon it will become a rule that you can't violate. That if you're not butch or femme enough, people will be upset. And then there'll be another backlash. I feel the same thing about s/m. I go to the bars and I look at some of these women who are running around in all this leather and all these chains, and I'm [saying to myself], 'Who the hell are these people, and *what* are they doing? And who do they *think* they are?' Not so much as in, 'Who do they think they are to be wearing it?' but what is their self-concept? I look and I think, 'What are they doing to each other? And do they understand enough about this to be doing it? Do they just think this is how to be cool?' If they're doing it just to be cool, I hope they're not. I wish they wouldn't. So I'm worried about butch/femme and s/m becoming new fads for people to feel miserable about."

Me, Myself, and I: Double Takes

Meet Eriko Yoshikawa, a twenty-something U.S. resident, middle-class, Japanese, able-bodied, one-time Catholic, contextually lesbian, not particularly butch but not exactly femme woman. There's very little you can understand about Eriko, or what happens to her day by day, if you insist upon examining these tags one at a time. Even she couldn't separate them. Even she had to speculate in order to explain the bad treatment she experienced at the women's bar in her California town.

What made the bartender refuse to serve Eriko a second drink? Racism that would have targeted any person of color? Class resentment? A West Coast legacy of anti-Asian political agitation? Was the bartender scapegoating Japanese for the way that multinational corporations had shifted jobs out of the country? Could she have felt squeamish about public kissing? Opposed to interracial sex? Disdainful of femmes across the board? And why did most of the white women at the club immediately take Eriko for femme? The gendered effects produced by long hair? The cut of her clothing? Stereotypes that divide Asian women into Dragon Ladies and China Dolls? Three of the above? All of the above?

In Japan, where the Western concept of identity has a short history, Eriko might not have thought about herself in quite the same way. In the United States, she accepted identity tags provisionally. How else could she proceed in a society where what you "are" has become every bit as important as where you fit and what you do?

Juggling so many identities tends to throw people into quandaries. Chris Parker nearly drove herself to distraction with the question, "Can a person be shy and still be butch?" Does timidity move a middle-class white girl "toward femme" (the old sliding scale model), or does it combine with age to make her feel more like a boy than a butch? And what could be more boyish—in WASP terms—than roaming the streets of San Francisco at the ripe old age of twenty-eight, her pockets invariably crammed with "stuff"?

Part of Cynthia Murray's rationale for switching from butch to femme involved the sense that she was getting too old to be butch. Other women talked about lesbians turning stud with the passing years. But Cynthia associated butch with an energetic, "truck-driving type mama." How could she sustain that level of activity as time went on? Wrapped up in Cynthia's decision to go femme were more than a handful of assumptions about gender, age, sexuality, physical ability, and culture.

The fact that identities are bound up together does not mean they always come into play together. Different identities have different significance in different contexts. Sometimes they hardly operate at all. When Diane Kunin walked into a working-class men's store to buy a pair of jeans, she violated a very specific blend of classed, raced, and gendered expectations. She may even have pushed the limits of ethnic and religious propriety. Young middle-class Jewish girls just didn't dress that way in the South during the early 1960s. Yet age had little do with this particular transgression. Jeans were no more acceptable attire for Diane's mother or grandmother than they were for her. A young African-American woman might have worn denim to work in the fields, if not to a job in domestic service. But the teenage son of white *or* African-American farmers could have bought a pair of blue jeans in the same town without attracting much attention—so long as the African-American man went to a shop that sold to blacks and waited patiently behind every white customer in the store.

Histories of conquest can encourage people to highlight or downplay particular identities. Carolyn Fisher grew up emphasizing German over Cherokee ancestry. European was better than Native American, right? Didn't the Indians always get slaughtered in those old Hollywood movies? When classmates ridiculed her for being German American after watching a documentary on the Holocaust, Carolyn finally turned her attention to her American Indian heritage. If Germans could have done something that horrific, maybe there was more to being Indian than she'd thought.

To work through stereotypes of "lazy, no-good," drunken Indians, Carolyn revisited a great-grandmother who was none of these. As she began to take pride in being Cherokee, she integrated race into her search for a lover. Maybe she could find someone "like me": not only relaxed and female and athletic but with the same chestnut hue to her skin. In Carolyn's case, "like me" also left out a few things. Age, for one, was not an issue. She hated the fact that many older lesbians refused to go out with her because of her youth. Where was a baby dyke to find a partner?

Identities do not simply meet at some mythical point of intersection. People have a hand in mixing them up. If Carolyn had responded to social pressures to declare a single "race," or gotten caught up in the post-1960s romanticization of all things Indian, she might have identified as Cherokee to the point of ignoring relatives who had crossed the Atlantic. And in her search for a racially "like" partner, she didn't have to cast the net of affinity so widely. White girls were pretty much out, but Carolyn considered both Native Americans and dark-skinned Latinas date material. In the pursuit of likeness, Carolyn could have gone only for American Indians, or other Cherokee.

Sometimes identities become transparent. That means people look right through them. Many people in the United States deny the difference that class makes, preferring to locate everyone somewhere in "the middle." But for every transparency there is a moment when the glass that separates people comes into view. There once was a lesbian paralegal who mistakenly opened the paycheck of the gay lawyer who employed her. After noting with shock the $10,000 discrepancy between the lawyer's monthly income and her own, the paralegal's queer buddy became "the boss." "I just couldn't think of her the same way again," she explained.

As Ruth Frankenberg's studies on whiteness and identity have shown, many white women think of race as something only people of color have to deal with. And in a dealing sense that can be true. White femmes are not often put in the position of having to explain, "Uh, most of the cosmetics in this store won't work for me." It's easier for Anglos to imagine the world to be white unless otherwise specified. The institutions around them converge to create that impression. Cosmetics companies hire white consultants, stores carry products developed for white consumers, and ads carry pictures of smiling white faces. With the exception, of course, of the occasional "ethnic" line.

So Judith Mayer's contention that race had nothing to do with her sexuality was not unusual. Even though Judith could tell you that walking down the street as part of an interracial couple could get your ass kicked in the Village of the 1950s. Even though what propelled her on her youthful quest for the big orgasm was a thoroughly white legacy of female sexual passivity. Even though Judith identified as lesbian and Jewish and white.

But there's more to handling multiple identities than selecting some, neglecting others, and holding a few close to your chest. Depending upon the situation some identities can assume greater significance than others. When the topic was friendship, Diane cared more about age than religion or gender. She liked younger people but was appalled by their ignorance about even the very recent past (*her* past!). When the topic turned to sex, gender became more important, because Diane preferred butch partners. Yet if she had to choose between a butch bottom and a femme top, she swore she'd pick the femme every time.

Identities can also get lost in the translation. No matter how well Teresa Cruz dressed, she kept running into Anglo women who assumed her class because they couldn't conceive of a Latina with money. Or think of all the white lesbians who read any African-American woman with dreads as femme. African-American queers would be more likely to pay attention to the style of the dreads and how she wears them before making that particular judgment call. A simple object like an earring can style you girly-girl white, black male urban chic, homie material, suburban heavy metal, leather queer, or a casualty of MTV. Neither the earring nor its interpretation occupies neutral ground. Gender plus race plus age plus class plus sexuality, sure, but that doesn't tell you how to read the signs.

The notion that all these identities, and then some, coincide at a single point doesn't allow for much tension, conflict, or contradiction. How is it that Misha Ben Nun could have felt like a class traitor when her family moved into a rambling house with no furniture? Was she the middle-class girl she had always known herself to be, an upper-class girl like the kids at her new school, or an impostor, pure and simple? If Misha had felt comfortably ensconced at the point where American met wealthy and Jewish and white, she wouldn't have had to work so hard at teaching her parents how to *be* American. She might have stayed home instead of going out for cheerleading. She might have come out to her parents without worrying that the threat of losing family ties would call up memories of the Holocaust. Eventually Misha decided that as a second-generation immigrant, as a Jew, as the product of her parents' upward mobility, she could forget about joining "the mainstream." She would always end up betraying somebody's aspirations, or something left behind. No way to graph these betrayals onto intersecting axes.

So far class, ethnicity, sexuality, and the like have shown up primarily in the guise of identities. But these integral aspects of the ways people gender themselves are not only about identity. Sometimes they don't come close to anything coherent enough to make you say, "I'm this" or "I'm that." Nothing you would print out as a label and stick on your back. Yet that doesn't make them irrelevant to gendering. That just opens them up to subtlety and throws them up for grabs.

Diane, for example, occasionally had sex with men. But these every-so-often encounters didn't automatically make her redefine herself as bisexual. She could have. Instead, she treated these male-female trysts as interludes in an otherwise lesbian sexuality. Bisexuality may have been the practice, but Diane didn't adopt it as an identity. Did that mean the gender of her partners had no bearing on her sexuality? Of course not. If Diane hadn't made any distinctions on the basis of gender, she wouldn't have ended up with mostly women for partners. Not to mention women who gendered themselves butch and eroticized themselves top.

When Eriko failed to satisfy her lover's concept of butch by screaming at the sight of a lizard, she defined her response as "childish" rather than "femme." Her lover, however, insisted that age had nothing to do with it. Screaming at creepy crawly little animals was just not part of the butch repertoire. So Eriko decided that two could play at that game. In the next phase of her argument she tried to take apart the notion of what it means to be butch by driving a wedge between gender and sexuality. I don't mind getting things rolling in bed, Eriko insisted, but why should I have to play the strong silent type? This lovers' quarrel centered on whether femme and butch should be taken seriously *as* identities. And the two women highlighted different aspects of gendering (age versus sexuality) to make their respective cases.

None of the women in this chapter was inclined to sit at an intersection of identities with the engine idling, waiting for the light to change. Any one of them could run figure-eights around the parking cones marked, "Who are you?" "Who am I?" and "Who are we?" They didn't have much choice. None of them fit the dominant profile of a straight, white, middle-aged, middle-classed, Christian male, gendered and coifed accordingly.

Some of their identities put them in the driver's seat. Some relegated them to the trunk. Some were likely to get them dragged by a rope behind the car. Taken together, these multiple aspects of gender force people to negotiate constantly as they travel from one context to another. Eriko even had to slip in and out of the concept of identity as she moved between countries. No wonder she felt like she was "shifting gears all the time."

But if crossings are many and cruise control nonexistent on this particular journey, what's a good way to think about all the shifting and grinding of gears? Maybe "renditions" is a better term than "intersections." Like an intersection, a rendition can encompass age, sexuality, nation, or what have you. But unlike an intersection, a rendition implies no geometric point where all identities meet, no preassembled axes of race or class, each defined in isolation and coming together after the fact.

Diane's "determination to look like a working-class male" is a rendition. When she marched up to the counter to order a pair of blue jeans, she had in mind a specifically classed rendition of male, a specifically gendered rendition of class. And if she had thought about it, she might have put a race to her fantasy. When she envisioned herself in denim, she had to picture something more than the abstract equation "gender plus class." There are all sorts of men, just as there are all sorts of ways to work for a living. The Mexican-American working class has had a different history from the Chinese-American working class. Poor white men and black working-class men lived in completely different sections of Diane's small Southern town. To envision a working-class male style, you have to color in the picture.

Imagine what could happen if you forgot to look for renditions and started treating gender as a thing unto itself. You could end up like Eriko's lover, giving your girlfriend an aqua nightgown that turns her complexion green. You may think you're doing it all in the name of femininity and frills. But where has ignoring skin color in your approach to femme gotten you? If you're lucky, just momentarily kicked out of the house. Could be worse, though. You could be Eriko: disembodied and called out of your race by the person who's supposed to love you most.

Chris was initially taken aback at the thought that she couldn't aspire just to be butch. She had to decide what class boy to be. When Chris shaded "butch" into "boy" in her story, she was looking for laughs. But her dilemma was serious. If no pure version of butch existed, Chris would just have to cast about until she came up with a classed rendition of "stud" that she could live with. Repelled by her father's version of suit-and-tie male, but not knowing the first thing about white working-class masculinities, Chris didn't know what to do. Suddenly the answer came to her: I know, I'll be a cowboy.

Chris's solution didn't exactly get her out of class hierarchies. Historically, some cowboys may have hit the frontier looking for a classless society, but they still had a class location. It wasn't the Eastern bankers who were chucking it all for the chance to herd those little dogies. And it wasn't just white boys, either. Plenty of Latinos and African Americans hit those dusty trails.

Of course, Chris wasn't planning to go back in time or even sign on for a job at a working ranch. Like Diane, she was searching for a "look." Her decision to be a cowboy butch raises the issue of whether you can select your identities with more regard for style than circumstances. Or, when the dust settles, will you be just another middle-class boy-girl in boots?

Renditions are very specific and very concrete. You run them through your body every time you make gorditas or throw on those jeans or brush your lips against her neck. But with all the imagery that renditions bring into play, it's easy for them to edge over into stereotype. Judith's initial rendition of "lesbian" got in the way of seeing herself as queer. How could she be a lesbian, when "lesbians were only interested in playing cards, going to bars, watching TV . . . whereas we socialized with writers and poets and publishers"? For years she saw gay women as exclusively working-class, making them, relative to herself, a lower class.

White women in the bar saw Eriko as femme for reasons that had more to do with race/gender typing than the length of her nails. Eriko knew that she was no China Doll. Since when had she been passive, available, and therefore deserving to have her sexuality policed? Under the circumstances she did not have the luxury of gendering herself in response to an idle question like, "What shall I be today?" She needed to stake out a position that could head off this kind of harassment. "Femme" wouldn't do because the term was already raced and sexualized in specific ways by the time these white women affixed it to her body.

Renditions are not always about mis-takes. Misha described herself feeling like a teenage girl rather than feeling femme in some generic sense. Diane peppered her descriptions of studliness with modifiers. Sissy butches, macho butches, screaming butches: even a gendered term such as "butch" could accommodate differently gendered renditions. Judith interpreted womanhood through the elegance and reserve of Greta Garbo's screen persona. Butch, on the other hand, had something to do with age. Although Judith didn't call herself butch, she thought others might take her for one "because I don't have grown-up clothes." And those rather unadult clothes had class ramifications, as well. How could she dress for dinner with such a wardrobe?

Class, age, gender, and such come together not only in the doing but in the perceiving. They can be separated in thought but seldom disentangled in practice. You may not encounter all of the combinations all of the time, but renditions give you at least some of the combinations all of the time. And when these terms do come together, the reason they combine this way rather than that often has something to do with power.

The assumption that Eriko enters a bar to be taken and touched seethes with a racist sexism, a sexist racism that becomes palpable in "the way they put their arm around you, the way they talk to you." When Eriko gets ready to shout, "I'm not femme!" in this context, she also means, "Take your hands off me! I'm not your 'Japanese girl'!" Her statement is one part identity, two parts resistance.

Political struggles over identity and entitlement complicate things further. Eriko had to deal with Japanese who thought her too American, and Americans who found her not American enough. Some Asian and Asian-American lesbians portrayed her as a race traitor for pursuing an interracial relationship. Yet she wanted to feel community with other women of color. And she could hardly leave race behind. It wasn't her white girlfriend who panicked at the sight of an anti-Asian bumper sticker. "If I cut in front of him," Eriko worried, "he might shoot me." Regardless of what identities Eriko claimed for herself.

A person doesn't shift gears all the time unless she has to weave her way in and out of categories already littering the roadway. Yes, she can make the choice to jam that transmission into third or fourth. But she's in trouble if she thinks she can freewheel it around the corners. Most choices about identity are constrained by inequality or historical circumstance. And more than a few are forced.

Chapter 8   Power, Power . . .

Fired from your job. Jeered at by passersby. Drop-kicked. Sucker-punched. Forced into a drug program where they strip you naked and make you call out your sexual "sins." Photographed by tourists. Undermined in love. Whited out on "women's land." Targeted by right-wing posters that want you gone or dead. Accused of genocide by your own family. Surrounded. Alone. Pummeled with rocks and fists till you can't get up again. Assaulted by the assumption of heterosexuality. Brought into line by threats. Accused of violence, ignorance, or insanity if you try to respond.

These are just a few of the more destructive manifestations of power in a society that discards, disrespects, and dismisses its queers. Sometimes there's a recognizable culprit: institutions that call gods or the law over to their side. State agencies, employers, and religious organizations have all been known to aim a stake at the heart of gay relationships. At times these institutions have entered into shifting alliances with white supremacist groups, the religious far right, and the more conservative elements of queer communities. Every once in a while, they take a stand that supports lesbians.

But the power brokers who have such an impact on queer lives are not just social workers, immigration officials, grand wizards, bosses, or deacons.

They're also: Straight men who come onto you because they refuse to see femmes as "real" lesbians. Straight women who station themselves at the entrances to public restrooms to keep passing women out. Gay organizations that tell you to meet the press in a dress. Gay clubs where the women stare you down if you enter the place in a dress. The neighborhood kids who so thoughtfully repainted your car. (Couldn't they at least have spelled out "dyke" instead of "faggot"?)

They are the coworkers who grumble about your pay raise because they can't imagine you supporting a kid. Relatives who acknowledge your sexuality but keep sending you dangling earrings for your birthday. Relatives who want to show they accept your sexuality by sending you cufflinks for your birthday. Relatives who refuse to send the dangling earrings you requested for your birthday because they're afraid to do the wrong thing. Lesbians who assume you're femme because of your race. Lesbians who assume your class because you're butch. People who are more than happy to share their identities with you without ever inquiring into your own.

Each of these scenarios is part of the ordinary dangers and everyday affronts of living queer. Yet these scenarios generally are not the first things that come to mind when people think about power in relation to femme, butch, androgyny, chameleon, or other modes of gendering yourself lesbian. Most of the discussion of lesbians, gender, and power confines itself to interpersonal—usually relationship—dynamics. There's no denying the importance of power dynamics in couples, a topic central to the next chapter. But this chapter focuses on power relations in a society larger than two, from local communities to the United States as a whole to the global political economy. None of these contexts exists apart from gender, which means that none exists in isolation from race, class, or sexuality, either.

Gendering has an impact on who gets hurt, who gets work, who fights back, how, when, where, and why. But what exactly is the relationship between visibility and power? Do gender tags target you or protect you? Is the closet a femme's "natural" ally? Are butches always as easy to pick out of a crowd as people say? Can you answer these questions without also asking what kind of femme or butch you're talking about?

Is a white middle-class butch the same kind of lightning rod for gay-bashing as a white working-class butch? Can a working-class femme always pass? If a Latina goes high femme, does she pass over into something called "heterosexual privilege," or does she pass over into a stigmatized category called "whore"? Does it matter who's doing the reading?

Over the years much ado has been made about the cultural politics of androgyny, butch/femme, and gender-fuck. When it comes to policing and performing gender, is it always obvious who's subverting whom? Wearing fish-nets with galoshes may speak gender to power—it's a no-no that hasn't made it onto Paris fashion runways (yet). So may talking your way into a job as a sheet metal apprentice, or refusing every gendered label someone wants to paste on your forehead. But how effective are these strategies? Do they get peo-ple to stop assuming you're heterosexual? Do they get other lesbians off your back? Do they keep anyone from getting beaten up? Does gender change? Do the questions change? As time passes, as jobs shift, as the world twists in the wind?

Power plays can be as mundane as they are frightening. Sometimes they're frightening precisely because they *are* so mundane. Even the blood trickling onto the sidewalk turns out to be the most ordinary thing, glistening in the sun-light of another day. And power relations leave so very little untouched. All of us find ourselves implicated at one time or another. How free are your "choices" about how to gender yourself when this is what you're up against?

Gina Pellegrini: "The Tourists' Eyeballs Were Hanging Out of Their Sockets"

"Men in straight bars don't take no for an answer. You say no to a woman in a women's bar, she says, 'Okay,' and walks away. These guys have to get really raunchy: 'Whatsa matter, gotta problem?' I just turned around and said, 'One asshole in my pants is enough.' He finally got the drift and left me alone.

"The job I have now, they don't know [I'm gay], because my boss is such a redneck. He looks out the front window about two months back and said, 'Gina, come here!' I thought somebody had an accident or fell or something. He goes, 'Where did all these black people come from?' I said, 'Excuse me?' I just looked at him and said, 'You're really fucked.' I just walked away. What kind of damn question is that? You know, I really took offense by it.

"Then he calls them 'little faggy queens' when they come in, or he calls the women 'little bulldykes.' He always has a comment for somebody, but he should look in a mirror. If I didn't need the money—I've never worked for six dollars an hour since I was eighteen—if I did not need that money and I was-n't so broke right now, I would have told him to shove it up his ass. But I need the money. I'm really in a lot of financial trouble right now, so I can't afford to. I have to walk on eggs.

"The first neighborhood I lived in was kind of poor. Then my father's busi-ness took off, so we moved to another neighborhood that was real suburban middle-class. And then after they got divorced I moved to a not-so-nice neigh-borhood where I was probably the only white person. There was Hispanic and black. Then my mom got married to this guy who was pretty wealthy and we moved to an even better neighborhood than the first one."

When Gina's mother discovered that her daughter was in a sexual relationship with a girlfriend from high school, she sent Gina to a psychiatrist. "He was trying to play little mind games with me. Like, 'What does this look like?' 'It looks like a tit. What do you think it looks like?' Or, 'What does this look like?' 'Well, you have one between your legs. What do *you* think it looks like?' Just because I was gay they thought I was stupid, I had no intelligence. Or I must have been emotionally damaged. Or somewhere I must have been screwed up so badly that it made me that way. It wasn't like it was a preference that I chose that I was happy with. They considered it a sickness and I should be cured."

Because Gina "felt so strong about not letting them get me down and try to mold me into something that I wasn't," she continued to come into conflict with her parents. At the age of fifteen she found herself in a girls' home. "There was junkies there, there was drug addicts, there was unwed mothers that were separated from their kids. So it wasn't that they cared that much [that I was gay]. It was that the counselors didn't know what to do." Although Gina was not addicted to drugs, the counselors referred her to a drug rehabilitation program for lack of an alternative placement.

After taking away all Gina's possessions, the supervisors of the drug program attempted to strip-search her. She refused. "That's why I got in trouble from Day One. They were so sadistic in this place. One night they found out I was

Italian and they wanted me to make Italian bread. It's like French bread. So I decided I was going to get creative and I made pizzas. I made like twelve huge pizzas for all these people. That's what I did wrong. Everybody liked the pizza (they fed you mush in this place). But [the counselors] got really pissed off and told me I'd have to spend twelve hours on a 'dummy line.'

"If you did something that they considered 'dummy,' you had to stand perfectly straight against a wall but not leaning on it. And then there was this door over there that was the office. The woman, she would be in her office, and she would say, 'All right, who goes there?' and you'd have to scream your name. And she'd say, 'Louder, louder, louder!' until you're screaming until you're hoarse. And then she'd say, 'Okay, back to the end of the line.' Isn't that weird? And she seemed to be kind of normal, so I didn't understand what she was into. Sadistic, I guess. And then you'd go to the back of the line and the next person would have to do it. And you'd have to stand perfectly steady. You were not supposed to move unless when they told you to advance one spot on the charts that they used. 'Advance one spot!' It was like you were in the military.

"One night finally I fell asleep or passed out or something. I ended up on the floor, and they told me I'd have to go sit on a rock. I said, 'I have to go sit on what?' They make you sit on a rock that's this pointed shape. They made you sit on that till your ass is black and blue. I wished I was high like most of the people in the place, because I was seeing all this realistically, and half the other people were so high they didn't know what the fuck was going on.

"This one guy was caught masturbating in the shower. And they brought him downstairs in the middle of the living room and shaved his whole, entire body. His pubic hair, his head, his legs, his arms, mustache, beard. He was a nice-looking guy, you know: blonde hair, blue-eyed, looked like a little football player. And they shaved him. He had to scream twenty-five times what he was doing in the shower, and what it was like. To all these people, he had to scream this whole story. The guy had a nervous breakdown right there.

"In that neighborhood it's so bad that none of the doors are locked. Because the weirdos outside know that there's weirdos inside, and the weirdos inside don't want to go outside. Because those guys will kick your ass, rape you, just beat you up, steal whatever you have on you. They'll roll you just for your clothes and leave you bare-assed. It's junkie heaven. There's so many people out there that need so many things that they'll just do anything to get it. And what I did was, I just left one day.

"I went to my lover's house. I started crying. I was a mess. I'd hitchhiked all the way home and some guys tried to get fresh with me. I jumped out of the car; I think it was a red light or a stop sign. I was too scared to hitchhike anymore. So I walked the rest of the way, and it was twenty miles.

"Well, that was the only thing that kept me strong, was my own identity. Because otherwise I would of went nuts in those places. That was my only focus, was that I *do* have somebody I love in the outside world, and I don't care what anybody [does]. You can call me anything you want, and I'll kill you. I was just so . . . angry. I was so angry at the people for not understanding, or not even wanting to listen. I didn't expect them to accept it, but I at least wanted them to hear me out. As soon as you said, 'I'm gay,' or someone else said you're gay, the door was closed. There was no discussion. That's it."

After going to court to have herself declared an emancipated minor, Gina rented a room in a boarding house. "Most of the women there were really lost. And I probably at that time was, too. Because I had no place to stay. I had lost my job. I didn't know what to do. I was living off like fifty cents a day. I was panicking. I didn't want to ask my folks for money. My mom wouldn't give it to me, and I didn't want to ask my dad—he was too broke.

"I got to be friends with one of the boarding house manager's daughters, and I admitted to her that I was gay. She didn't understand it that well, because she was only fifteen or sixteen. So she went and talked to her older sister about it, who was totally homophobic. Told everybody in the place. Well, they all ganged up on me and they were going to kick my ass from here to hell and back. The funny part was, no men were allowed to stay over, but *women* were allowed to stay over. So of course they all got pissed off at me, because my girlfriend could sleep over but their boyfriends could not!

"They would break into my room and steal my stuff. They would steal all my food. They'd let my cat out. One girl did actually try to beat the crap out of me. She came pretty close. She was throwing dishes at me, and she hit me on the head with a hairdryer. The mother had to come upstairs and break it up. That was pretty nasty. I was scared to go out of my room at night to use the bathroom.

"It takes a little bit longer [now] to trust people with certain things. I've really realized how prejudiced people are. It didn't matter if you're black or what. Like in high school, when 'the black people started coming,' quote-unquote, everybody got all pissed off because it was this little white neighborhood. Except they didn't know to be prejudiced against me, because I didn't let them know [I was gay]. But I identified more with [the African-American kids] than the other kids. I just stayed away from [the white kids]. Because they all had money and the best drugs and the best clothes. They were all very wealthy and they were more interested in materialistic things than what people were really like.

"God forbid if they found out that you were gay. Forget it. Black kids, they made sure that the black kids didn't get to sit in the front of the school bus. I mean, that's how bad these people were. One day they attacked me because I was talking to this guy who happened to be black, and they literally ripped off my shoes, threw them out the bus window, along with my books. They just didn't like anybody who didn't look perfect [or] act the way you're supposed to go in society.

"There's so many labels on everybody. You know, that one's a butch and that one's a femme. You're still a woman. It doesn't matter if you weigh two pounds or if you weigh four hundred pounds, or if you wear leather or not. Unless they're real jerks. Like I know a couple women who act like my grandfather used to. I mean, then I think that they should be labeled a butch, if they can go snort and spit. It's like they're helping stereotype themselves or something. I don't understand what they would get out of that. It's not just butch, but crude.

"I mean, they think that crude goes with it, and it doesn't. Like the one woman I'm talking about, who happens to be a bouncer, who on a one-to-one thing when we're just talking, I love her and she's great and we get along, but as soon as we're out in a crowd, all of a sudden she puts on the black leather and snorts and spits. While you're eating she does this! I'm like, 'Oh, stop it!

Just knock it off! I can't stand it.' And then she gets angry. When you say it nicely, she doesn't listen. But she doesn't do that if we're alone talking.

"It's like they have to protect themselves. They put on their little armor. My ex-lover went through a stage like that for a while. It would drive me nuts. 'I have to wear my cowboy boots just in case.' Just in case what? If there's a cockroach on the floor? We used to call them 'corner cockroach kickers,' because she had little pointy toes on them.

"A lot of women used to give me a lot of pressure, saying that I was too feminine or I should do this or not act like that. To this day, some people give me a hard time about it. Because I carry a purse. What am I going to do, carry things in my pockets and chains hanging off me with keys on it? I don't think that looks attractive on a man *or* a woman.

"My father always had tuxedos and I always used to wear his stuff when I was a kid. When I didn't fit into it, it was playing; when I started to fit into it, it wasn't play. It was serious. [Years later] when all of us quote 'dykes' were walking across the street to Pier 43 ½ for a boat party that never happened, the tourists' eyeballs were hanging out of their sockets. 'That's them, that's them!' They must have heard about it. They were all waiting for us to show up. Some women were in tuxes. A lot of them had the whole thing, you know, with boutonnieres and cummerbunds. I had cufflinks on. I had a little black teddy underneath my bright red tux shirt! Some had mink stoles with long gowns and slits up to here.

"It was a mixture of everybody. But the tourists were definitely saying, 'That's all the dykes in San Francisco. They must all be in the same spot!' There must have been three hundred of us, all walking across the street at the same time, so it was like a parade. One woman just shined a moon at them. They deserved that, though. The guy said something weird. He was yelling out his car window, something about his kids were in the car. We were like, 'So what are you on this street for? You knew we were here. What are you doing in San Francisco?'"

Jenny Chin: "A Carload of Teenagers Screaming at You"

"Society is one big closet. As far as our not being able to just be who we are, have that readily known and accepted. I mean, even if you dress a way that they think you might be [gay], people will hurl epithets at you on the street. I've been walking with a friend, and she might be dressed a certain way, and get a carload of teenagers screaming at you, 'Dyke!' It's so ridiculous! I think it's easier to be with a man. You can just go anywhere in public, and people leave you alone. [Men] are in different positions of power in society.

"The real work, I think, is bringing up men differently. Because when they're treated and pampered and served and waited on as boys, they turn out to be that kind of man. My brothers could just come home, sit down, and watch TV. And I would make dinner, because my mom worked at night. I set the table, I laid out the dinner, I called them, they would come and eat, and they would leave and go off and do their own things and watch TV. And then I would do the dishes and I would clean up. They didn't lift a hand. They still don't.

"Society is so totally polarized about men are like this, women this, and white people this, and black people this. So I wouldn't say that in my lifetime I have a great vision of how it's going to be changed. There are so many strictures of feminine behavior that you're just hemmed in more and more. You can't fold your legs like that; you can't wear this combination of clothes because it's too masculine; you can't speak up so much because it's being too brassy. I mean, just everything! My mom told me you can't be too smart. No one's going to want to marry you. You can't be too capable. You can't speak your opinions. You can't deviate off this narrow little path. I think it's a good thing that I became a feminist and a lesbian at the age I did, because I would probably be very unhappy in that role. You know, if I'd stayed straight. Very frustrated.

"When I got to be in high school, I got very close with this woman. Matter of fact, it fit more the mold of what they always said that you feel when you fall in love with somebody else. I mean, the opposite sex. You know, your knees get weak, and you blush, and you just want to be around them all the time. It got to a point where it flashed in my mind that I was having physical desires for her. When it flashed in my mind that I might be gay, I just totally dismissed it. Because I said a gay woman is this dyke, and she's got chains on her ankle, and she weighs three hundred pounds, and she's got this scowl on her face, and she's just an angry whatever. That's just all I knew of what lesbians were. And because I wasn't that, I said, 'Oh, well, I guess I don't have to worry about that.'

"When I was nineteen, I was unburdened as far as I was still allowed to kind of be a kid. There was a certain freedom there. If I had grew up in a real poor, different class, and I got pregnant when I was thirteen and had this kid and I had to drop out of school, and we didn't have any money, it'd be very different. Even the whole fact of me being a single Chinese woman in America. You know, in my grandmother's time, she couldn't just go hitchhike with a backpack on her back and go up to live in the woods. It's unheard of. But because of these times, and the age in which I live, and that I was middle-class, I just decided that I wanted to go [be with] all these women [who were part of a women's land collective] in the woods in the Northwest.

"I had friends, black friends, who are afraid in the Northwest. Because the

Ku Klux Klan and all that kind of very intense racism is still alive in backwoods counties. [They were] really afraid to get out of the van because somebody would see them, think they're black, think they're trying to steal their horse, or break in their house. And take out their shotgun. In other words, what I'm trying to tell you is, to a certain extent being Asian is like [being] an 'okay' minority. Nonthreatening.

"But in the Northwest there are no people of color. That, after a while, created many grave problems as far as my living in the Northwest. And then living in that [white women's] community. In my family you weren't really supposed to trust white people. They were somebody that . . . well, they were just different. With women friends, they're just thinking they're girlfriends, so it doesn't really matter. When it got to be high school dating and stuff, my parents—especially my mother—were very much concerned that I date Chinese boys.

"See, one thing about the people that I hung out with [growing up]: we were all not real established middle-middle class. We were all lower-middle class. Our families had just struggled to get a place where they had a house in a nice neighborhood. We didn't have all the [middle-class] trappings and all the attitudes. Because they were still kind of struggling, and we were their offspring. So this friend of mine came from an Armenian family that was very close. And when she dated a boy, one of our close friends, who was Jewish—who also came from a *very* Jewish family that was *very* close—it was a scandal. Because she wasn't Jewish; he wasn't Armenian. And that's how it was. It would be the same if I was really, really close to somebody who wasn't Chinese. It would be very upsetting.

"In the Northwest it was very easy to be a separatist, because a lot of these people had no strong communities, as far as an ethnic cultural community. So when I came down to San Francisco, I really saw how much all these things cross, like Third World people's movements, and the poor, or single mothers. That we have a common oppressor, or a common whatever you want to call it. I mean, you can't just say, 'Well, the La Raza movement, I don't identify with that at all because you're straight.' Of course I identify with that, because they're not white. And they've been screwed over in this quote-unquote 'equal' society because they're not white. It's not like I say, 'Well, I'm not going to back you, because you aren't a radical lesbian feminist.' I mean, these people are still trying to get eight-hour work days.

"Eventually, after all these years, for me it's a lot easier to relate to just my close friends, a lot of whom are Asian. Because we have the same background. The whole Asian-American community, we're such a minority in the larger white society, that just the fact that you're a lesbian and you're Asian is enough [to make you] somebody that's like us.

"Sometimes I've tried to figure [butch/femme] out, but I don't think that I'm more one than the other. And matter of fact, you know, I think it's good to strive for that. [My friends] don't think I'm either, either. When I first came out [in the 1970s], everybody was more into being butchy. But I was always sort of a femme butch. I was always sort of . . . not real. I just played at it. One time, in a bar, this [white] woman starts talking something about a kimono. To the extent to which I am butch, it's probably wanting to rebel against that whole feminization of Asian women. Which totally denies our strength."

Deborah Gauss: "They Would Have to Publicly Denounce Me"

"I see myself as a professional woman. I'm forty-six years old; I'm not nineteen. There's something about a person who comes out at sixteen and just tells their family. That's another thing [from] someone who gropes as I have and then deals with a professional career where you could lose your job. How do you deal with the fact that you don't feel akin to the dykes on bikes? I just don't look at them as professionals. It's like a world that I don't . . . well, anybody who's into the bike culture, I don't identify with. I don't have any friends who are leather people, who are s/m people. Maybe some of my friends are and they don't tell me, but I doubt that.

"For a person my age, it's a little more difficult. For someone who's been born into the world before there was all these gays and straights. Well, I wasn't born into that world, and neither was my family. And they aren't reborn yet around that, either! They really punish people who step out and question the way they've put their lives together. My race, being German, comes into it a bit in terms of that kind of embarrassment of not being like you're supposed to be. My parents are second generation, so they're real close to that. And I was around my grandparents, who made me do things right. You don't embarrass people. You don't embarrass your family.

"In Catholic school, you do have a way out: you can become a nun. Which I did. In the novitiate, I was so naive. I didn't even check out, well, what is the process? It was a three-and-a-half-year program, the first six months of which was totally cloistered, mostly in silence. Mostly study, prayer, meditation. They give you a lot of time. All you deal with is other people from the order and your superiors. You're watched, and all your mail is read, and everything is totally monitored. And you do have, after the three and a half years, a very intense identification. There's this kind of community feeling, and you don't special- ize it.

"When I was in the novitiate, if they saw you together with a person a number of times, you were called in, and you were both told to avoid that person and not to develop a special relationship. It used to be called 'particular friendship.' It was very structured, and I was very young, and I followed *everything*. It was going to lead me down the path of mysticism. Some of it did, and most of it didn't. Most of it was pretty rigid. And pretty empty. I'm just [now] in the throes of dissolving that relationship [to the religious community].

"Because of my adolescence, dealing with sexuality is a little disgusting. Because it's so hard not to sin. It's hard to think of myself as a lesbian. It's been very painful, actually, to have it come out. I can understand why one would not let themself get behind that title. There's *no* affirmation in my family, in my background, or the community I'm in. [At my last job] they had a specific instance that they saw, that they knew that I was lesbian. It got reported to my superior. It was a real horrible kind of a thing to deal with. To be a nun, to have this ultraconservative superior telling you, you could either get some other sisters to move in, move away from my lover, or quit my job. It was very humiliating to have this asshole giving you these three choices. I had prepared my whole life for this career in ministry, and I couldn't do it.

"I think of myself as being very closeted. Especially with my new job. When people find out that you're lesbian, because it's a subculture and it's a weak place, people like a priest on our staff would find that a really powerful piece of information that could put me on the line in terms of my job. If it were made public, they would have to publicly denounce me. So the closet gives me an ability not to give him that power.

"If I were independently wealthy and invulnerable financially, I think I would feel a lot freer. If I wasn't doing this job. If you're the first person out, you're the martyr. People that are the first people out are the prophets whose heads will roll. I'm afraid that this now-known fact that you can lose your job, change your career, has shaken me up. You'd rather not have who you are create such a tidal wave.

"My mother's had a few breakdowns, and my family has this attitude that her breakdowns are because I'm living with a lesbian. So, that's a lot to carry. Before she has a breakdown, she starts focusing on the fact that I'm living with a lesbian. *I'm* a lesbian, but she announces to the family that I'm *living* with a lesbian. And I like feminine women! More than the masculine type. Leather, all that stuff, motorcycles, it just grates. It makes me walk away.

"I've seen people that are more femme than I am, so I wouldn't say that I'm a one [on a one to ten scale]. Hardly quite the two, either. I'm in between two and three. I just ran a thing on class: I always think of [butches] as lower-class. Not that I would mind being in a relationship with a person of another class, up or down, but I do find myself mostly in relation to middle-class or upper-middle-class [women]. I don't see the butch type looking for antiques for their house, or reading feminist spirituality, or drinking nice, good wine."

Cheryl Arthur: "I Wanted to Say, 'This Is Who I Am, You Fuckers'"

"This is silly, but I used to hate Paris. Because I thought Paris was real feminine, and I didn't want to have anything to do with it! Part of it has to do with sexism. Who wanted to be a girl, and have to do these boring things all the time? Playing dolls, and not being able to wear pants and climb trees and ride bikes and get in fights and play ball.

"When I'm in a relationship with someone, it goes back and forth, and I don't feel like there I play a role. I have certain preferences, let's say. You know, I like to fix things, or something like that. But that's just a preference of something I like to do. Except for . . . I can see the things that I've read about people who were into butch/femme roles in the 1940s and 1950s, or even the 1930s, when it was much more an affirmation of who you were. You know: 'I'm a lesbian and I'm going to dress this way so that it's clear to you that I'm a lesbian.'

"Because I felt like that when I was teaching in the Midwest and this moral majority kind of group came in and was putting up these antigay slogans all over the campus. I felt like going home, getting dressed up in the absolute butchiest outfit I could find, and coming back and walking through that campus. Not because of any stereotyped ideas about who I thought I was, but because I wanted to say, 'This is who I am, you fuckers. And I'm going to be who I am no matter what you say.'"

Sarah Voss: "A Slap in the Face of Heterosexuality"

"I went to the bar in the pictures I showed you, I went to Gianni's, and I waited there for two weeks for someone who was not my college friend—you know, little dorm buddy—to pick me up to fuck. And for two weeks no one paid any attention to me because I had long hair and love beads and fringe and I was a pacifist, and they were all butch/femme. At the end of two weeks someone picked me up. She was an older woman; she was probably twenty-five! She took me uptown in New York to her apartment, and she put out a plate of milk and cookies and locked herself in the bedroom and said, 'You're too young to get in the life.' And I was so furious I almost broke the door down. I was just really irate, because I was already in the life. I'd been in the life since I was three!

"So I went back to the bar and finally one day someone picked me up, but she did it literally. The biggest, meanest, ooogliest, scariest butch there picked me up so that my little toes were dangling above the floor and she said, 'Are you butch or femme?' I had been saying, 'Neither, I mean, that's irrelevant, I mean, I'm a . . . I'm a feminist, I'm a pacifist, I'm a free spirit. Ah, I don't ask what gender you are!' And this time, with me up in the air, and me knowing that if I answered 'femme' I would be married to this . . . this . . . this garbage truck on wheels for the rest of my life, I went, 'Aaargh!' and she put me down. I thought about it and thought, 'Yeah, that's probably accurate. From tomboy to butch, sure.'"

Not long after that encounter in the late 1960s Sarah Voss and her girl-friend, Shawn, found themselves "hanging around these kinds of liberal straight couples our age, and they more and more pushed us into a butch/femme role. That was the easiest way they could deal with us and acknowledge our relationship, but put it in terms that they could understand. Shawn would get grabbed by the women and dragged off to the kitchen, a room in which she had never spent any time in her life, and I would be grabbed by the men and hauled off into what I considered a very enjoyable discussion of the inner workings of the internal combustion engine. So I was happier in it, because it more suited my tastes, but we were both real unhappy because we didn't want that to happen to us, to our relationship.

"The bar we were hanging out in was an old-fashioned butch/femme bar. That's all there fucking was." Women at the bar could not understand how Sarah, a pacifist opposed to the Vietnam War, could be "a butch who wouldn't fight for my woman. And Shawn wouldn't let me fight for her; she could fight for herself. Until she decked a woman, we really were despised."

After that incident, "they tried to make me into the femme. The butches talked to the butches and the femmes talked to the femmes, first of all, because any violation of that was regarded as a flirtation and trouble. And also, it was what most people preferred. So a whole bunch of people who had been talking to me didn't talk to me any more. They tried talking to Shawn, but Shawn didn't like them. And a whole bunch of femmes who had trusted her suddenly put her on the other side, you know, as a batterer, as a person who hits. So she could no longer be confided in. You know, the way women don't talk to men.

"They really couldn't understand what we were doing because we dressed alike and we looked alike. I got tired of people hitting on her. It was like our status as a couple wasn't being recognized. So I thought, there's an easy, old-fashioned gay way to handle this. I made us wedding rings. My nonfeminist wife hit the roof. 'I'm not going to wear that badge of slavery and servility!' she said. 'It would keep both of us from getting beaten up at the bar,' I said. We wore them.

"We were both unhappy about it. But it made life in the bar distinctively easier because committed couples were honored. So the issue of which of us was butch and which was femme wouldn't come up, because it was only relevant to us. It made our lives easier, but it ruined our relationship. It really fucked us up. Everyone was pushing us into this butch/femme couple, and we ended up there. We ended up there. I'd come home and drink a six-pack of beer and go to sleep. That was life."

Eventually Sarah discovered the Duchess, which tended to attract a working-class clientele although it was not a "roles" bar. At the Duchess she remembered women who were "all about forty years old and really, really at the most miserable stage of their gay lives. You're losing your looks, you're old enough to realize that you're not going to be a success in the material world. For obvious queers even in New York there were not a lot of jobs. It meant you were never going to be an editor at Harper and Row. You might have your own hair salon, but if being an editor at Harper and Row is what you wanted. . . . Those kinds of dykes never showed up in the bars, that kind of uptown dyke. They met in each other's living rooms. They would *never* have been seen in a bar because it was a kind of exposure. Plus, they'd have to talk to a lot of scum in bars like us.

"There was the class aspect [to butch/femme]. It was a very lower-class thing. It was associated with working-class bars. It was associated with replicating working-class familial violence." The biggest change in butch/femme as practiced in later years, Sarah felt, is that "it's crossed class lines in a more permanent way. In the general movement to empower everybody, say to everybody, even a faggot in a gold lamé dress, 'You have the right to exist.'

"I don't think that 1950s butches really believed they had the right to exist except as maimed men. If you read the literature of the time, that comes in very, very clearly. And don't ever say it's just a book, because where American cultural identities come from is often the media. There were no Hell's Angels, there were no bikers, in the modern sense, until a movie. There were no butch/femme couples, *exactly*, until *The Well of Loneliness*. If you read that book, and it doesn't matter whether you're in Houston or San Francisco or Oshkosh, that is how you learned to be gay. Because even in San Francisco chances are that you're not going to know where the gay people are who are not like that."

The renditions of "femme" and "butch" developed in the 1980s may have appealed to middle-class women, but they still featured working-class styles, "in the same way that the young of America tend to take working-class styles for the period of their youth. Because that's where the juice is. Bruce Springsteen is exciting. Frank Sinatra is boring. Except that Frank Sinatra, when my father was young, was working-class and terrifying. He was a razor's edge of working-class sexuality. We're not allowed to say that 'Negroes have more fun' any more, but we're still allowed to say that the working class are sexier than the rest of us, right?"

In contrast to the working-class symbolism associated with butch/femme, Sarah believed that professional organizations such as Bay Area Career Women (BACW) promoted the "lipstick lesbian" because "that's the one that is going to win us civil rights, or at least that's the conservative thinking. That is the most comfortable one: a yuppie who's appropriately garbed in the garments of the appropriate gender. The BACW would like to see every lesbian who rides a motorcycle disappear off the face of the earth.

"And yet the professional woman is, you know, Mr. and Mrs. America's terror butch. This is the classic butch image. It's from the 1920s and 1930s and the 1940s: the corporate butch. She's an heiress in the early decades. In the later decades she's got a mentor in General Motors or something. But she's that businesswoman and she fires men and she takes their wives. Tsk, tsk, tsk, she's so bad. So she's still *out* there. You see her on the soaps all the time. I think, 'Where were you when I was young? I kept looking for you!'

"[In the Jewish community] queer is so bad that butch doesn't make any difference at all. My father thinks you can either be gay or Jewish; you can't be both. You know any Jew born after, say, 1945 is supposed to repopulate the world with Jews because of all the ones that had been killed. It's not just the black community, it's not just black women who get told they're committing genocide by not having black babies and being lesbians. Jews also get told that, and so, probably, for all I know, the Puerto Ricans and every other ethnicity on earth.

"Most of America doesn't think there are working-class Jews. Jews are all rich, Jews are all educated, da-da-da. So to find somebody [like me] who's a middle-class Jew wearing black leather riding a motorcycle is a terrible shock, both to other Jews and to the other people on motorcycles!"

Given her initially negative impression of what it meant to be butch, I asked Sarah how she came to adopt that term for herself. "It's a hindsight call, I think. It's realizing that every man you've ever picked up has been extremely femme, and about half of them came out later. And it's realizing that other people consider you butch. And saying in perfect innocence at seventeen, 'Well, yeah, I was my dad's son until something terrible happened when I turned thirteen. I could ride, I could shoot, I could fix motor vehicles. I'm responsible. I take care of women.'

"I don't think anybody has ever seen me as femme, including my family. Even when I had long hair. I grew my hair out a couple of years ago, and you know, it didn't fool anybody then and it didn't fool anybody now. And now men have long hair, so it just means you're becoming a rocker. I haven't owned a dress in twenty years. I used to own a black dress for my father's funeral and then one day I realized, 'He'll be dead. What can he say to me?'"

Sarah considered butch "something you are. And I think some people aren't. I mean, I think for some people that this is not an issue and it's not an identity. When butch, unacknowledged butch, was the politically correct uniform in Iowa City, from say 1970 or 1972 through about 1978, I did see people who were organic, natural femmes squeezing themselves into that uniform, because without it you weren't acknowledged. You weren't listened to. Iowa City, Iowa, then was the most politically correct boil on the ass of America I've ever seen. It made Berkeley and all the Berkeley dyke jokes look like mild salsa.

"Everyone who was heavy, both large and heavy in terms of being important in that community, was butch even if they didn't admit it, even if they were sort of a lipstick butch, but they were butch. The one time a femme tried to do a little 'power in the community' trip, we were building a women's restaurant, and this femme comes bouncing up. She's got long hair and she's real bouncy and she's wearing a skirt. We were doing heavy construction. We go, 'Well, hi!' She's got this butch with her. And so we try and assign her to painting and assign her butch to working with me building a wheelchair ramp. And they switch on us! We go, 'Uh-oh, why are you switching?' And they go, 'Well, because the femme is an engineer.' And we went, 'Oh, we are such good feminists!'"

Did Sarah still think of herself as a feminist? "Yes and no. Yes, because when people say no, they're not a feminist, they're giving in to that whole right-wing backlash, and I'm real tired of the little girl saying, 'I'm not a feminist but I believe in *everything* that the feminist menu presents.' On the other hand, in my own life, every feminist I've ever known who was straight, and quite many of the gay ones, their primary function in life has been to fuck up other women. To say, 'You can't do this,' and, 'Don't hurt our revolution.' Just insane. The feminist movement has a fascist streak.

"So when I'm with my closest friends and we say 'feminist,' we mean the kind of woman who tells you you're 'male-identified' and then wants you to teach her the skills that you learned rather painfully from men, so that she can be high status. Blue-collar jobs are very high-status, still, in the lesbian community, although they're growing less so, and it's about time. But it used to be that if you were a carpenter or a plumber or a pressman, you were just hot shit, because it was penultimate butch. And you know, you can't buy it. You can't pick it up off the ground. Your mom can't make you one. It's like buying a Harley doesn't make you a biker. Riding a bike makes you a biker.

"Straight women love a nice, safe butch, especially if they're coming out of a bad relationship with a man. They *adore* butches. Because we will do all the good stuff that men do. We will fix their tires, da-da-da. Plus, they get all the woman stuff. We will listen to them bitch. Plus, we won't rape them. (This is the one thing that butches have never been accused of.)

"We all participated in that nonsense [in the 1970s]. They always wanted a big, bad butch to take care of them. First they'd tell you to take out the garbage and talk to the landlord, and then when you got back they'd say, 'And by the way, you're into roles and roles are bad.' You'd go, 'Then why am I taking out the garbage?'

"A lot of us go through this thing of, 'Am I a man?' Like Gertrude Stein, who would get up every morning and say, 'Thank god I'm not a woman.' I think by that she meant, 'Thank god I'm not some straight, dizzy broad.' It certainly would be easier to be heterosexual. All the things that are objectionable about me for most people would be positive if I were a man, even exactly the same sort of man that I am woman: kind of short, kind of wimpy. It would be okay to have attitude, it would be okay to have a motorcycle, it would be okay to have a butch job, it would be okay to have a girlfriend. But I don't want to be heterosexual.

"I don't think that butches are transsexuals. I don't even think that butches are transvestites. Some are both and either, but I think there is this other thing that is butch. You're presenting as a man to the most naive heterosexual from Indiana, maybe, but in the city where you probably live, you're presenting as butch. You're a slap in the face of heterosexuality. You're putting yourself in a position where you may at any time be killed by the nearest man, and his woman would probably applaud, if she doesn't go home with you.

"I had a lover who didn't allow it [being butch]. I tried very hard, for her, not to be anything, but I was. Why do they do this? They fall in love with you because of who you are, and then they want to change all of it. Nothing makes me feel more in a traditional butch/femme thing, than to get in this kind of marriage where the wife is saying, 'Well, ah, I wish you'd sell the motorcycle. I wish you'd grow your hair out.' Then she'd talk in a high voice: 'Wish you'd get a [different] job.' You know, why did you marry me?

"I think the femmes [today] are much more empowered and the butches are much more willing to experiment." At a certain point Sarah began going out with women she perceived as butch. Although she described most of her ex-lovers as femmes, she also said she had decided not to get involved with some women because she had perceived them as "too femme. Femme in the old-fashioned, to me pejorative, sense of that they wanted to be a kind of dependent person that I don't want to be around. It's the kind of femme that my mother would have considered herself, where she, partly as a joke, would say stuff like, 'Women made a big mistake getting the vote because they had more power, real power, when they influenced men's votes. Now they can't do it because the man can turn and say, "Well, if you feel that way, why don't you vote?"'

"It's a kind of old-fashioned femme behavior which I don't think represents the Joan Nestle school of new, powerful, empowered femmes. A lot of the stuff Joan Nestle talks about is stuff that I had thought was the province of butch, and I'm glad it no longer has to be. Things like taking responsibility for yourself in bed, saying, 'Hey, I'm here to have fun, and I'm gonna tell you what I like.' Because part of the old-fashioned femme thing was to be a tease, to make the butch do all the work. Roles interlock. Nobody is a villain, I think, in a dyad.

"There is an old kind of manipulative femme, and an old kind of Archie Bunkerish butch. Those roles do exist, and I spent some time in those roles. [That kind of femme] wanted to do an 'Ozzie and Harriet.' They wanted to turn me into the old-fashioned butch who doesn't take off her clothes and doesn't have emotions. Even my father doesn't have to live up to that, so why should I?"

Power, Power: Double Takes

It doesn't take long to turn up a story of job discrimination or violence directed at someone because she's gay. Meaning Afro-Caribbean femme. Or Laguna Pueblo chameleon. Or backwoods baby dyke. Or unemployed Chicana professional, lately of the working class. Or white girl in borrowed leathers. Or South Asian Indian waiting to get off work to go to the club. Or middle-class Jewish butch on a bike. Or whatever particular rendition of lesbian happens to elicit uncontrolled anger and fear.

Memories of covert injustice bring forth another kind of story. When gay women make jokes about the lesbian thought police, or make fun of white folks who never suspect they're queer, they're trying to get at less formal modes of power that go hand-in-hand with institutionalized discrimination.

What does it mean to speak gender to power? To wield a cultural politics of gendered resistance? To look to gender for shelter from the worst of all that's antigay? First, you have to understand what's at stake. For starters: the integrity of your body (no beatings, no rape), a chance at employment, ability to travel, the freedom to pursue relationships and to hold onto life itself.

Popular wisdom says that it can be dangerous for a lesbian to wear gender on her sleeve. Or at least, the kind of gendering that's susceptible to interpretation as butch. After losing the job she had trained for all her life, Deborah

Gauss was determined to stay in the closet. "The closet" can mean different things to different people. To Deborah it meant presenting herself as a reasonably feminine professional who associated primarily with others "of her kind." What could butchy women know, she wondered, about the "finer" things in life: antiques, good wine, or her own passion, feminist spirituality? (Obviously Deborah hadn't met Sarah Voss.) Working as a nun in a church that condemned homosexuality only heightened Deborah's sense of urgency about leaving any tomboy ways behind.

The idea that "femininity" will protect you works best for lesbians such as Deborah who are white and middle-class. But no version of femininity is guaranteed to transform every onlooker into a chivalrous knight. Reality check: even buff-skinned women open themselves up to (hetero)sexual harassment when they try to avoid antigay harassment by going femme. Femmes of color have to deal in addition with the racist legacy that casts them as prostitutes or loose women. This, in a society where working the streets renders a woman a legitimate victim for any predatory impulse ("Who cares, they're only whores"). Not much protection there. Conscious of the stereotype, some lesbians of color take great care in choosing the length of a skirt, the cut of a blouse, to downplay beauty or sexual attractiveness. So much for the freedom and unalloyed privilege in traveling femme. Or they refuse to change for the stereotype and have to field whatever obnoxious behavior comes their way.

"Femininity" in any key can make a lesbian's competence as invisible as her sexual identity. Good to look at, so how can she be any good at her job? That doesn't mean women have it any easier traveling butch. Jenny Chin knew that the threat of street violence escalated when she walked down the street with a friend who "dressed a certain way." But was the violence aimed solely at the masculine edge to her friend's apparel? Would people have taken Jenny for butch in the same outfit that marked her white friend as a stud? That depends upon the viewer. An Asian/Pacific-American lesbian might gender her very differently than a white lesbian or a straight Chinese-American would.

Many women believed that the butch posture so often targeted for violence offered the best possible—sometimes the only possible—response to persecution. Like Lourdes Alcantara, they whipped out their toughest stance when someone gender-typed them. "Hey, *marimacha!*" You want it? You got it. You fear it? You face it.

In-your-face moves were not limited to the street. Cheryl Arthur, a nonbeliever in butch/femme if ever there was one, ended up tearing apart her closet one day in a search for "the absolute butchiest outfit I could find." What got into Cheryl? She needed a quick response to the antigay organizing drive on her college campus, and butch seemed to promise the greatest visibility. But what did she settle on? Not the chinos and blazer she considered everyday wear for teaching her classes—an ensemble many queers would have characterized as already (middle-class) butch—but the tie, vest, boots, and slicked-back hair that evoked the classic working-class butch of the 1950s. There went Cheryl, speaking stereotype to power.

Even Jenny took refuge in butch on occasion, although she understood clearly that fighting antigay attitudes entailed facing down racism. Bad enough that a white woman should come on to her by mumbling about a kimono. Couldn't the girl at least get the difference between Chinese and Japanese right? Jenny remembered her parents' advice not to trust white people, never to date non-Chinese. At such moments she felt inclined to go butch "to rebel against that whole feminization of Asian women." No way that butch could ever be a purely gendered rebellion.

Gina Pellegrini didn't separate racist from antigay attitudes, either. Her stories moved from one scene of violence to another: fighting words hurled at pedestrians by her employer; an attack by other white kids for talking to an African-American student on the school bus; an assault by women in her boarding house who resented Gina for being gay. Institutionalized power lurks in the margins of these stories. The bus driver doesn't intervene. The school administration doesn't care. Gina gains a rare advantage over peers due to heterosexist assumptions built into the boarding house rules ("No boys allowed"). There's class conflict in the stories, too. The students at Gina's school hate "anybody who didn't look perfect" (that is, white and middle-class like them). The young women in the boarding house are down and out before they've had a chance to grow up, filled with rage that gets channeled Gina's way.

What would regendering butch have done for Gina in any of these situations? It might have made her a little more intimidating to her attackers, but probably no better able to defend herself, and certainly no more determined to make her own way. She would have been no less the fighter or the race traitor or the queer. As it was, she filled her handbag with makeup and her head with visions of a world where race and class would matter about as much as a pair of corner cockroach kickin' boots.

So femme is not always about hiding, just as butch is not always about physically overpowering the opposition. You go "guy" as a mild-mannered office worker and you're likely to get filleted on the street. You go out into the street as a working-class white check-out-my-muscles stud, and you'll be no match for working-class African-American verbal repartee. If you mistake any of these modes for the whole of butch, you'll be completely unprepared for the ways that Latina *indigenismo* and Native American traditionalism can infuse spiritual power into the physicality often associated with stud.

The circular association of butches with violence, butches with "the" working class, and the working class with violence has historical roots in the oppressive conditions lesbians encountered in the 1950s. According to the research of Elizabeth Kennedy and Madeline Davis, street butches of that period did a great deal to counter anti-gay violence and build lesbian community. Sarah Voss's account of how her lover Shawn became known as "a person who hits" after a fight in a "roles bar" of their youth complicates this picture in some interesting ways.

Sarah's story gives the lie to the cliché that butches are by nature more aggressive. Nothing natural about it. To uphold the link alleged between studs and violence, the rest of the women in the bar transferred Shawn from femme to butch. Yet they did not reclassify her because femmes don't fight. If Shawn had "fought like a girl," she might have remained peacefully on the femme side of the bar. In gendered terms there's a world of difference between slapping a cheek, or pulling out hair, and decking someone with your fists.

A few decades later, or in another neighborhood, Shawn could have slugged away without anyone necessarily casting aspersions on her reputed femininity. She'd simply be a femme who surprised everyone by packing a mean punch. Just as there are plenty of working-class butches who would rather go out dancing or read a book than get into a physical altercation. What it takes to kick a person over into another gendered category can differ with race, class, religion, and time.

In the end there's no simple relationship between visibility, self-defense, and butch or femme. A femme who comes out as a way to reject heterosexual advances may confront an anger more explosive than if she had presented as butch all along. When women like Deborah did try to pass, they created a very fragile zone of safety. Deborah saw the femininity demanded by "the closet" as a way of seizing power rather than being seized by it. As a lesbian nun going up against her religious community, she had good reason to fear sanction. But even with the best cover middle-class money could buy, she had already been forced to resign once.

It's not always obvious how to wield gender to power because each particular rendition of gender lends itself to more than one reading. Sarah knew that long hair could make her a rocker rather than a femme. Carrying a purse did nothing to dispel the judgments leveled at Gina. "Just because I was gay they thought I was stupid." Stupid dyke overlapped with dumb broad, idiot spic, half-witted worker: all versions of the kind of elitism that casts people on the bottom—any bottom—as utterly lacking in intelligence. Jenny noticed that walking with a man tended to curb the insults routinely hurled at her on the street. Without any change whatsoever in the way she gendered herself, having a man on her arm encouraged people to read her as heterosexual.

Some women believed that gendering makes for a more effective politics if you deliberately mix it up. When styles of gendering seem "natural," they allow people to assume that you have always been and forever will be one way. A politics of gender-fuck tries to shake that assumption by combining things that don't ordinarily go together. In Gina's description of the boat party that never happened, hundreds of gay women stream down to the docks dressed up for a night on the town. So far, so predictable: many of the women arrive looking every bit as butch as the diesel dykes that tourists came prepared to see. Not to be left out, Gina has her cufflinks, too. But peeking through her tux shirt is a black teddy, disrupting her otherwise studly attire. That's gender-fuck. Women are not naturally feminine, dykes are not naturally butch. Tourists, take note.

And these tourists need to take note. When a man in a car challenges the women's right to be there, the partygoers respond, "What are you doing in San Francisco?" If there's a spectacle here, you tourists are it. The object is to turn the gaze back on the gazer, with gender or whatever comes to hand.

Sarah understood that the politics of gender-fuck could not be confined to gender. Guess what else isn't supposed to go together? How about a middle-class Jew in black leather on a motorcycle? It's not every day you see a Jewish girl with a steady income adopt the signifiers associated with white gentile working-class boys. Just by turning into a parking lot, she made people stop and think.

Still, there are limits to what gendering can do when it comes to power. Gina's confrontational approach to handling sexuality and gender got her kicked out of her home, sent to social services for "rehabilitation," and remanded to an abusive drug program because cuts in government funding had eliminated more appropriate placements. The language Gina used to describe these experiences—having a lover on the "outside"—says "prison" all the way. What happened to Gina is not so different from the fate of teenagers today who are assigned to psychiatric facilities against their will to be "cured" of homosexuality.

Gendered rebellions can be short-circuited by class and race relations, or by a legal system that limits rights for people of a certain age. As an adult Gina finally gained the power to live wherever she wanted. But she still couldn't always dress the way she wanted, or take issue with her boss's racist and anti-gay comments, for fear of losing her job. Class is about resources, not just the symbolism of driving a BMW or a bike. Even Deborah, with financial assets beyond Gina's wildest dreams, thought that she would feel less guarded about gender and sexuality if she were independently wealthy. Jenny believed that changing times and middle-class resources had given her "a certain freedom . . . to kind of be a kid" well into her twenties. Would her immigrant grandmother have hitchhiked up the coast in jeans without a thought of looking for a "real" job? Maybe color had something to do with it, too. Most of her African-American friends wouldn't have tried for fear of being raped, beaten, or shot.

Even with the most creative attempts to regender themselves, people cannot always extricate themselves from stereotypes. Jenny could spend a lifetime attempting to refute the cultural illogic that leaves her, as an Asian-American woman, always and already feminized. But how seriously would people take her attempts to fight back by transforming herself into a stud? Many women — especially white lesbians — will find subtle ways to dismiss her middle-class Chinese-American rendition of butch. She will have to fend off the laughter that implies she doesn't quite make it as a stud, and the indulgent smiles that cast her as an eternally baby dyke. Switch, and the stereotypes switch with you.

Now imagine an African-American lesbian who embraces butch, stereotype or no, because it seems to offer some protection. The effort it takes her to slip into stud may differ, depending upon whether her skin is chocolate or yellow or light brown. Because of the race-typing of gender (or the gender-typing of race, depending upon how you look at it), she will probably find it easier than Jenny to command respect. But a butch presentation may also give her more than she bargained for. Maybe she won't have to fend off unwanted arms around her shoulders, but she will have to deal with the hurt created when people keep their distance. In more than one mind's eye, she will appear too close for comfort to the stereotype of the menacing African-American man. The fear that dogs her steps is a product of white racism that has become so culturally pervasive it can influence people across the board. What will it take to make common cause with people who read her "right"? And how will she deal with the people who get her "wrong"?

Gendering is complicated in its effects, and not only because the "same" moves that set some white people to giggling at a butched out Asian-American body find them cowering in a corner of the room when the body is African-American. It's also complicated because class opens up options for regendering to some women that are closed to others. It's complicated because many women don't feel capable of regendering at the drop of a hat. It's complicated because power is never just about style, and gendered performances are never strictly under individual control. Class/race/gender relations go beyond individuals.

The same gendered look that Cheryl proudly assembled to throw in the face of the right-wing group on campus might have felt coerced in another context. What if she had been picked up by the same "garbage truck on wheels" who challenged Sarah to declare her gender (femme or butch) in the 1960s? What if Cheryl had said "no way" to Madame Truck and tried to evade these community policing maneuvers by going androgynous? Like Sarah and her girlfriend, Cheryl would have ended up isolated in the bar culture of the time. Yet if she had gone for femme, within a few years she would have run headlong into the shunning of femmes ushered in by lesbian-feminism. For her part, Sarah believed that peer pressure to conform to a very simplistic model of a femme/stud couple had wrecked her relationship with Shawn. Yet butch/femme had also given her terms to help explain her personal history of gendering and attractions. Two different contexts: disempowerment in one, empowerment in another.

Jenny too had discovered that the shifting relationship of gender to power had to be negotiated inside as well as outside lesbian communities. Her standing as a member of a so-called model minority did not protect her on "women's land." (Never mind that the model minority myth, which asserts that Asians have "made it" in the United States, ignores the many Asian Americans still perilously close to the bottom of the heap.) Regendering wasn't much help in a situation where Jenny was the only lesbian of color and African-American friends wouldn't visit for fear of their lives.

Although the Pacific Northwest was never as thoroughly white as Jenny portrayed it, her comments underline the importance of paying attention to racial specificity. The "respectable" whites who posed the real danger to Jenny and her friends were more likely to cast African Americans than Asian Americans as criminals who deserved to find themselves at the other end of a gun. But that did not make Jenny immune to the anti-Asian sentiment that had been so formative in shaping racism on the West Coast.

From Gold Rush land grabs to immigration restrictions to the internment of Japanese Americans during World War II to waitresses who never show up at your table, Asian Americans have confronted racism aplenty. Use that background to interpret Jenny's wish to share "women's land" with women who shared more than a lesbian identity. Jenny had grown tired of cultural exchanges in which she stood in for all women of color, and the cultural currency most often exchanged was white. Under the circumstances, it would have been remarkable if this rural separatist retreat had afforded Jenny the same comforts as it did her white "sisters."

If power systematically works its way through institutions such as communes and courts and synagogues, if the shape of power changes as the times change, if power infiltrates the tiniest crevices of everyday life, then it can't ever be contained in bodies or controlled through performance. Likewise with differences. They may involve gender, but they aren't exclusively about gender. They may draw upon every fantasy and stereotype in the book, but they aren't played out exclusively in people's heads.

When push came to shove, Sarah located gender in the doing, not just the dreaming. "Buying a Harley doesn't make you a biker," she declared. "Riding a bike makes you a biker." You can pick up that construction worker look, but that won't necessarily get you a "nontraditional" job. You can style yourself like a church lady, but that won't necessarily make you any middle-class African-American friends. Depends upon where you start, how you identify, and how you back it up. Depends upon a society that tends to locate class in the occupation and race in the genes. A delicate negotiation at best.

In wielding gender to power, there are many times—most times?—when stance is not enough. If there are no jobs this week for a femmed out Chicana/South Asian Indian girl, you may be out of luck. You can't afford to ignore a little thing like racism, or rapid-response capitalism, or the way employers hire only certain "kinds" of people for certain tasks. As you make those moves for change, you have to do more than walk it like you talk it. You have to take the world around you into account.

Tell that to Gina's old girlfriend: the one who refused to head out the door without her cowboy boots. Attired in footwear that radiated "tough," she cut quite a figure for her peers. More important, she expected to keep hostile members of the straight public at a respectful distance. Gina found the entire ritual silly. Why? Because Gina, who had survived more than her share of violence on and off the street, knew something her ex-lover didn't. Power doesn't always come through profiling.

Chapter 9   Who's Got the Power?

Does the woman in trousers always wear the pants in the family? What if neither or both of the women in a couple wear them? In the mating and dating game, is there any fixed relationship between gender and power?

When people say they don't want to hear about butch/femme, their reasons often have something to do with the impression that femmes get a raw deal from butches who call the shots. The classic (lesbian-feminist) critique of butch/femme focuses on the way that couples negotiate power. Like most critiques, this one makes some major assumptions: Gendered differences, by definition, upset the balance of power in a relationship. Butches dominate femmes in practically all the ways that count. If a femme says that she likes going under to a butch, her statement only serves to confirm what the critics suspected all along. Talk about false consciousness! How deluded can the girl be?

The concerns that ignited this critique—from lesbian battering to the mindless tyrannies of habit—are serious. Try as they might, queers have not managed to rid themselves of the capacity to inflict damage in the guise of romance and affection. Like heterosexuals, they sometimes hurt the ones they love. It's hard to resist the temptation to appeal to gender occasionally in order to latch onto a prerogative or lord it over a partner. But the critique of butch/femme tends to reduce its characters to stereotype in order to sustain what is, after all, a melodrama: helpless femme tied to the tracks of heterosexual convention seeks rescue from villainous stud.

To get the audience to hiss and cheer in all the right places, some pretty one-dimensional characters have to trot onstage. Casting "the femme" as always and everywhere the hapless victim smuggles a rather anemic picture of white, middle-class femininity into the script. (Not again!) Casting "the butch" as forever the oppressor leaves studliness to muscle-bound, working-class brutes. Femmes and butches in thrall to heterosexuality? Working-class people as violent lugs? Every femme girl a good girl, every good girl a white girl? Colored girls as butch or nothing? White girls as incapable of standing up for themselves? Please! Who left the stage door open to such nonsense? What happened to the entire range of differently raced and classed renditions of gender?

If you come across a woman who identifies as butch giving orders to a lover who identifies as femme, the easiest and most misleading thing in the world is to assume you know exactly what you're seeing. This was Jerri Miller's point when she tried to separate issues of power from issues of gender. Just because you can find couples in which a butch dominates, she argued, doesn't mean you can't find others in which a femme sets the agenda. Just because a few femmes and studs settle their differences with their fists doesn't mean women who call themselves androgynous never beat each other up. Maybe gendering is gendering and abuse is abuse.

But suppose for a minute that gendering and power turn out to be inseparable in relationships. Are the two joined in any predictable fashion? Is "the butch" always the one on top? Is the person on the bottom necessarily under someone else's control? What does it take for a femme to have the upper hand? What happens to power in femme/femme and butch/butch relationships? In interracial and cross-class relationships?

Do you have to change your gendered identity—femme, butch, chameleon—to change the way you handle power? What if you acknowledge gendered differences in your relationship without identifying as anything in particular? Can the links between gender and power change with the times? Over the course of a relationship? Over the course of a lifetime spent in and out of relationships? On the day your lover loses her job? When she comes home after one too many run-ins with racism?

And what exactly do women mean when they talk so freely about power and control? Is power in relationships here to stay? If I have less, do you have more? It's a long way from power as domination to power as the capacity to create. Can you play with power, sharing it like your favorite sex toy or tossing it back and forth like a hot potato? Can you do so without consequences for the balance of power in a relationship? Is there such a thing as a balance of power in a relationship? Or are most people stuck in some tired old ways of thinking: good guys versus bad guys, oppressor versus oppressed, top-down and bottoms up?

With very few exceptions the women interviewed for this book wanted equality with their partners. But when it came to the question of what makes for equality in a relationship, they often parted ways. Did it matter who took out the garbage? Was sex a good place to look to see who's leading whom? What about physical force? Education? Decisions? Desire?

How do you recognize power when you see it? By the take-charge attitude, or the access to money in a dog-eat-dollar world? Unless you come up with some answers, you'll never know whether that girl hauling boxes around the apartment is strong, in command, out to prove a point to her lover, or just plain pussywhipped.

Richie Kaplan: "The Point of Invulnerability"

174

175

"I happen to have a charge card and my [middle-class] lover's been really poor according to her own income. One time I was taking her out to eat and I paid with my charge card. And the waiter gave it back to her, even though she's clearly femme and I'm butch. So it's like there the obvious power dynamics in the world around roles didn't come out. What came out was, this guy picked up on the class differences and gave *her* the charge card back, assuming it had to be hers.

"Because of the way stuff is in the lesbian community, it would be hard having a relationship between a working-class femme and a middle-class butch. Not that I think that there aren't middle-class butches in the world, but I think in a relationship it would be just really intense. Because I feel like the power in the community is given to butches, whereas the power in the world is given to middle-class women in mainstream society.

"Whether or not one's in a quote-unquote 'butch/femme relationship,' there does have to be some kind of equivalents. I mean there has to be some . . . I won't use the word 'equality,' because it's not exactly the same. But it does have to be give and take."

Was there anything Richie did around the house that her lover would not do? "Not really. Each of us does half of the house. We do it when it gets dirty. No, everything's split pretty evenly. Except when we get gas. I guess there are things that [only] I do. For example, even when I didn't drive, I would always go around the car and open the door for my lover! It just seems the right thing to do. Carrying boxes—I always do it. Just taking control. Except when I get panicked. Like when I'm trying to put the stereo cords up and they didn't match, and everything was a mess!

"Maybe sexuality around butch/femme has not to do with who has power over whom, but different ways of having power. I don't think about secretly seducing someone—and to me, femmes do. You seduce someone to make love to you." "What would you do in a similar situation?" I asked. "Seduce someone to make love to them," Richie grinned.

"Let's start out with how I feel when I make love. It's not just taking initiative. That's too simplistic. Maybe it's almost like leading in a dance. Part of how I feel—and I'm not so sure if this is different than femmes—is like this woman's body is entrusted to me. It's sacred, almost. And there's a lot of trust being given to me in being able to have that power, sexual power, over her. In our world, where women have allowed themselves to be sexual, so often that has meant being hurt. And if I'm going to have that kind of power over another woman, it's also part of that to be protective. I laugh sometimes: in fact, I have almost no self-esteem in almost anything I do, but I know I'm a good lover. I don't know where that comes from, and I don't know if that's part of being butch.

"Compared to Christian friends of mine, where women's sexuality is definitely not allowed, I came out of a tradition where women are supposed to be sensual. Sexuality is a very big part of Jewish culture. I mean, for instance, supposedly you're supposed to have sex every Shabbos. It's part of life. So those things, even in nonreligious homes, get filtered down.

"I always joke: I say if I had been a boy and been a faggot, I probably would have been femme, because my mother is really tough and my father is really a softy. You know, in Jewish culture there is such a tradition of strong women and women's leadership. As much as my mother probably wanted me to be feminine, she's not very feminine! And so there were very mixed messages growing up. It's like to survive you have to be tough, but in order to get along in this world you should know how to be feminine. She wanted me to be dressed up in little cute skirts with Mary Jane little shoes. Now *that* felt like a costume to me.

"To me the issues around gender in this country are very painful. Because if you don't fit into certain roles, then you're an outcast. And it's hard not to internalize those views. Gender discrimination and oppression has been a big part of my life. And who knows what I would have been if that didn't exist? And how that affected my self-esteem? I totally relate to drag queens, probably more than any other people. The way I always saw camp is, [it's about] changing that hurtful stuff into something that is funny but is also something positive. But it wasn't talked about in terms of butch/femme sexuality of women.

"When I'm on my own territory and my own terms, I know I play around a lot with gender. And those are the times I can laugh and feel good about it. There are times, for instance, when I've almost been picked up by boys in gay bars. I'm kind of amused by it, in some ways, and I almost like to do it on purpose. Because I like it—not the getting picked up part but knowing that I can pass. But when I'm in the world, and even sometimes around my lesbian friends, those are the parts of myself that I hide. The little bit of it that I show usually is enough to get people upset. That's maybe an eighth of what I am. I don't dress in my drag as much as I used to. Tie, vest. And part of why I think I stopped doing it is because it wasn't accepted.

"In the past I've always had to be really tough. Not because of outside pressure but because of inside pressure of, like, being afraid to be too vulnerable. Vulnerability being, for me, a sign of weakness. Which also probably has to do with growing up working-class. It's too dangerous to be vulnerable on the streets. I used to fight all the time as a kid. Which is why I don't fight as an adult. But I know if I had to I could defend myself. I don't have any question about that. Physically I'm pretty small. But the experience of myself in my body isn't very small.

"My sexuality was constructed around not just being an initiator but being almost totally in control to the point of invulnerability. Which was more of a reaction than anything else to how I perceived a woman's sexuality. As I become older, it's easier for me to become softer. And if that's what people mean by feminine, then yes, there are feminine parts to me.

"Part of that, too, has to do with my own history of being sexually abused. And once I started dealing with that, that really blew open a lot of my own perceptions of myself. One of the things was [the belief] that if one was vulnerable then one can be hurt, and I would associate that with being butch. I've been out for almost fourteen years and it's really only been in the last year that I have felt, in my own body, my own desire attached to my own body, instead of wanting to make love to someone else. To this very day and probably for the rest of my life—although one can never say—I start being sexual and my first response is to make love to a woman, not to be made love to.

"I'm definitely top, 95 percent of the time. [My lover and I] took some pictures of ourselves nude with my [camera] timer, and I was on the bottom in the pictures. My lover says, 'This is probably the only time I'm getting you on the bottom. We'd better save these pictures!' I think tops and bottoms are more metaphoric, and when people tried to apply it literally, it got very boring.

"When we first started talking about butch/femme in the 1980s, Joan Nestle talked about this one time where a woman who picked her up was very butch. How her hand trembled at the softness of her lover. I think that for those of us in the 1980s—my generation—we ignored those parts of ourselves as we created what it means to be butch. I know for myself, I always hated these women who would get up there and talk about how many women they had fucked and how many women they had picked up. That was their interpretation of butch. And to me that was a reconstruction of what straight men do.

"I don't really believe in [butch or femme] 'sides.' If one interprets butch as simply meaning masculine, then it makes sense to talk about it as being a side. But if butch is a particular way of experiencing being a woman, then that doesn't mean there's no feminine part to that. I think we've dichotomized things— either you're feminine or you're masculine—and we've made that too much what butch/femme is. I do not experience butch as being simply masculine. Butch means that maybe I have permission, at least in the privacy of my own home, to be contradictory."

Nicole Johnson: "All You Got to Do Is, You Take a Woman and You Kiss Her"

"My mother used to give me to people. Like I remember one couple she gave me to was a white couple, a doctor and his wife, and her reason for giving me away was because she couldn't afford to feed me. There were four children at home." After Nicole thought about it, however, she realized that she was the only child her mother had sent away for years at a time. "I guess because I was light-skinned. My family is very black, very dark, and I didn't look anything like them. So these were white people, so she gave me to these people and they took good care of me. They gave me clothes and they gave me food.

"I stayed with them maybe a few months and then I was going into the third grade and she sent me to live with my grandmother. Because now I found out that she somewhat owed a debt to my grandmother, because my grandmother adopted my mother. My mother ran away from home and she really broke my grandmother's heart. My grandmother was in this rage, still, about how bad my mother was. I was just a kid—I was just turning seven—and my grandmother was blind, so they sent me there to take care of her. My aunt was there and she lived around the corner from my grandmother, and my grandfather lived with my grandmother, and my uncle lived with my grandmother.

"So there I was, this little kid, with all these adults. And they didn't like me. You know, I couldn't go any further than the porch. I wasn't allowed to play. They didn't feed me. They fed me, but I could only have little portions and there was a lot of food. I mean, these people weren't hurting for money. So I had to sit there and look at all the food. I had to take care of my grandmother and do all the housework and do all of that. They used to beat me, too. They liked that. I guess because they thought I was a horrible person. They never talked to me. You know, they talked to me by telling me what to do. I was never allowed to speak or anything.

"I lived with my grandmother until the ninth grade and then she died. As mean as my grandmother was to me, when she died I was devastated, because she protected me somewhat, since at least I had a house. It reminds me of a rapist. You know, if a rapist keeps their victim for any length of time, they begin to believe and love that person no matter how sick that person may be. It's all they know. It seems like they're the one that are keeping that victim alive.

"I discovered alcohol when I was in the third grade. I stole a bottle of whiskey from my uncle and took it somewhere and started drinking it. I got beat really bad for that one, but that was a beating I really deserved! And I loved the flavor. I drank a ton from the time my grandmother died in ninth grade. That's when I got my freedom to do whatever I wanted to do. The people I ended up with then did not mind me drinking, so I drank. I drank from the time I got up in the morning until I passed out at night. But I held it very well. And then I discovered glue, so it was glue on top of my alcohol and just anything else I could get my hands on. So that's how I felt all this pain: I escaped through alcohol.

"I guess all I wanted was my mother. I just wanted to be with my mother. I wrote her, and there's only one thing in my whole life that I've ever asked her for, was a pair of boots that I wanted for Christmas. And she never sent them to me. She never communicated with me all those years. It was just a total shutdown.

"I started playing around with little girls. When I was seven, I showed them how to masturbate. I don't think I had a crush on any of them, but I may be wrong, because I started liking girls and I just fell in love over and over again with girls. And then I was about fourteen or fifteen when I went to New York and I started hanging out with a group of women who were . . . 'bulldaggers,' they called them. One of them knew my brother. They were real masculine. They really looked like men. And that's the only type of women that I knew that liked other women, so I got really attracted to them. My brother didn't like that at all, so there was some commotion over that. They didn't want me to turn into a bulldagger. I knew that it was something wrong—I mean, you weren't supposed to look like these women. But they really fascinated me.

"You certainly are getting a lot of my history! Then my eleventh grade education. That's when I met a gym teacher, a white woman from New England, who fell in love with me and I in love with her. I lived for this woman, I just loved her so much. She was married, too—married to a military guy. At the end of the school year, she convinced my mother into letting her be my guardian. And then she took me to New England to live with her and her family and her husband, and we were still having this love, this romance, kissing and making love.

"While I was in New England I had a lot of struggle with her, because she was trying to be heterosexual, and that's the image she was putting out. There I was, in love with this woman, and seeing her get pregnant by her husband who she claimed she didn't love. I believe she did not love him, that she in fact loved me, but she couldn't show that. So I was very hurt and crushed and drank a ton. And maybe that's where I developed this thing, this desire for a variety of women, that has stayed with me up until this point. I was never satisfied after that with just one woman. Whenever I saw a woman I wanted her, and I'd go after her no matter who I was involved with or how much supposedly commitment I had to them. And so I loved double standards. The women I hooked up with were not going to go out and be with anyone else except for me, and they agreed to it.

"These were straight women that became my lovers, so therefore they weren't straight anymore, technically. I started to take on this butch look, real butch. I don't think I ever thought of myself as a bulldagger. No, I know I didn't. Because I really didn't want to be a man. Yes, I did—I did want to be a man! I wanted that freedom that they had with women. You know, that they could have many women. And I thought in order to get that, I had to be a man. So for a while there I started looking like a man, dressing like a man, wearing men's pants. I don't think that I went to any further extreme than that. They weren't exactly men's pants; they were like painter's pants, things like that. I didn't want to pass.

"And then I got turned off when I started to bars, eighteen years old. I got turned off when I saw the really hard women. It was the women they were with that I wanted, the feminine women. And I still am that way. I really love feminine women, and consequently, because of my taste, I have to go after straight girls. I love the challenge, and like I said, those are the types of women that I usually get attracted to because they are prettier, they dress better, they smell better. And just because they're bisexual or straight . . . it just goes along with them. But that doesn't turn me off at all. I'm cautious how I am with them sexually—you know, like oral sex—but I like being with them.

"There are just too many butches out there. Now there's butches that are turning into femmes. There aren't many of them and they aren't doing it fast enough. I think it's a marvelous idea: if women feel like being feminine, that they can. Nobody should stop anyone from that. My ex-girlfriend, she's very femme, and her friends are very femme. When they came out—they would often talk about this—they would go to bars and nobody would talk to them. People would turn their back on them. These are women's clubs! Think that they were straight and what the hell were they doing there. They were really treated bad.

"I think the word has got around that you will not be accepted in our community if you look a certain way. So I think a lot of women who would probably have been femmes, who were femmes when they were out there in the straight world, in order to be loved by women thought they had to look ugly as sin—the combat boots and the whole works—and become dykes. I'm not a dyke. I hate that word. I think it's associated with bulldagger, and I'm not going to fight for that word.

"I think women—feminists or political, strong women—around here who say, 'Well, you should be downwardly mobile,' or, 'You should look ugly and fat and not look pretty, so that men will be turned off by you,' they should have their tongue snatched out of their head for that stuff. Why would they want to make women ugly? That's, to me, very, very wrong. Shave your head, and if you have a house, sell it and go into poverty, and all of that. I guess maybe because I've seen all of that, and I know what poverty is. I've tasted it. I've eaten watermelon and biscuits for weeks and weeks on end when I lived with my mother. I know what it's like, and to make someone go through that just because of politics is beyond me.

"I don't think anybody in the community has a right to tell women what they should do. And there's not a lot of strong women out there like I am. I mean, if the community starts swinging this way, they become that way. If the community goes back, they are inside the whip. Where I'm not. I'm a self-made person. I'm such an individual. If they ask me what [race] I am, I'll tell them. I'm proud of that [being African American]. But when I was a kid, I didn't belong to the white race, I didn't belong to the black race. All of those pushed me away from them. And I was hitting center, trying to belong to someone, and I didn't—they wouldn't allow it. So I had to become this one unit, this whole unit. I know I didn't belong to anything, so my sexuality was also part of that. The most important thing in my mind was that I was a woman. I guess that's all I knew. That I was a woman. A female. A strong female. So I stand outside of [the community] and I do what I want to do. Especially when I'm feeling my sexuality and who's in my bed.

"I've had everything else, it seems like, and what I really, really want is a family and a wife. If there's kids around, adopt some. Women who don't identify as being lesbians are temporary, in my experience. They're very temporary. Which has always been fine with me, because I never wanted any long-term relationship. I always used to seem to get into these things and they were against my will. I was in them, so the other party somehow kept me on the line, but I'm well aware that if they're thinking that they're straight but having sex with a woman, that's the way it is. There's no converting. And I know that it's just a one-night trick or whatever, and we'll see each other a couple times a year or something, but it's a trick. I would like to get married and settle down now.

"I see myself as being probably a six or seven [on a butch/femme scale]. My friends don't see me as being that. They think I'm very feminine. It was work that made me change. If I'm somewhere in a warm climate, I think nothing of putting on a skirt or a dress, and as a matter of fact, I would prefer it rather than wearing pants. And I like being attractive to both sexes. I like being desirable by men and women, and I love women who are that way, too. If I'm with a woman that I know men want, too, that just fills my ego. Like there's no tomorrow. That just feeds into me. Makes me feel fat.

"I don't like my lover to carry anything heavy and I like her to look real pretty all the time. Even taking out the garbage, gosh, I'll take out the garbage! When I come home, I want her to, if she wears makeup, just look really feminine or ready for me. Most of the women that I've gone with, if they wanted to dress like a boy, then they couldn't be my woman. I don't think I'd be attracted to a mechanic. I have to be with a woman who has those typical jobs, female jobs, whereas if I'm with a woman who's in the trades, then I think, well, shit, why don't you just go be with a man? Because she's not as soft as I want her to be. She doesn't smell like I want her to smell. She'll smell like a man. She'll feel like a man. She won't be thin and fragile, emotional. Maybe she will after I take off all those clothes! [But] I don't want to have to do all that stuff.

"My last girlfriend and I had a little trouble in the beginning with [me liking] to wear dresses. She didn't like that. I stepped over the line with her. But she got used to it, I think. (Maybe she didn't!) She liked me to look butch. And sometimes she liked me to even dress butchier, when we were alone. Put on something like a dark T-shirt, or something that really, really turned her on.

"Although I don't dress really, really butch and I wear dresses and skirts, what I feel inside, how I handle a woman when I'm with her, the way I make love to her, the way I romance her, is very so-called masculine, but it is very butch. There's no doubt about it. I was always the aggressor. A lot of women have a lot of difficulty because there's no aggressor. Like they'll be saying, 'Oh, gee, I really like this woman,' and both of them will be really liking each other, but will they go to bed with each other? Will they kiss or anything? All you got to do is, you take a woman and you kiss her, and then one thing leads into the other; but noooo . . . 'Oh, I will, I will,' and they go on for months. I'm not that way. I take women. You see, it doesn't matter if they're straight or gay. If I want them, I'll take them. And women like to be taken. So that's where my advantages come in.

"I used to wish that our community was like the men's, the gay guys, that sexual freedom. But that was just another thing that men had that I wanted. They always had a lot of money, they had power, they had a lot of sex. [Lesbians are] kind of old-fashioned in that way: 'Oh, let's meet for coffee first and then we can go to bed.' I'm not. I don't have those beliefs. If you like someone, by all means have them, and as soon as possible.

"I guess some people feel like, oh, geez, they don't know how to do it. I know I'm good at making love, so that gives me a ton of confidence. I don't have trophies and I don't have anything to really show for myself, so to speak, and so I think that knowing that I can have that power over someone's emotions and their body has made me strong in that area. It's a way to control a person. Even if they do something when you're outside of the bed, you know, if they think you're stronger and they do something that you don't like, then you may wait until this moment [in bed] and then that's just another way of showing them who the boss is.

"Used to be, you had to be all in the roles, the real strict roles that we're not involved in at all, that our sisters used to be with. So that's where I see the major change, and we're not going back to that. We're still remaining women. And we know that we can enjoy each other sexually without becoming a man. It's okay now for women to switch. Like to cook, in a butch. They switch roles more often. I don't switch, I'm telling you right now. I don't switch! But there's almost this understanding when I go in, like sometimes it's okay if I become passive.

"I'm not an untouchable person. I'm not the untouchable butch. I love to be made love to. But only to a certain point. I don't like penetration that much. Well, like a woman wants to eat me, make love to me that way, then I can have an orgasm that way, but taking them is where I get off the most. And now I use a vibrator and I put it between both of us and I still want to be on top. Having an orgasm at the same time with someone is fantastic. So maybe I'm wrong saying . . . I guess I have to be passive once in a while. If I let a woman make love to me, that's being passive."

What did Nicole think of the idea that partners should relate as equals? "Can't be that way. It's all fine and dandy to say. You know, people say those things, but when you get cornered, then your mind kind of changes. It's just a matter of whoever is the strongest.

"I don't like to humiliate anyone. So that makes it difficult for me to be a top or a bottom in s/m, because I have too much pride in myself and I respect people too much to want to belittle them and call them ugly names. I don't mind making a woman beg a little bit, but not . . . well, I don't mind tying a woman up. If the bed has posts, I don't mind tying her up that way and then making love to her. I like holding them down and forcing them to kiss, and I like playing games like that.

"There were a couple of times I did that. A woman that I didn't know—I never saw her before or anything, and I really liked her at a party. I forced her into one of the bedrooms and pinned her down on the bed and started taking off some of her clothes. Totally dominating this woman. I ripped off her panties and I ripped her bra off and I get so aroused doing this. I don't come totally; I haven't orgasmed at that moment, but that is my foreplay, is forcing a person. And biting. If I'm involved in a relationship, I use words that are safe or [tell her] what to say if I'm going too far so we'll be able to stop. There's nothing to make me really stop even after she says the word. It depends on how I'm feeling, if I feel like stopping. I still am the one that's in total control.

"Especially this last woman, she loved being dominated. She loved it, and I loved taking her. And when I would start making love to her, you know at first maybe I'll be gentle, and then I'd work into a frenzy of starting to hurt, give her pain, biting her nipples, biting breasts. All over her body, licking and biting, forcing, holding her arms down. And then when I start to get into the right position, then I start putting my hand inside her, and then my fist, and that I love more than anything. To have total dominance and to be able to fist-fuck someone is the ultimate to me."

Roberta Osabe: "I Only Wanted to Do It Through Looks . . . I Didn't Want to Do All the Dishes"

"I've really come full circle on butch/femme. Because I knew I was attracted to really butch women when I first came out. And at first I thought, well, I should just be *like* that, because then they'll like me. And then I realized I wasn't *getting* them, the ones I wanted! So I thought, well, maybe I'd better be more feminine, then. So I started doing that. I really got into butch/femme relationships."

After graduating from high school, Roberta Osabe made herself a fake ID to gain entry to gay bars. "I took my driver's license and I color Xeroxed it and I screened the photograph. Then I laminated it on Kodak paper, this double plastic, so it looked really good. I started hanging out in this bar in southern

California, and I fell in love with the bartender there. When I first was kissing this girl Chris, I went crazy! I became really into her life and her lifestyle.

"She was very tough. I decided to be much more feminine. It was very exciting, because I wasn't supposed to be doing this—you know, my feminist ideas were kind of a contradiction. Chris was—well, she was an alcoholic, [one] in a succession of alcoholics after that. But she was my first alcoholic. She was in jail and I would go visit her on weekends, and then she got out of jail. She had a motorcycle. She was just all these things that I had never [encountered]. I was really fascinated by that. She was ten years older than me. We lived together for a short period. I also was devastated when we broke up. She left me because she felt that I couldn't deal with her drinking. It's true: I couldn't. And I'm real glad she did, now. But at the time, I wanted to commit suicide. It was just awful. I was with her on such a romantic trip. I wanted to be with her until we were old.

"She always wanted to do better, but she worked in a factory, and she tried to do a couple other things, but she kept fucking up. So she just gave up. And even though I was really into her, I really wanted to be a survivor. I had really shitty, horrible jobs at that time. I knew I couldn't last doing those, whereas she might have resigned herself to just doing what she was doing, and she pretty much did. She pretty much is still there, and I've since gone to college and graduate school.

"I've always been in tumultuous relationships. And a lot of my friends have been in tumultuous relationships. I guess what I mean by that is—I don't know—sometimes women get crazy, and I know I get crazy! Just in the last few years, I've realized that getting really violent and dramatic and stuff is something that I want to get rid of. But it was definitely part of the coming-out years. Ten years ago I remember at the bar we had brawls between the old crowd and the new crowd. It seemed like all the people I knew, when you were fighting, you were really fighting. And when you were loving, you were really passionate. Kind of either/or. Now, I'm tired."

With a degree in fine arts and a job as a waitress, Roberta Osabe described herself as "working class with middle-class aspirations." For a time during her childhood, Roberta lived "back East, where racism was really bad. I remember the kids just treated me really different, actually called me 'nigger' and all this stuff, and I didn't even know what that was." Although she considered herself a feminist, Roberta had made a point of distancing herself from the women's movement. "Divisions between race and class drove a wedge right through it. And I felt that it's really too bad, because I didn't think it had to be. But everybody's learning about each other."

At a certain point in her life, Roberta explained, butch/femme relationships "became not right. I only wanted to do it, really, through looks, and certain small little behavior things. But not any big deal. I didn't want to do all the dishes, or the laundry, or the cooking—all that stuff that all these women kept *expecting* me to do! And at that point, I thought, 'Uh-oh. This isn't right.' So I made a change, a personal change. I still became attracted to really butch women, until, actually, I moved up here. Then I started going out with different kinds of women, and I started feeling more like *I* wanted to be more butch. Now that's how I feel. I feel much more butch than I feel femme.

"With [my girlfriend] Jennifer, we have some kind of differences. She dresses kind of like a tomboy, and she relates like a tomboy, but *really* she's much more femme. And I dress more feminine and kind of put out that image, but *really* I'm much more butch. Sexually and personally. In the beginning, when I was first experiencing lesbianism, I wanted to *feel* it from another woman. I wanted to be made love to. And now, I feel like I want to *give* it. Much more I want to give it.

"I think there's all kinds of people. As long as they're doing [butch/femme] and they dig it, and they feel right about it, then that's cool. I still have friends that are totally into that. But they've *always* been into it, even before all this revival got started. That was just the way they *were*, as gays. It was their image of what they were supposed to do, based on sort of a heterosexual model. So they don't see anything wrong with it, and they just do it how they feel.

"One complaint I have about the women's movement and the lesbian community, is that they always ('they' meaning me, too, in some ways) seem to grab onto trends. Things are in for a while, and then it's out for a while. I really get suspicious of that. So what I would say about butch/femme roles is that, if that's how the people really feel, then to me that's fine to do. But to say that that's the most liberated thing, or to say that that's the goal. . . . it's not the goal for me."

Toni Williams: "You Can't Always Be the Aggressor"

The first time Toni Williams went to a gay bar, she was nineteen years old. "My friend and I, we were both sitting, parked right in front of Maud's. My other friend was twenty-three at the time, so she bought us a six-pack of Michelob. We sat there drinking our beer and saying, 'Aw, I bet you're not gonna go in there.' 'Aw, I *know* you're not gonna go in there.' Very scared, because for one thing, we weren't twenty-one. So we knew we could have got carded somewhere.

"The whole fact that we're gay, that's even a double whammy. It's like you want to be accepted. It's different [than] if you were straight and you were going to a bar and they carded you. I mean, we would take it as more—more than just, 'You're not twenty-one so you can't come in here.' We'd be more sensitive to it. And thinking also, maybe, 'Oh god, I'm gay. I can't even get into a gay bar and meet gay people.' We didn't know where to meet these people. We always thought bars, when we were younger.

"So we started drinking up, and we got through our six-pack of beer. She says, 'Well, let's get out, and let's just walk by there.' So we walked by the bar. And she says, '*You're* not gonna go in that door.' That's all it took. She was daring me. BOOM! Open the door and walk right in. Try to act real cool, you know? Like, 'I've been here before.' Real tough. I really put on the butch role, because it's a protectiveness, sometimes. 'What'll you have?' 'Oh, I'll have a Bud.' I knew the terminology. You don't say, 'Can I have a Budweiser, please?' You say, 'Can I have a Bud?' I assumed all these things of how to act in a bar. Even though I had never been to a bar. So that was my first experience. Drinking beer, walking around and watching everybody.

"Even at age twelve years old, my father had a very long talk with me. 'You've got to start looking more feminine. You're a girl. You're not this little boy any more, this little tomboy in the family. You have to wear dresses, maybe, and put some makeup on and fix your hair.' My father's giving me this lecture here! I'm like, 'I think this is what *mom's* supposed to be talking to me about.' He attempted to try to persuade me to change myself. And we did go out and get my hair cut. Did go out and get myself a dress. But I never wore that dress! I think that they realized I had made up my mind.

"I came off as, and I probably still do come off as, this very aggressive butch type of person. But once you get to know me, you know that I'm not that way. I'm probably more femme than [my lover], Marta, is in this relationship. Or just in dealing with people, and talking to them, and getting to know them. I do wear dresses every now and then. I'm not the stereotypical butch that *always* wears jeans and wears her hair slicked back and has a pack of cigarettes rolled up in her sleeve.

"Sometimes we just reverse the roles. She's going to take care of things. Which is typical of the butch. And then the femme just sits there and looks pretty, or whatever. Can't make up their mind what they want. So I would say I'm right in the middle, cool with it. I can go either way. I'm not afraid to act more feminine, and I'm not afraid to act more aggressive. But only through the *relationship* do I learn that.

"I didn't have that before. I played the very aggressive butch role. I'm going to take the lady by the hand, and we're going to go do this and this and this. Drive the car. Marta, she rarely drives the car when I'm in, but we're trying to change that so that she has more of an opportunity. I shouldn't *always* drive the car. I see that as very manly, or butchly, or whatever the word is.

"Now, like I say, we're working on a lot of things. Before, Marta would never make love to me. I would be always the one that was on top, so to speak. I mean, you got tops and bottoms. But I don't think that it was a matter of butch; I think it was a matter of trust. I was very afraid. But everybody said that that was the butch role, so I was like, 'Hmm. I guess I'm being really *butch.*' Because you heard: butch is always on the top, and femme is always on the bottom. I don't know who made those rules up, but somewhere along the line, you hear this.

"I don't know how it would be if I wasn't in a relationship. If I would be the one to sit there and go up and ask this woman to dance. I don't know. Because when Marta and I got together, I told her that I was gay. And it went under the water, so to speak, for about two months. She says that I approached her, but I say that she approached me, so it's like even at that point. Once I knew that I had a relationship with Marta, even though it wasn't a physical and a love relationship right then, I knew that I didn't *have* to pursue Marta. And that she didn't *have* to pursue me.

"Plus, society now, you know, we're changing. The butch doesn't always look so masculine. I think that people are trying to get away from that. At least, *I'm* trying to get away from that. Even though I still relate back to it. Sometimes.

"You can't always be the aggressor. You can't always be the one to initiate. And so that's where fantasy comes in. You fantasize that this older person—a teacher or whatever—is going to sweep you off your feet. I played a lot of those kind of games with my head. Because I didn't like being such a butch. In a relationship you have the opportunity to explore both issues. What do you want to be: femme or butch? Or you can be both. When you're outside a relationship, you've got these walls protecting things."

Vicki Turner: "Just Because She's Butch Doesn't Mean She's My Master"

"I know a lot of butch women that strip. Ones that are in shape, because you've got to have a certain look. And they're good. See, it's a character. Even I become different. It's not Vicki walking in there; it's Aurelia. And it's like a role, an acting role. I used to play the boop-boopy-do bimbo, dumb blonde bimbo person. And I'm *not.* I get in the mirror and I put on this different kind of makeup. I do my hair different. I put on this costume. And I become Aurelia.

"I see butches get off their Harleys, and their boots, and their leather jackets, and their jeans, just butched out, and walk in there, strip it all off, shave their legs, throw on makeup, and become Miss So-and-So. I'm not saying they're the ultrafemmes of the world, but they change and they become their little character. Makeup comes off after their shift, they put on back their boots, and they're—vrooom—on their motorcycle and gone. Butches are not ugly. But if they go on [as] what they're supposed to look like [as a butch], as opposed to what a man would like to see, yeah, they [have to] clean up.

"It's all in the hustle. I really don't think it's a beauty contest, in that kind of a place. It's more of just knowing how to work the men there. Sometimes if you come out knowing that you're really pretty, and you carry yourself well, they get scared. I think if you're gay, you've got it made there. Because I go in there, and I don't think of them as men. I just think of them as [an] 'I'm going to get your money' kind of thing. I'm sure they look at us the same way. It's kind of an addiction. We're their drug.

"I'm burnt out in my business. I liked stripping. I liked more the burlesque. And now it's becoming more hard-core. That's a dying thing, the burlesque, in stripping. Now it's totally nude, and they're there to see tits and ass. They don't give a shit how you perform. I hope I can make it another three years in my business. I think my job will allow me to do what I want to do, like going to school and not starving.

"I get a lot of flak for what I do. They just don't understand how I get into it. But if they only knew how much [money] I was taking home, they'd go, 'Oh. Maybe that's why.' Women are still fighting with each other, in many ways. They still put out 'good girl/bad girl.' I don't think that's women standing next to each other. I really don't.

"I'm a stripper, so they think, well, she *likes* men. And it's *not* true. I can't *stand* men. *I* see what they're really like. I mean, there are men that walk through my place—they are not perverts that have these coats that open up. No, no, no. They are white-collar, blue-collar. Some of the top mayor men, that are next to the mayor, they come in, they have their seat there. They're *all* kinds. They look like every Joe Schmoe. They're so normal-looking, okay? And they're all coming here for something, for something that we give them. Who knows what that is. I don't know.

"I think men really feel between their legs, you know what I mean? I think it's funny how they call women sluts. Because that's a man-made word. It's a man-made word to put us down. If anything, men are the animals. They're the sluts. Because I'm not there because I need to be, or I need to fix something. I'm there because I'm making money off of it. But *they're* the ones paying for it. I don't understand the thing that if women sleep around, they're whores, and if men do, they're really men.

"I've always been femme. I couldn't be butch if I tried. I think even if I was in combat boots and a T-shirt and jeans, I still would be feminine. I look femme. I act femme. I take care of things, like a home. My personality's not submissive or anything as a quote 'femme.' I have a strong personality, but I'm really the high point of what they consider femme when I get in my full get-up. I used to live in pumps. I've mellowed out a little bit, I'd say. I've gotten casual. But I think that's the style of the times now. I've realized that I'm still feminine, but I can wear jeans and boots and not feel that to be feminine is to be really primped.

"I always said that my lover couldn't ever wear a dress around me, and that's true, because I'd feel like I'm competing with her. I used to go out with really, really, *really* butch women, that sometimes looked like men, literally. I don't like that any more, because I do like *women*. And sometimes I find that really heavy butch women tend to not let their feminine side out. So I'd say my girlfriend's butch, but she's still a woman as to lookswise and everything. She's soft. Kind of baby butch, you would say.

"I do admire feminine women, and they do turn me on. But not as a relationship, to carry it through. I think there's more than fucking in a relationship. My ex-roommate, she goes with a butch girl. We haven't figured that one out, either. Because she talks about blondes and bimbos—you know, girls. We haven't seen her with one yet! Here they are, they put this butch presence out, but they don't hang with the femme girls. I know a lot of girls—women—who are like that. (I hate using 'girls'; I don't know why I'm using that word.) They talk about blondes and skirts. Kind of like men do, in that way. But who they end up sacking with, in bed, is really different. So it confuses me.

"I stay in my role. Because that *is* me. You know what I'm saying? It's not something that I have to work at. I just came out, and said this is who I like to sleep with, but I'm not changing this look. Because I like this look.

"When you become lovers, you start setting up house and try to play house. I don't know if it's from childhood or whatever happens, but you just automatically do. I don't feel like I'm imitating. I could be imitating my mother. But that's just how we were raised. I don't think my girlfriend's imitating her father! I don't think we're trying to have the white picket fence, and she's daddy and I'm mommy. For me it's like, you do what your thing is, and I do my little thing, and we don't get it in the middle. It's just an easier way to live.

"Now, when I first started, I was really very, very femme. I wanted to be like Ozzie and Harriet. I'm supposed to cook, and clean, and make sure that my girlfriend comes home, and that her dinner's ready, and everything like that. And I did that for a long time. And I felt weird when my girlfriend would do it to me. I thought, 'Something's not right.' After a while, I couldn't do it *and* work. So slowly, in my relationships, we'd split it. But that's like one extreme.

"I, at one time, was the only person that cleaned the house. Today I don't have time to do that. Just like a straight woman doesn't have time to do it and work, too. I don't see any difference with that, [no reason for] making it a femme kind of thing. I know butches that go, 'I don't clean and I don't cook. My old lady does that.' That's, to me, a typical stereotype of a man-woman relationship. The old 1950s thing! This is 1990, and even straight couples, they take care of the kids [together]. It's an equal thing.

"I work. I can't cook all the time. Nor would you want me to cook all the time! In actuality, I'm the worst cook there is! We have chores together that we split in half. And I do only work part-time, so sometimes I do clean more than she does. But it balances. That's a hard one to do. It's just keeping a balanced household. But if I had enough money, believe me, I'd have a maid.

"I never take the garbage out. Actually, it's my turn. Because we have this new chores, and I *hate* taking the garbage out. I never have! But I *am* the aggressor. I know what I want. Because I think being feminine is not being submissive and doing the dishes. It's just that's what a woman did, even ten years ago. And that's where, in my head, you got this role act. Maybe I do more what's considered feminine around the house, and she does more of the nailing and hammering. But I do that, too, if she's not around. I'm just as strong as her. [Butch/femme is] just more of the way I *feel* and the way we *look*.

"But when it comes to, like, discussing bills or going out to dinner or things like that, or who pays, I take my lover out because I make more money. That all has nothing to do with butch or femme. That just has to do with someone's money arrangements. And we're both a part of this household, so we both make our decisions. One doesn't say, 'Yes, we're doing this.' I say, 'No, we need to talk it over and come to a happy medium.' Just because she's butch doesn't mean she's my master.

"I'm aggressive out of the bed. And I'm submissive *in* the bed. But that's another whole different kind of thing. I don't bow down to my lover if we're having an argument. Though sometimes I do. But I think that belongs to our personalities. I don't think that has anything to do [with] if you're butch or femme, if that means the butch daddy gets everything she wants. No.

"Could you be a femme and a top? Yeah, definitely. And make a good living at it, too! I don't do it in general in my private life. Because I enjoy being a bottom. And I enjoy my *girlfriend* being a top. She's a really good top. And it kind of takes that fantasy out of it, if she bottoms out on me. But she doesn't like to, either. I mean, sometimes she'll a little bit bottom out for me, because I'll have little fantasies. I'll go, 'Gee, I was thinking about this thing . . .' But it's not the same. I'm still submissive, but I'm on top, in a way. If you can figure that out. But the complete control thing, no. I do that at work. At work I am really the top controller. And I like it, when I come home, to be [different]. Even though I think I wear the pants in the family. But in bed, I take them off!"

Who's Got the Power? Double Takes

After years of struggle, Nicole Johnson had finally made it, no thanks to other people. Shuttled from family to family and house to house, she had learned young about differences of culture and extremes of wealth. What bothered her was not so much the moving as the conviction that nobody really wanted her. Her break from heterosexuality into queerness seemed all of a piece with her childhood sense of belonging to neither "the white race" nor "the black race." As an adult Nicole claimed a racial identity as "African American plus ?" and a sexual identity as a lesbian. But as a child only her identity as a woman had seemed indisputable.

Nicole considered herself a self-made person. But take a closer look. Skin color was central to her own explanation for why she, rather than her siblings, ended up being "given away." Nicole's mother didn't have the money to keep all the children at home. So she followed the time-honored practice among poor African Americans of having several adults share the responsibilities of childrearing. That's where Nicole thought color came in. Being the light one, she got sent to a white family. Except, of course, for the times her mother shipped her off to her grandmother for another installment of abuse.

Multiple parenting arrangements usually work for kids, not against them. "Other mothers" spread resources around in situations where there's not much to go around. According to researchers such as Patricia Hill Collins and Carol Stack, they also give children adults to turn to when things don't work out with their primary caretakers. Even a story of victimization as bleak as Nicole's has its bright spots, not to mention its ironies. If Nicole never received the show of affection she wanted from her mother, she did have a brother who cared enough to warn her away from the bulldaggers in the neighborhood.

When Nicole took stock of her relationships with women, it was with a backward glance toward these early experiences. Her sense of herself as an outcast—a highly desirable outcast, but an outcast nonetheless—informed the ways she gendered herself queer. As far as Nicole was concerned, empowerment only came at someone else's expense. A self-styled rebel, she could talk all afternoon about forcing femmes, laying down the law in a skirt, instituting double standards, or picking up straight girls to get the look she wanted in a lover. Flouting the conventions of "the lesbian community" just added a chapter to a much longer story about finding her way in a world that refused to find a place for her.

Paradoxically, the childhood experiences that organized Nicole's story had everything to do with society-made, not self-made, power. Who's got the money? Who goes without? Which color counts for more? A person can't begin to answer these questions without paying attention to factors beyond individual control. Even a rebel has to have something to rebel against. As long as she fixes her eyes on the conditions she's trying to escape, they continue to hold her in thrall.

Nicole was not the first or the last person to believe that she had evaded subjection because she had managed to pick herself up every time something or someone knocked her down. But is it ever possible to get beyond striking range? If you should be so inclined, can you take your girlfriend along to a place where power can't touch you?

The evidence in even the few accounts included in this chapter argues against it. For one, people do not pursue their relationships in a vacuum. Nicole's history of going out with "heterosexual" women developed because of her taste but also because "the lesbian community" had shunned femmes for so many years. During the 1970s lesbian-identified girl-girls were hard to find! As community policing of gender relaxed, Nicole watched and waited for more "androgynous" women to go femme.

Changes in the economy had made it increasingly difficult to run a household on a single income. Although Vicki Turner began a relationship playing Harriet to her lover's Ozzie, she ended up too tired to do all the housework and work for wages, too. Gay or straight, more women in the work force meant more demands on partners to do "their share" at home.

Richie Kaplan associated the need to protect herself on the mean streets of her youth with her inclination to guard against vulnerability in a relationship. Even when she wanted to, she found it difficult to abandon her customary stance of wary self-defense. Alertness to the nuances of power intruded upon her most intimate moments. If she had wielded a fraction of the power white middle-class men do outside the bedroom, she might have had an easier time dressing (and undressing) to please her lover. But as it was . . .

Richie could scarcely imagine a working-class femme and a middle-class butch surmounting the difficulties they would face in a relationship. Wouldn't the femme be doubly disadvantaged: little respect from the lesbian community, and no middle-class cachet outside it? Yet putting a working-class butch together with a middle-class femme didn't necessarily balance things out. What about the time the waiter returned Richie's charge card to her lover? At a fancy restaurant class differences sometimes overshadowed the two women's strongly gendered presentations, leaving Richie's well-heeled partner in charge. If gender had been the only factor operating, Richie figured she would have gotten the card back—as its bearer, if not "the butch."

Get out there in the nine-to-five world, and the ground can shift under your feet. Richie believed that pressures to assimilate were compounded in relationships with women like her lover who were Jewish and femme and middle-class. Or bent upon improving their working-class prospects. Or hooked into a private version of the immigrant dream.

Roberta Osabe described herself as "working-class with middle-class aspirations." When she decided to leave butch/femme behind, she hoped to leave with it an entire world of hard-drinking women who despaired of ever "bettering" themselves. But look how many things she carried forward. She hadn't moved seamlessly into the middle class. She remained an aspiring artist who waited tables to make ends meet. She couldn't separate hard times from racism from the way she gendered herself when she encountered barriers to getting ahead. And she still resorted to terms such as "femme" and "butch" to explain life with her current partner.

Like nearly everyone I interviewed except Nicole, Roberta wanted equality in her relationships. Not that Roberta or most of her peers would have called themselves feminist activists. When Roberta realized that the white women running the women's center in her California town hardly spoke to folks in the neighborhood who looked like her, she withdrew from the women's movement in frustration with its race politics. Yet she still flirted with the feminist credo that gendered differences in lesbian relationships can only oppress.

The 1980s was a decade for looking over the shoulder at lesbian-feminism. Shimmering in the distance, its well-intentioned critiques sometimes looked more like farce than reasoned arguments. But shimmer they did, which meant they had to be addressed. Women who craved a more complicated thesis than "butch/femme is bad" or "butch/femme is good" developed some new ways of thinking through gender and power. They began by dividing the coupled life into domains and went on to distinguish top and bottom from butch and femme.

Critiques of butch/femme tend to separate partners into controller and controlled, the person with the power and the person without. Since "the butch" presumably has the power, "the femme" doesn't stand a chance. Way too simplistic, many women responded. In a relationship that stretches out over time, that much consistency becomes impossible. Like Toni Williams said, from her no longer quite so butch perspective: "You can't always be the aggressor."

Heated discussions flared. Lovebirds may not be consistent, but power has to be there somewhere. Have you ever seen a femme who fixed motorcycles, or a butch who admitted to a passion for knitting? Different capacities, different kinds of power. Others said butch/femme had more to do with sex than hobbies or work. A person who bottomed out in bed was femme, end of story. Still others contended that only manner and appearance really counted, because no one would ever know what went on behind closed doors. Borrowing terminology from s/m, they saw at least four different possible combinations of gender and erotic power: femme top, femme bottom, butch bottom, and butch top. No reason femmes couldn't orchestrate the action. (Vicki: "And make a good living at it, too!") The result? Sexual possibilities that don't begin to be covered by a term such as "fluff."

With three different domains—work, appearance, and sex—organizing relationships, debates about gender and power became much more interesting. In theory a woman could reap the benefits of power in one domain and let her lover hold sway in another. Or she could try to share power in every domain. Privilege didn't have to follow directly from a particular style of gendering or belong to only one person in a couple. Roberta could act debonair on date night, dress like a girl, control major economic decisions, outclass her partner, get pulled over by traffic cops more often than her light-skinned lover, initiate most of the moves in bed, and still get stuck doing all the dishes. Vicki could live as femme as you please in almost every department but insist that her lover split the chores.

By adding complexity the questions change, and with them, the proposed solutions. Forget about asking, "Who's got the power?" You're better off with: "What makes for equality in a relationship?" Forget about getting rid of power differences by tossing out gendered differences. Think instead about how to do gender in ways that keep you and your lover on a par.

If only the answers could have been more obvious. Of all the domains, appearance seemed easiest to divest of any predictable relation to power. Sporting muscles says nothing about how you use them. Just because you have big hair doesn't mean you can't make all the moves when you sex someone up. And a woman can always maintain a playful attitude toward whatever figure she cuts. Wear those three-inch heels, but do so more as burlesque than as an expression of some diehard identity. Be as quick to trade them in for a pair of wingtips as you'd drop your drawers if Tina Turner or Melissa Etheridge walked into the room. Or wax consistent, and get your kicks from thwarting your girlfriend's best efforts to get you into a skirt. Confront every stranger who's out to hit (on) you just because of the way you're dressed. Remind your friends that looks aren't everything. Looks can be deceiving. Look twice.

The real trouble began with work. How were partners supposed to evaluate labor? Maintain equality? By dividing everything down the line? Then what were they counting—dollars earned, windows washed, readiness to take on the jobs a lover hated? Did it help to keep track? Or was keeping track itself a controlling behavior?

Lovers often agreed to split the chores "fifty/fifty," but what that meant on a day-to-day basis was by no means a fixed proposition. They might rotate everything ritualistically. Or they might settle upon a 1990s variation of the old "femmes cook while butches fix things" schtick. Which might look like no variation at all, given, say, a middle-class Jewish stud without a penchant or cultural injunction for home repair. Whether or not they divided tasks according to a gendered logic, they generally expected "doing my share" to square things.

Still, cleaning "half the house" can translate into vastly different amounts of time and effort. Depends if you happen to draw the half with the clutter from last night's party. Depends if you can afford to bring in someone to help you mop up. Depends whether your partner notices how you sacrificed your ball game to the greater good of sparkling floors. It's common enough for people to differ in their perceptions of who does how much, underestimating their partner's efforts and overestimating their own. This an old story, with which heterosexual couples are also well acquainted.

Children make things even messier, literally and figuratively. Their care and feeding activate all sorts of cultural and economic arrangements. Partners have to negotiate who will dispose of the diapers, who will nurse, who's got friends and relatives that can help out, who wants to stay home for the first few months, who can't afford to stay home because she's got the better-paying job or the insurance covering the kids. In making those decisions, people take gendering into account. But there's a lot more to consider than who's feeling androgynous or femme or butch.

As for the kind of work that yields cold, hard cash, well, a steady job never provided a clear indicator of gendering in a relationship. (The *kind* of job might provide a few clues, but that's something else again.) It's always been difficult to support someone else on a woman's salary, even in the heyday of the family wage. Segregated labor markets made the "you-stay-home-I'll-work" pattern even harder to achieve for people of color. In years gone by it was the rare woman who managed to talk her way into a corporate boardroom or weld her way into a unionized, blue-collar job. In most cases her partner also had to work for wages.

In a country with privatized health insurance, financial resources give you access to medical care that could save your life. They allow you to eat. They give you the means to walk away from a bad relationship. But earning the money and controlling the money can be two different things. Some couples pool unequal incomes. The person who manages the money isn't always the one who earns it. And plenty of unemployed folks, queer or otherwise, have taken out their frustrations on the girl who's bringing home the bacon. So raking in the big bucks provides no ironclad guarantee of power on the home front.

And then there's sex. Fucking, penetrating, starting something, going down, initiating, seducing, grabbing that cherry, lighting that fire, topping, teasing, taking, going under, bottoming out are all potentially gendered terms. Or not, if you can separate the positions and the moves from the way a woman genders herself.

Here's where counting as a way to strike a balance really starts to look silly. Like Rona Bren, Richie wondered what's achieved by trading orgasms. "Tops and bottoms are more metaphoric," said Richie, who considered herself a top. "When people tried to apply it literally, it got very boring." Some girls can use their hands from underneath in ways to make the most disciplined body squirm. It's perfectly possible to direct from the (literal) bottom, submit from the top, or roll around in bed without giving an inch when it comes to control.

Even the famous acid test used to pin girls down with respect to gender creates false dichotomies and, with them, false consistencies. The exam question goes like this: If you were marooned with only one other person on a desert island, would you rather make love to her or have her make love to you? But what if you can't decide? Or you place less importance on what the other girl does than how she does it? Even then there's always room for interpretation. Did that glint in her eyes beckon or command?

Besides, these days it's supposed to be okay to switch, even if you strongly identify as femme or butch. That's what Nicole thought. Yet when she tried to *do* something about it, she ended up questioning the gendering of her own erotics. Did it make her more "passive," less butch, to let her partner go down on her? But remember, this is the same girl who got off on force. If fistfucking someone represents your ultimate in sexual pleasure, can you be any more butch? Or should you leave "butch" out of it and call yourself a top? Likewise, how "passive" is the power femme who holds, grabs, and unzips to beg for—or was it demand—more?

Suppose you put away your stopwatch, and with it the idea of "equal time" in the sack. What's important to consider, then, in terms of power? You could start with cultural differences. Richie suspected that attitudes toward eroticism might differ for lesbians who came from a religious background in which people expect to have sex on the Sabbath. Not that the women in her Jewish neighborhood had avoided exposure to those puritanical throwaway lines. ("Let's get it over with." "I guess it's time." "Pull up the covers first." "Tiffany, don't touch me there.") But at least Richie's neighbors had other histories to draw upon.

Nicole reacted with amazement—and amusement—to the popular notion that women shy away from making the first move. What's to figure out? Just take the girl and kiss her! Likewise with the idea of "lesbian bed death." Why would gay women stop having sex two years into a relationship? Not everyone was raised to fit that middle-class white ideal of a good girl as a bending over to be obedient girl. Just as not everyone who was raised to become an Ice Queen became one.

Factoring in class and culture only highlights the vagueness of terms such as "active," "passive," "bottom," and "top." On the plus side, though, ambiguity leaves room for play. A girl doesn't have to get overly literal to flirt with the erotic possibilities of me up, you down. Changing places. Changing partners. Power can be sexy, in and of itself. But that leaves the question of whether power play in the boudoir inevitably turns into power struggle outside it. Is the bedroom connected to the other rooms in the house? If you're under her body, are you under her thumb?

Of course, it all depends on what you mean by power and equality. Easy enough to confuse equality with sameness. Look at the young Nicole, wavering between wanting to be a man versus wanting the power that men seemed to have. Or witness the ubiquitous chore wheel: a cardboard device affixed by magnets to the refrigerator doors of budding lesbian-feminists to yield a perfect, mechanical rotation of chores, without respect to preference or ability. A few spins of the wheel ensured that everybody in the household had a chance (and an obligation) to do everything.

If you aspire to equality, do you really have to dress the same, work the same, eat the same, fuck the same? It's one thing to live with your partner in your duplex, trailer park, or seaside estate. It's another to pass those years together in a house of mirrors. But if equality isn't sameness, then what? Richie set her hopes on the give-and-take of reciprocity over time. Fairness required equivalent, but not identical, contributions. Vicki said she felt equal in her relationship because she knew she was capable of doing anything her lover could do. "I'm just as strong as her," explained the self-described ultrafemme. Knowing her abilities freed her to "play house," which sometimes meant using a gendered rationale to divvy things up.

Then there's the kind of equality worked out in the endless negotiation of trust and resources that spells "relationship." No foregone conclusions here, either. You can abuse the woman who entrusts you with her body. But you may also find yourself trembling in the presence of a lover with the guts to place her body in trust. You can equalize your income with your partner's by passing up the opportunity for a good job. But you'd end up looking foolish to someone like Nicole who had known poverty from the inside out. Besides, your magnanimous gesture of turning down the job won't extricate you from power relations. You still had the option to say yea or nay. Your partner didn't even have a job offer to reject.

Difference is no more intrinsically about inequality than sameness is about equality. And neither turns exclusively upon gender. Because Vicki made more money than her partner, she paid more of the bills and frills. But she insisted that the arrangement had everything to do with the practicalities of finance and nothing to do with butch/femme. This from a woman who identified strongly as femme and earned her money in a gender-coded job. A case of defining away inconsistencies (a girl-girl picking up the tab)? Or an indication of the latitude couples have in negotiating gender and power?

Richie's devil-may-care approach to gender surfaced in memories of opening the car door for her lover even in the days when Richie didn't know how to drive. Can't you just see her: bowing ever so slightly as her lover seats herself behind the wheel, then walking back around to the passenger side? Sure, Richie did some "taking control things" like carrying heavy boxes. But outside the bedroom, there were few gendered terrains she would defend to the death. Richie freely admitted to incompetence in a whole host of white working-class butch talents. By laughing about her inability to set up the stereo system, she tapped into another sort of power: the power in humor to get a person through.

Not all gendered differences are created equal. Richie, who would jump out to put gas in the car faster than you can say "lesbian dildo fetishism," refused to count the number of femmes she'd fucked. That, she said, wrinkling her face in disgust, would be like "what straight men do." She liked to think that butch/femme, unlike masculine/feminine, left room for contradictions. "If butch is a particular way of experiencing being a woman, then that doesn't mean there's no feminine part to that." Especially for a nice Jewish girl. She wanted an equal relationship that didn't begin and end with gender.

Despite women's best efforts to attain parity, life and love turn out to be made up of inequalities, large, small, and variously conceived. What to do? Lock in struggle? Work out terms? Concede the fight? After years of working with her girlfriend to disentangle gender from power, Toni sheepishly confessed to being the one who drove the car. Could driving steer clear of gendering, given men's propensity to take the wheel when straight couples hit the road? Nicole and her last girlfriend had wrangled over Nicole's preference for skirts. Why wouldn't Nicole dress butch to complement her partner's femme attire? Why did she get to flaunt a hemline when her lover couldn't appear in pants?

Admitting inequality is one thing, embracing it another. Nicole was the rare person who acknowledged a love for a well-turned double standard. Her girls had to look pretty, smell good, stay away from heavy work and other women. None of these requirements applied to Nicole herself, of course. Whether Nicole got what she wanted or just bragged about getting it, she located her "advantages" in the very qualities that made some women equate studs with domination.

Roberta turned against butch/femme to fend off restrictions on what she should or shouldn't, could or couldn't do. Enough with the laundry already! But many other women traced inequalities to circumstances rather than gendered differences. A butch doesn't have to be your master, Vicki reminded anyone who cared to listen. Neither, she might have added, does a femme have to be someone's doormat.

Although relationships can foster inequalities, inequalities don't begin and end with relationships. There are plenty of things outside a couple's control that can challenge even the strongest bonds. Try making an interracial relationship work in a racist society. Or dealing with relatives who refuse to accept your partner into the family. Or telling your lover about coming up positive on an HIV antibody test.

As far as Toni was concerned, the world out there wasn't changing fast enough. Nowadays, she observed, "the butch doesn't always look so masculine." But Toni still found it easier to experiment with things she considered femme inside the perceived safety of a relationship. Walking down the street on her own, she flipped into a more "aggressive" mode.

As women got older, many began to suspect that they could spend a lifetime running after equality. At that point they generally made some adjustments. A more experienced Nicole stopped getting together with "hard" butches once she discovered other ways of living queer. Roberta went femme when she realized that presenting butch wasn't getting her the studs she wanted. Ten years later she saw herself moving out of butch/femme but also away from "feeling it" toward "giving it." Meanwhile she had learned to pick her battles. Richie searched for power in an unexpected place: the vulnerability that allowed her to feel "my own desire attached to my own body." Vicki learned that femme didn't always have to mean high femme. What a relief to kick off her heels, throw on a T-shirt, and sit back while her lover cooked.

In a world of compromise and constraint, is freedom where you find it? Ask Vicki Turner. The wages from stripping that got her off the streets gave her the freedom to eat well, live high, and help support a lover. She might have gone for another job if there had been money in it. But jobs were few and far between for a girl without a college degree. As it was, she had done better for herself than most of the women in her high school class.

Dancing had everything to do with cash and very little to do with femininity or desire for the guys. Hell, she could have been butch and stripped too. Yet Vicki's stage character was more typecast than self-determined. Under the lights she radiated cold, blonde, take-charge sensuality. Men paid to watch. Little did they know she regarded her moves as a performance, nothing more. Little did they know they were being emasculated right there in their seats. (Vicki: "I don't think of them as men.") They thought they had bought her. She regarded them as dupes willing to part with good money for a look-don't-touch arrangement.

After playing the dominatrix all night at work, Vicki was more than happy to come home and bottom out in bed. In the morning she and her lover would clean the house together. If they were lucky, they would finish in time for Vicki to button up her girlfriend's tux shirt and take her out for an evening on the town. So who's inside the whip?

After Words

Kris Lindquist was a twenty-something firebrand who did and didn't think of herself as butch. A woman who could say in one breath, "My mother is a butch," then just as quickly retract her statement because her mother identifies as heterosexual. Speaking boy-girl to boy-girl, white girl to white girl, theorist to theorist. A woman prepared to turn guessing games right back on her interviewer.

"If you put someone in a category," she explained, "then you can deal with them. I can say you're a butch and it makes it easier for me, and when you go outside those perimeters, well, then we're going to have to rethink. But for now, it puts me at ease to call you butch. Because then I know what you're going to do next. You're predictable."

Just how predictable I wasn't ready to put to the test. I thought about pulling out my own tattered history. Speaking as been-there dyke to baby dyke, professor to clerk, daddy-was-a-mailman to daddy-owned-the-business, researcher from a multiraced and racist family to . . . who knows, I just met you, Kris. You really expect predictability from someone who once thought that upward mobility required learning what "femininity" meant to a WASP and dressing accordingly? Of course, you did catch me tucking that notebook into the back pocket of my regulation black jeans. I let it go. The girl didn't miss a beat.

"I have a friend I went to school with and she's adamantly opposed to the whole butch/femme idea. Which is odd, because we spend a whole lot of time talking about it! See, butch and femme is a funny thing, because butch and femme, to me, don't really exist. They're not real things. But radical lesbian feminists who say, well, butch/femme is identifying with [a] male hierarchy— it's like atheists who talk about God. I'm always worried about them. If you don't believe in it, why are you talking about it?"

And why are all of you out there reading about it?

"[For] women who say butch and femme doesn't exist, it's just role-playing . . . it's a fascination to them. Because everyone, at one time or another, has said, 'Well, I'll bet she's butch,' or 'I'll bet she's femme,' or 'I'm more butch now than you.'"

Right. But who said what? And what did they say next? What did you understand when they said it? Was anything accomplished in the saying? What did they notice and what did they "forget"? Last but not least, why the fascination here and why the fascination now with this gendering that is not one? What was that about real wages on the wane, credit and hate crimes on the rise?

"If someone's going to a special occasion—if it's the inaugural ball—people change. They have this whole way of thinking: 'Okay, we're going to the inaugural ball and we'll shake the president's hand.' You act differently than if you were going to go to the ballpark and eat hotdogs. So dressing up in a skirt and pumps, it certainly doesn't change who I am, but I will act different because of how I look."

Suppose that after working your way throught these some-odd pages, you agree with Kris that gendered concepts ("virile," "vamp," "*macha*," "mannish," "femme," "delicate," "cooperative," "stud") are "totally permeable." In a society built upon the sands of identity, compounds of race/class/age/religion/ nation produce gender as always and everywhere a different thing, forever open to conflicting interpretations. Which is to say, not a thing at all. Does that make renditions of gender meaningless? Has understanding gender as a social creation divested it of power, contradictions, effects? But wait, the girl's not done.

"If I was given ten things to list as what I am, butch would not be in the top ten. I'm white, or I'm a woman . . . butch doesn't come up. Yet people circulate around me differently. They will offer my roommate drinks [at a party] but will expect my lover to get her own. There's this whole kind of energy that surrounds a femme, an aggressive femme, and someone like me or someone like my lover who's butch. People will walk through my roommate and walk around my lover. For those people who say, 'I don't even believe in the whole thing, it doesn't exist,' they certainly act on it a lot. They will inevitably act the same way that everybody else does who believes in butch/femme."

Try it sometime. While you're at that party, ask yourself which of the women in this book would have been invited. Then you can start to figure out who you mean by "they."

Background Material on the Women Interviewed

Each woman interviewed completed a brief fill-in-the-blank–style questionnaire about her background. Some of the terms used to describe identities have changed since I began my research in 1985. "African American," for example, entered common circulation in the late 1980s, and "queer" only began to be widely reappropriated as a positive designation in the early 1990s. I have retained whatever usage individuals preferred at the time of their interviews. The specific terms that designate race/ethnicity and religion are those the respondents themselves supplied. To help ensure anonymity, I have substituted more general categories of employment for the jobs people listed on the forms. Income figures are not strictly comparable because of inflation and changes in employment markets over the five-year span of my research. Keep in mind that a salary of $20,000 purchased considerably more in 1985 than in 1990.

Name	Age	Race/Ethnicity	Occupation	Income	Father's Occupation	Mother's Occupation	Religious Upbringing	Religious Beliefs
Lourdes Alcantara	34	Latina	Housework	None	Self-employed	Education	Catholic	Catholic
Cheryl Arthur	41	White	Education	$15–20,000	Military	Nurse's aide	Catholic	"Force greater than humans"
Misha Ben Nun	26	Jewish	Student	<$6,000	Engineering	Therapist	Atheist	None
Julia Benoit	28	French Canadian American	House cleaning	<$6,000	Sales	Housework	Catholic	Agnostic
Rona Bren	34	Jewish	Skilled trades	$30,000+	Management	Housework	Jewish (Reformed)	Culturally Jewish
Jenny Chin	29	Chinese-American	Unemployed	<$6,000	Social services	Nursing	None	Spiritual
Teresa Cruz	31	White/Hispanic	Media services	$10–15,000	Doctor	Housework	Catholic	Agnostic
Paulette Ducharme	33	Franco-American	Skilled trades	$15–20,000	Self-employed	Housework	Catholic	?
Rose Ellis	30	Black	Unemployed/ Skilled trades	$15–20,000	Farm work	Farm work	Baptist	Baptist
L.J. Ewing	32	White	Student	<$6,000	Skilled trades	Therapist	Baptist	Zen agnostic
Carolyn Fisher	19	German and Indian	Student	<$6,000	Self-employed	Self-employed	None	Higher Power
Helen Garcia	32	Latina	Education	$15–20,000	Law	Clerical work	Antireligious	Higher Power
Deborah Gauss	46	German	Education	$20–25,000	Trades	Housework	Catholic	"No way to describe"
Charlyne Harris	25	Black	Skilled trades	$15–20,000	Trades	Day care	Baptist	Baptist
Nicole Johnson	34	Black and ?	Sales	$20–25,000	?	Education	Catholic	"A goddess and me"
Richie Kaplan	34	Jewish	Education	$25–30,000	Factory work	Clerical work	Atheist	Atheist
Diane Kunin	36	White/Jewish	Self-employed	$25–30,000	Doctor	Contracting	Jewish	None
Judith Mayer	48	Jewish/American	Publishing	$20–25,000	Pharmacist	Housework	Jewish	Mountains
Jerri Miller	32	Caucasian	Clerical work	$15–20,000	?	Clerical work	Semi-Catholic	Agnostic

Edith Motzko	40	White/German-Spanish	Skilled trades	$20–25,000	Skilled trades	Housework	Catholic	Catholic
Cynthia Murray	34	White	Management	$30,000+	Self-employed	Art	Catholic	Personal
Paula Nevins	39	White	Self-employed	$10–15,000	Food service	Factory work	Catholic	Spiritual
Roberta Osabe	28	Third World-mixed/Japanese-Native American	Food service	$10–15,000	Engineering	Nursing	Protestant	Agnostic/Pagan
Chris Parker	28	WASP	Student	<$6,000	Management	Housework	Lutheran	Undecided
Gina Pellegrini	26	White/Italian	Media services	$10–15,000	Entertainment	Sales	Catholic	None
Raye Porter	39	African American	Social services	$25–30,000	Custodian	Custodian	Baptist	Jewish
Jeanne Riley	37	White	Education	$30,000+	Skilled trades	Clerical work	Baptist	Agnostic
Connie Robidoux	28	Caucasian	Art/Food service	<$6,000	Research	Housework	Catholic	Spiritual
Louise Romero	30	Brown	Skilled trades	<$6,000	Skilled trades	Housework	Catholic	None
Marta Rosales	27	Hispanic	Nursing	$20–25,000	Factory work	Housework	Catholic	"Still sorting out"
Elaine Scavone	28	Italian-American	Media services	$20–25,000	Sales	Clerical work	Catholic	Eclectic
Melissa Simpson	46	White	Writing	$10–15,000	Trades	Housework	Disciples of Christ	New Age
Sid Stein	30	Caucasian/Jewish	Management	$25–30,000	Sales	Clerical work	Jewish	Culturally Jewish
Yvonne Taylor	26	African American	Clerical work	$6–10,000	Government	Government	Little	Pagan
Rachel Tessler	27	Caucasian	Education	$25–30,000	Law	Education	Secular Jew	Atheist
Yoli Torres	37	Puerto Rican	Social services	$15–20,000	Factory work	Garment work	Catholic	None
Vicki Turner	24	White	Entertainment	$30,000+	?	Housework	?	None
Sarah Voss	40	White	Education	$20–25,000	Engineering	Clerical work	Jewish	?
Toni Williams	24	White	Food service	$10–15,000	Marketing	Housework	Catholic	None
Eriko Yoshikawa	32	Asian	Student	$6–10,000	?	Housework	Catholic	None

Bibliography

Allison, Dorothy. 1994. *Skin: Writing About Sex, Class, and Literature*. Ithaca, N.Y.: Firebrand Books.

Anzaldúa, Gloria. 1987. *Borderlands/La Frontera: The New Mestiza*. San Francisco: Spinsters/Aunt Lute.

Ardill, Susan and Sue O'Sullivan. 1990. "Butch/Femme Obsessions." *Feminist Review* 34:79–85.

Baldwin, James. 1985. *The Evidence of Things Not Seen*. New York: Henry Holt.

Barale, Michèle Aina. 1992. "When Jack Blinks: Si(gh)ting Gay Desire in Ann Bannon's Beebo Brinker." *Feminist Studies* 18 (3): 533–549.

Beck, Evelyn Torton, ed. 1982. *Nice Jewish Girls: A Lesbian Anthology*. Watertown, Mass.: Persephone Press.

Beffon, Julia. 1995. "Wearing the Pants: Butch/Femme Roleplaying in Lesbian Relationships." In *Defiant Desire: Gay and Lesbian Lives in South Africa*, ed. Mark Gevisser and Edwin Cameron, pp. 202–205. New York: Routledge.

Bender, Debbie and Linnea Due. 1994. "Coming Up Butch." In *Dagger: On Butch Women*, ed. Lily Burana, Roxxie, and Linnea Due, pp. 96–112. San Francisco: Cleis Press.

Benjamin, Walter. 1969. *Illuminations*. New York: Schocken.

Bhabha, Homi K. 1994. *Location of Culture*. New York: Routledge.

Blackman, Inge and Kathryn Perry. 1990. "Skirting the Issue: Lesbian Fashion for the 1990s." *Feminist Review* 34:67–78.

Bornstein, Kate. 1994. *Gender Outlaw: On Men, Women, and the Rest of Us.* New York: Routledge.

Bright, Susie. 1992. *Susie Bright's Sexual Reality: A Virtual Sex World Reader.* Pittsburgh: Cleis Press.

Brown, Jan. 1990. "Sex, Lies, and Penetration: A Butch Finally 'Fesses Up." *Outlook* 7:30–34.

Burana, Lily, Roxxie, and Linnea Due, eds. 1994. *Dagger: On Butch Women.* San Francisco: Cleis Press.

"Butch or Fem? The Third World Lesbian's Dilemma." 1975. In *After You're Out: Personal Experiences of Gay Men and Lesbian Women,* ed. Karla Jay and Allan Young, pp. 68–69. New York: Links Press.

Butler, Judith. 1990. *Gender Trouble: Feminism and the Subversion of Identity.* New York: Routledge.

——. 1993. *Bodies That Matter: On the Discursive Limits of "Sex."* New York: Routledge.

Cahn, Susan K. 1994. *Coming On Strong: Gender and Sexuality in Twentieth-Century Women's Sport.* New York: Free Press.

Caldwell, M. and L. A. Peplau. 1984. "The Balance of Power in Lesbian Relationships." *Sex Roles* 10:587–599.

Carby, Hazel V. 1992. "Policing the Black Woman's Body in an Urban Context." *Critical Inquiry* 18 (4): 738–755.

Case, Sue-Ellen. 1989. "Towards a Butch-Femme Aesthetic." In *Making a Spectacle: Feminist Essays on Contemporary Women's Theatre,* ed. Lynda Hart, pp. 55–73. Ann Arbor: University of Michigan Press.

Chauncey, George Jr. 1983. "From Sexual Inversion to Homosexuality: Medicine and the Changing Conception of Female Deviance." *Salmagundi* 58/59:114–146.

Clark, Danae. 1993. "Commodity Lesbianism." In *The Lesbian and Gay Studies Reader,* ed. Henry Abelove, Michèle Aina Barale, and David M. Halperin, pp. 186–201. New York: Routledge.

Cohen, Ed. 1991. "Who Are 'We'? Gay 'Identity' as Political (E)motion (A Theoretical Rumination)." In *Inside/Out: Lesbian Theories, Gay Theories,* ed. Diana Fuss, pp. 71–92. New York: Routledge.

Collins, Patricia Hill. 1991. *Black Feminist Thought: Knowledge, Consciousness, and the Politics of Empowerment.* New York: Routledge.

Cordova, Jeanne. 1979. "Are Roles Really Dead?" *Lesbian Tide* (July/August): 4–7.

Creet, Julia. 1991. "Daughter of the Movement: The Psychodynamics of Lesbian S/M Fantasy." *differences* 3 (2): 135–159.

Crenshaw, Kimberlé. 1995. "Mapping the Margins: Intersectionality, Identity Politics, and Violence Against Women of Color." In *After Identity: A Reader in Law and Culture,* ed. Dan Danielsen and Karen Engle, pp. 332–354. New York: Routledge.

DancingFire, Laura Rose. 1984. "Meditations of a Possible Femme." *Common Lives/ Lesbian Lives* 14:10–19.

de Lauretis, Teresa. 1987. *Technologies of Gender: Essays on Theory, Film, and Fiction.* Bloomington: Indiana University Press.

——. 1990. "Sexual Indifference and Lesbian Representation." In *Performing Feminisms: Feminist Critical Theory and Theatre*, ed. Sue-Ellen Case, pp. 17–39. Baltimore: Johns Hopkins University Press.

——. 1994. *The Practice of Love: Lesbian Sexuality and Perverse Desire.* Bloomington: Indiana University Press.

D'Emilio, John. 1989. "Gay Politics and Community in San Francisco Since World War II." In *Hidden from History: Reclaiming the Gay and Lesbian Past*, ed. Martin Duberman, Martha Vicinus, and George Chauncey Jr., pp. 456–473. New York: Meridian/Penguin.

Desmond, Jane C. 1993. "Where Is 'The Nation'? Public Discourse, the Body, and Visual Display." *East/West Film Journal* 7 (2): 81–110.

Douglas, Susan J. 1994. *Where the Girls Are: Growing Up Female with the Mass Media.* New York: Times Books.

duCille, Ann. 1994. "Dyes and Dolls: Multicultural Barbie and the Merchandising of Difference." *differences* 6 (1): 46–68.

Duggan, Lisa. 1992. "Making It Perfectly Queer." *Socialist Review* 22 (1): 11–32.

Echols, Alice. 1989. *Daring to Be Bad: Radical Feminism in America, 1967–1975.* Minneapolis: University of Minnesota Press.

Epstein, Julia and Kristina Straub, eds. 1991. *Body Guards: The Cultural Politics of Gender Ambiguity.* New York: Routledge.

Faderman, Lillian. 1991. *Odd Girls and Twilight Lovers: A History of Lesbian Life in Twentieth-Century America.* New York: Columbia University Press.

——. 1992. "The Return of Butch and Femme: A Phenomenon in Lesbian Sexuality of the 1980s and 1990s." *Journal of the History of Sexuality* 2 (4): 578–596.

Fausto-Sterling, Anne. 1993. "The Five Sexes: Why Male and Female Are Not Enough." *The Sciences* (March/April): 20–24.

Feinberg, Leslie. 1993. *Stone Butch Blues.* Ithaca, N.Y.: Firebrand Books.

Ferguson, Ann, Ilene Philipson, Irene Diamond, Lee Quinby, Carole S. Vance, and Ann Barr Snitow. 1984. "Forum: The Feminist Sexuality Debates." *Signs: Journal of Women in Culture and Society* 10 (1): 106–135.

Findlay, Heather. 1992. "Freud's 'Fetishism' and the Lesbian Dildo Debates." *Feminist Studies* 18 (3): 563–579.

Foucault, Michel. 1980. *The History of Sexuality.* Vol. 1. New York: Vintage.

Frankenberg, Ruth. 1993. *White Women, Race Matters: The Social Construction of Whiteness.* Minneapolis: University of Minnesota Press.

Fuss, Diana. 1989. *Essentially Speaking: Feminism, Nature, and Difference.* New York: Routledge.

Garcia, Norma, Cheryl Kennedy, Sarah F. Pearlman, and Julia Perez. 1987. "The

Impact of Race and Culture Differences: Challenges to Intimacy in Lesbian Relationships." In *Lesbian Psychologies: Explorations and Challenges*, ed. Boston Lesbian Psychologies Collective, pp. 142–160. Urbana: University of Illinois Press.

Gay American Indians and Will Roscoe, eds. 1988. *Living the Spirit: A Gay American Indian Anthology*. New York: St. Martin's Press.

Golding, Sue. 1988. "James Dean: The Almost-Perfect Lesbian Hermaphrodite." In *Sight Specific: Lesbians and Representation*, ed. Lynne Fernie, Dinah Forbes, and Joyce Mason, pp. 49–52. Toronto: A Space.

Goldsby, Jackie. 1990. "What It Means to Be Colored Me." *Outlook* 9:8–17.

Gordon, Linda. 1991. "On 'Difference.'" *Genders* 10:91–111.

Halberstam, Judith. 1993. "Imagined Violence/Queer Violence: Representation, Rage, and Resistance." *Social Text* 37:187–199.

Hamer, Diane. 1990. "'I Am a Woman': Ann Bannon and the Writing of Lesbian Identity in the 1950s." In *Lesbian and Gay Writing: An Anthology of Critical Essays*, ed. Mark Lilly. New York: Macmillan.

Hamer, Diane and Belinda Budge, eds. 1994. *The Good, the Bad, and the Gorgeous: Popular Culture's Romance with Lesbianism*. Henley-on-Thames: Pandora Press.

Hammonds, Evelynn. 1994. "Black (W)holes and the Geometry of Black Female Sexuality." *differences* 6 (2/3): 126–145.

Haraway, Donna J. 1991. *Simians, Cyborgs, and Women: The Reinvention of Nature*. New York: Routledge.

Harper, Phillip Brian, Margaret Cerullo, and E. Frances White. 1990. "Multi/Queer/Culture." *Radical America* 24 (4): 27–37.

Hart, Lynda. 1994. *Fatal Women: Lesbian Sexuality and the Mark of Aggression*. Princeton: Princeton University Press.

Hebdige, Dick. 1979. *Subculture: The Meaning of Style*. London: Routledge, Chapman and Hall.

Hennessy, Rosemary. 1995. "Queer Visibility in Commodity Culture." *Cultural Critique* 29:31–76.

Herrmann, Anne. 1992. "Imitations of Marriage: Crossdressed Couples in Contemporary Lesbian Fiction." *Feminist Studies* 18 (3): 609–624.

Hewitt, Nancy A. 1992. "Compounding Differences." *Feminist Studies* 18 (2): 313–326.

Higginbotham, Evelyn Brooks. 1992. "African-American Women's History and the Metalanguage of Race." *Signs: Journal of Women in Culture and Society* 17 (2): 251–274.

Hollibaugh, Amber and Cherríe Moraga. 1983. "What We're Rollin' Around in Bed with: Sexual Silences in Feminism." In *Powers of Desire: The Politics of Sexuality*, ed. Ann Snitow, Christine Stansell, and Sharon Thompson, pp. 394–405. New York: Monthly Review Press.

hooks, bell. 1992. *Black Looks: Race and Representation*. Boston: South End Press.

Irvine, Janice M. 1990. *Disorders of Desire: Sex and Gender in Modern American Sexology*. Philadelphia: Temple University Press.

James, Stanlie M. and Abena P. A. Busia, eds. 1993. *Theorizing Black Feminisms: The Visionary Pragmatism of Black Women*. New York: Routledge.

Jay, Karla, ed. 1995. *Dyke Life: A Celebration of the Lesbian Experience*. New York: Basic Books.

Jeffreys, Sheila. 1987. "Butch and Femme: Now and Then." *Gossip* 5:65–95.

Jones, Lisa. 1994. *Bulletproof Diva: Tales of Race, Sex, and Hair*. New York: Doubleday.

Kang, L. Hyun-Yi. 1993. "The Desiring of Asian Female Bodies: Interracial Romance and Cinematic Subjection." *Visual Anthropology Review* 9 (1): 5–21.

Kennedy, Elizabeth Lapovsky and Madeline D. Davis. 1993. *Boots of Leather, Slippers of Gold: The History of a Lesbian Community*. New York: Routledge.

King, Katie. 1994. *Theory in Its Feminist Travels: Conversations in U.S. Women's Movements*. Bloomington: Indiana University Press.

Kite, Mary E. and Kay Deaux. 1987. "Gender Belief Systems: Homosexuality and the Implicit Inversion Theory." *Psychology of Women Quarterly* 11:83–96.

Kroker, Arthur and Marilouise Kroker, eds. 1993. *The Last Sex: Feminism and Outlaw Bodies*. New York: St. Martin's Press.

Langer, Nancy A. F. 1985. "The New Butch/Femme: The Eighties Answer to Astrology." *New York Native*, July 29–August 11, p. 28.

Laporte, Rita. 1971. "The Butch/Femme Question." *The Ladder* (June/July): 4–11.

Laqueur, Thomas. 1990. *Making Sex: Body and Gender from the Greeks to Freud*. Cambridge: Harvard University Press.

Lee, JeeYuen. 1996. "Why Suzie Wong Is Not a Lesbian: Asian-American Lesbian and Bisexual Women and Femme/Butch/Gender Identities." In *Queer Studies: A Multicultural Anthology*, ed. Brett Beemyn and Mickey Eliason. New York: New York University Press.

Leong, Russell, ed. 1996. *Asian American Sexualities: Dimensions of the Gay and Lesbian Experience*. New York: Routledge.

Lewin, Ellen. 1993. *Lesbian Mothers: Accounts of Gender in American Culture*. Ithaca, N.Y.: Cornell University Press.

Lim-Hing, Sharon, ed. 1994. *The Very Inside: An Anthology of Writing by Asian and Pacific Islander Lesbian and Bisexual Women*. Toronto: Sister Vision Press.

Lloyd, Michele E. 1996. "G.I. Joes in Barbie Land: Recontextualizing Butch in Twentieth-Century Lesbian Culture." In *Queer Studies: A Multicultural Anthology*, ed. Brett Beemyn and Mickey Eliason. New York: New York University Press.

Lorde, Audre. 1984. *Sister Outsider*. Trumansburg, N.Y.: Crossing Press.

——. 1982. *Zami: A New Spelling of My Name*. Trumansburg, N.Y.: Crossing Press.

Loulan, JoAnn. 1990. *The Lesbian Erotic Dance: Butch, Femme, Androgyny et al.* Minneapolis: Spinsters Ink.

Lugones, Maria. 1994. "Purity, Impurity, and Separation." *Signs: Journal of Women in Culture and Society* 19 (2): 458–479.

Lynch, Jean M. and Mary Ellen Reilly. 1986. "Role Relationships: Lesbian Perspectives." *Journal of Homosexuality* 12 (2): 53–69.

Marchetti, Gina. 1993. *Romance and the "Yellow Peril": Race, Sex, and Discursive Strategies in Hollywood Fiction*. Berkeley: University of California Press.

Martin, Biddy. 1994. "Sexualities Without Genders and Other Queer Utopias." *Diacritics* 24 (2–3): 104–121.

Martin, Karin A. 1993. "Gender and Sexuality: Medical Opinion on Homosexuality, 1900–1950. *Gender and Society* 7 (2): 246–260.

McCombs, Annie, Pauline Bart, De Clarke, Isabel Andrews, Karen Cameron, zana, Noretta Koertge, Judy Brow, and Cherie Lyn. 1986. "Femme and Butch: A Readers' Forum." *Lesbian Ethics* 2:86–105.

McKinley, Catherine E. and L. Joyce DeLaney, eds. 1995. *Afrekete: An Anthology of Black Lesbian Writing*. New York: Anchor/Doubleday.

Mercer, Kobena. 1990. "Welcome to the Jungle: Identity and Diversity in Postmodern Politics." In *Identity: Community, Culture, Difference*, ed. Jonathan Rutherford, pp. 43–71. London: Lawrence and Wishart.

Meyerowitz, Joanne, ed. 1994. *Not June Cleaver: Women and Gender in Postwar America, 1945–1960*. Philadelphia: Temple University Press.

Minton, Henry L. 1986. "Femininity in Men and Masculinity in Women: American Psychiatry and Psychology Portray Homosexuality in the 1930s." *Journal of Homosexuality* 13 (1): 1–21.

Moraga, Cherríe. 1993. *The Last Generation*. Boston: South End Press.

Moraga, Cherríe and Gloria Anzaldúa, eds. 1981. *This Bridge Called My Back: Writings by Radical Women of Color*. Watertown, Mass.: Persephone Press.

Mushroom, Merril. 1982. "How to Engage in Courting Rituals 1950s Butch Style in the Bar." *Common Lives/Lesbian Lives* 4:6–10.

——. 1983. "Confessions of a Butch Dyke." *Common Lives/Lesbian Lives* 9:39–45.

Nestle, Joan. 1987. *A Restricted Country*. Ithaca, N.Y.: Firebrand Books.

——, ed. 1992. *The Persistent Desire: A Femme-Butch Reader*. Boston: Alyson.

Newman, Lesléa. 1995. *The Femme Mystique*. Boston: Alyson.

Newton, Esther. 1985. "The Mythic Mannish Lesbian: Radclyffe Hall and the New Woman." In *The Lesbian Issue: Essays from Signs*, ed. Estelle B. Freedman, Barbara C. Gelpi, Susan L. Johnson, and Kathleen M. Weston, pp. 7–25. Chicago: University of Chicago Press.

——. 1993. *Cherry Grove, Fire Island: Sixty Years in America's First Gay and Lesbian Town*. Boston: Beacon.

Omosupe, Ekua. 1991. "Black/Lesbian/Bulldagger." *differences* 3 (2): 101–111.

Penelope, Julia. 1984. "Whose Past Are We Reclaiming?" *Common Lives/Lesbian Lives* 13:16–35.

——, ed. 1994. *Out of the Class Closet: Lesbians Speak*. Freedom, Cal.: Crossing Press.

Penn, Donna. 1991. "The Meanings of Lesbianism in Post-War America." *Gender and History* 3 (2): 190–203.

Phelan, Shane. 1993. "(Be)Coming Out: Lesbian Identity and Politics." *Signs: Journal of Women in Culture and Society* 18 (4): 765–790.

Podolsky, Robin. 1991. "Sacrificing Queers and Other 'Proletarian' Artifacts." *Radical America* 25 (1): 53–60.

Pratt, Minnie Bruce. 1995. *S/he*. Ithaca, N.Y.: Firebrand Books.

Probyn, Elspeth. 1993. *Sexing the Self: Gendered Positions in Cultural Studies*. New York: Routledge.

Ramos, Juanita, ed. 1994. *Compañeras: Latina Lesbians*. New York: Routledge.

Ratti, Rakesh, ed. 1993. *A Lotus of Another Color: An Unfolding of the South Asian Gay and Lesbian Experience*. Boston: Alyson.

Reich, June L. 1992. "Genderfuck: The Law of the Dildo." *Discourse* 15 (1): 112–127.

Robertson, Jennifer. 1992. "The Politics of Androgyny in Japan: Sexuality and Subversion in the Theater and Beyond." *American Ethnologist* 19 (3): 1–24.

Robinson, Amy. 1994. "It Takes One to Know One: Passing and Communities of Common Interest." *Critical Inquiry* 20: 715–736.

Roof, Judith. 1991. *A Lure of Knowledge: Lesbian Sexuality and Theory*. New York: Columbia University Press.

Rubin, Gayle. 1984. "Thinking Sex: Notes for a Radical Theory of the Politics of Sexuality." In *Pleasure and Danger: Exploring Female Sexuality*, ed. Carole S. Vance, pp. 267–319. New York: Routledge and Kegan Paul.

Rust, Paula C. 1992. "The Politics of Sexual Identity: Sexual Attraction and Behavior Among Lesbian and Bisexual Women." *Social Problems* 39 (4): 366–386.

Samois, ed. 1982. *Coming to Power: Writings and Graphics on Lesbian S/M*. Boston: Alyson.

Scott, Joan W. 1988. *Gender and the Politics of History*. New York: Columbia University Press.

——. 1992. "Experience." In *Feminists Theorize the Political*, ed. Judith Butler and Joan W. Scott, pp. 22–40. New York: Routledge.

Sedgwick, Eve Kosofsky. 1990. *Epistemology of the Closet*. Berkeley: University of California Press.

Segrest, Mab. 1994. *Memoir of a Race Traitor*. Boston: South End Press.

Silvera, Makeda. 1992. "Man Royals and Sodomites: Some Thoughts on the Invisibility of Afro-Caribbean Lesbians." *Feminist Studies* 18 (3): 521–532.

Smith, Barbara, ed. 1983. *Home Girls: A Black Feminist Anthology*. New York: Kitchen Table: Women of Color Press.

Solomon, Alisa. 1992. "Identity Crisis: Queer Politics in the Age of Possibilities." *Village Voice*, June 30, pp. 27–29, 33.

Spivak, Gayatri Chakravorty. 1987. *In Other Worlds: Essays in Cultural Politics*. New York: Methuen.

——. 1992. "Acting Bits/Identity Talk." *Critical Inquiry* 18 (4): 770–803.

Stack, Carol B. 1974. *All Our Kin: Strategies for Survival in a Black Community*. New York: Harper & Row.

Stein, Arlene, ed. 1993. *Sisters, Sexperts, Queers: Beyond the Lesbian Nation*. New York: Plume/Penguin.

Stevens, Robin, ed. 1994. *Girlfriend Number One: Lesbian Life in the Nineties*. San Francisco: Cleis Press.

Taylor, Verta and Leila J. Rupp. 1993. "Women's Culture and Lesbian Feminist Activism: A Reconsideration of Cultural Feminism." *Signs: Journal of Women in Culture and Society* 19 (1): 32–61.

Terry, Jennifer. 1990. "Lesbians Under the Medical Gaze: Scientists Search for Remarkable Differences." *Journal of Sex Research* 27 (3): 317–339.

——. 1995. "Anxious Slippages Between 'Us' and 'Them': A Brief History of the Scientific Search for Homosexual Bodies." In *Deviant Bodies: Critical Perspectives on Difference in Science and Popular Culture*, ed. Jennifer Terry and Jacqueline Urla, pp. 129–169. Bloomington: Indiana University Press.

Trujillo, Carla, ed. 1991. *Chicana Lesbians: The Girls Our Mothers Warned Us About*. Berkeley: Third Woman Press.

Vicinus, Martha. 1992. " 'They Wonder to Which Sex I Belong': The Historical Roots of the Modern Lesbian Identity." *Feminist Studies* 18 (3): 467–497.

Walker, Lisa M. 1993. "How to Recognize a Lesbian: The Cultural Politics of Looking Like What You Are." *Signs: Journal of Women in Culture and Society* 18 (4): 866–890.

Warner, Michael, ed. 1993. *Fear of a Queer Planet: Queer Politics and Social Theory*. Minneapolis: University of Minnesota Press.

Weeks, Jeffrey. 1991. *Against Nature: Essays on History, Sexuality, and Identity*. London: Rivers Oram Press.

Weston, Kath. 1991. *Families We Choose: Lesbians, Gays, Kinship*. New York: Columbia University Press.

——. 1993. "Do Clothes Make the Woman? Gender, Performance Theory, and Lesbian Eroticism." *Genders* 17:1–21.

Williams, Patricia J. 1991. *The Alchemy of Race and Rights*. Cambridge: Harvard University Press.

——. 1995. *The Rooster's Egg: On the Persistence of Prejudice*. Cambridge: Harvard University Press.

Williams, Rhonda. 1994. "Being Queer, Being Black: Living Out in Afro-American Studies." Paper read at the Thinking, Writing, Teaching, and Creating Social Justice Conference, University of Minnesota, Minneapolis.

Wilson, Elizabeth. 1990. "Deviant Dress." *Feminist Review* 35:67–74.

Wittig, Monique. 1992. *The Straight Mind*. Boston: Beacon.

Yamaguchi, Lynn and Karen Barber, eds. 1995. *Tomboys! Tales of Dyke Derring-Do*. Boston: Alyson.

Zita, Jacqueline N. 1988. " 'Real Girls' and Lesbian Resistance." *Lesbian Ethics* 3 (1): 85–96.

——. 1992. "The Male Lesbian and the Postmodernist Body." *Hypatia* 7 (4): 106–127.